THE scarpetta COOK BOOK

THE scarpetta COOKBOOK

SCOTT CONANT

WINE NOTES BY MASTER SOMMELIER
PAOLO BARBIERI

PHOTOGRAPHY BY BRENT HERRIG

Houghton Mifflin Harcourt
Boston • New York • 2013

Cover image by Melanie Dunea

Prop styling by Kira Corbin

Design by Vertigo Design NYC

Published by Houghton Mifflin Harcourt Publishing Company, New York, New York

Published simultaneously in Canada.

For information about permission to reproduce selections from this book, write to Permissions, Houghton Mifflin Harcourt Publishing Company, 215 Park Avenue South, New York, New York 10003.

ww.hmhbooks.com

Library of Congress Cataloging-in-Publication Data:
Conant, Scott.
    The Scarpetta cookbook / Scott Conant; photography by Brent Herrig.
        p. cm.
Includes index.
ISBN 9781118508701 (cloth); 9780544188051 (ebk)
1. Cooking, Italian. I. Herrig, Brent. II. Scarpetta (Restaurant: New York, NY) III. Title.
 TX723.C61728 2013
 641.5945—dc23
                                        2013005874

Printed in China

SZN   10   9   8   7   6   5   4   3   2   1

DAD

"Your job is to make your life better for your family, than I did for mine . . . ."
I can still hear those words ringing in my ears. I hope I have made you proud.

I love you, Pop.

FOR AYLA AND KARYA

I will always fight to succeed for you both.

CONTENTS

ACKNOWLEDGMENTS

THERE ARE SO MANY PEOPLE TO THANK FOR MAKING THIS BOOK A REALITY, AND SIMPLY TOO MANY TO NAME, BUT HERE GOES ANYWAY:

My wife, Meltem, for all the love, care and sacrifice she demonstrates on a daily basis so that I can pursue my dreams and passions. I don't tell you often enough just how lucky I am to have you. You are the reason why I can do what I do. I love you!

My core team at SCM: Nick Kennedy, Irene Chiang, Chris Cuomo, and Jorge Espinosa. You are the backbone; I thank you all deeply.

The rest of the players:

Nina Compton
Jennifer Fassett
Ben Kaplan
Todd Sugimoto
Gina Marinelli
Ryan Morrison
Gaetano Ferrara
Chris Wyman
Mike Pirolo
Freddy Vargas
Yssac Vargas

Alex Stratta
Yolanda Guererro
Jeremy Sung
Darron Lee
Joanna Zoldak
Nataly Herrera
Mario Di Si
Noe Alarcon
Kelli Binette
Marc Davis
Paolo Barbieri

The team at every one of my restaurants as well as the hotel partners in every property.

The team at WME: Josh Bider, Ken Slotnick, Bethany Dick, Jon Rosen, and Eric Lupfer.

All the judges I get to spend time with, great people and great friends: Geoffrey, Amanda, Alex, Aaron, Marc, Marcus, Maneet, Ted, and Chris.

The book's photographer, Brent Herrig, and prop stylist, Kira Corbin—without them this would not have been possible. Also Melanie Dunea for the cover photograph.

The ladies at Becca PR.

My editor, Justin Schwartz.

And, of course, Joanne Smart; as usual, she has captured the essence of my vision for this book. Thank you and your family!

INTRODUCTION

MY LOVE OF COOKING, AND ESPECIALLY OF ITALIAN CUISINE, BEGAN AT AN EARLY AGE. GROWING UP IN AN ITALIAN-AMERICAN FAMILY (MY GRANDPARENTS WERE FROM ITALY), I ENJOYED A LOT OF GOOD FOOD, AS EARLY PHOTOS OF ME AS A CHUBBY LITTLE KID CAN ATTEST. I ALWAYS FELT COMFORTABLE IN THE KITCHEN WITH MY GRANDMOTHER AND MY AUNTS, WHO DID THE BULK OF THE COOKING FOR MY EXTENDED FAMILY.

I first started cooking in a serious way when I was 15 and going to a vocational school. I wanted to be a plumber—I knew there was good money to be had there—but I couldn't get into the program. My second choice was culinary arts because it was the only thing other than gym that I ever got an A in. Around the same time, I started working at a family friend's restaurant as a dishwasher, just to make some money. I had always played a lot of sports, and what I loved about the kitchen was that same camaraderie I found as part of the baseball team: everyone doing their own thing but working together for the same ultimate goal.

After high school, I went to the Culinary Institute of America. In 1995, Cesare Casella asked me to be chef de cuisine at Il Toscanaccio, his Tuscan restaurant on New York's Upper East Side. A year later, I went on to revamp Barolo in SoHo and Chianti on the Upper East Side. When the chance arose to help open a new restaurant, I accepted the position of executive chef at City Eatery, where my modern take on Italian cuisine started getting some serious attention.

In 2001, I was approached about opening a restaurant in Tudor City. In preparation for what was to become L'Impero, I traveled all around Italy and cooked with some of the country's most celebrated chefs. (I also got the chance to reconnect with my mother's relatives in Benevento, which was just amazing.) L'Impero, which opened in September 2002, received a rave three-star review from the *New York Times*. A few years later, ready to strike out on my own, I left L'Impero as well as Alto, my upscale interpretation of northern Italian cuisine, to create Scarpetta.

If there is something that prompts a chef to truly define and refine his style, it's opening his own restaurant. Before Scarpetta, I had been involved in other restaurant openings as a chef and a partner, and I always made the decisions about the food and whom to hire. But Scarpetta was completely different. This was all on me. Every single decision, from the food to what kind of napkins would be on the table to which font to use for the menu to which florist we should hire to arrange the flowers, was ultimately mine to make.

And the sheer number of decisions that come into play when opening a restaurant is truly staggering. The only thing that kept me going at times was the desire to express my own vision.

The name of the restaurant says it all. *Fare la scarpetta*, "to make a little shoe," is an Italian phrase that refers to the act of tearing off a chunk of bread and using it to mop up any sauce that's left on the plate. And the intention of Scarpetta from day one has been to reflect that. Our logo incorporates the swipe that's left on the plate after you have dragged that bit of bread across it. It's an ever-present reminder of our whole corporate philosophy: not only to make food that people want to eat every last bit of, but also to create an environment that puts them at ease to do so. Yet this is not a casual dining experience, so it makes for an interesting and exciting balance that's exhibited in every facet of the Scarpetta experience.

The physical characteristics of the original Scarpetta in New York—elegant orchids rising above distressed wood paneling made from reclaimed flooring and white all-cotton napkins set on sleek, dark tables—telegraph that balance of style and comfort. Our waitstaff does, too. They may be stylishly dressed and impeccably mannered, but they're also friendly, approachable, and passionate about what they do. Then there's the food: simple dishes prepared with deliberation, classic techniques given an inventive edge, flavors that are sophisticated yet soulful.

Take my spaghetti, which has become a signature recipe. On the menu, it's described with just a few words: "tomato & basil." And that's pretty much all it is. Except the spaghetti is handmade. The tomatoes are carefully selected Romas cooked just until their flavor has become rounded and lovely. And the method, which you can read about on page 121, is simple yet deliberate, from the slicing of the basil to a finish of an infused olive oil before serving. I'm sure that most of our customers have no idea that so much care and attention goes into creating what ultimately looks simple on the plate. All they know is that the spaghetti makes them very happy.

Indeed, when I opened Scarpetta, it was with that one simple goal: making people happy. This very basic idea—that customers leave our restaurant happier than when they walked in—is my overriding mission. It's something I kept top of mind as I opened Scarpetta in different cities. In each location, I looked to balance the Scarpetta style with the locality of the place. Our diners have come to expect dependability from Scarpetta, yet each Scarpetta has been tweaked to make it a little different from the others while not losing its overall integrity. Scarpetta in Miami, for example, reflects the South Beach lifestyle, which has more of a cocktail culture than the neighborhood-bar feel of Scarpetta New York. Scarpetta in Toronto is a more elegant restaurant in response to its location in that city, whereas Scarpetta Las Vegas, situated in the magnificent Cosmopolitan hotel with a view of the Bellagio fountains, takes on a sexier atmosphere. (How could it not?) And while Scarpetta Beverly Hills in the Montage hotel may have al fresco dining on the patio and celebrities galore, it still retains an earthy and sophisticated feel, which to my delight the *LA Weekly* described as "very much in the Conant style."

How would I describe that style? Whether it's how I am plating a dish or decorating my office, I call it urban-Milan-meets-rustic-Tuscany in that it exhibits the clean, crisp lines and modern design you expect to find in that fashionable city while embracing the warmth and vitality of the Italian countryside. Walk into Scarpetta and you get hit with a vibe that's cool yet calm, sexy yet soothing. You're excited to be there, but you feel completely comfortable, too.

I'd love for everyone reading this book to enjoy the full Scarpetta experience, because so much of that experience is also about our hospitality. I'm the chef, so I know our food is great, but I also know that for us to succeed, the service just has to blow people away. I think that's true for home cooks to some degree when they're having friends over. Of course the situation is not parallel—your friends are not paying you for dinner—but I do believe that even more important than the food is that guests feel comfortable and well cared for. Because then, and only then, can they really appreciate the great food that's put before them.

HOW TO USE THIS BOOK

The intention of this book is to provide home cooks with the ability to re-create the dishes we serve at Scarpetta. We have a lot of regulars who would love to know how their favorite dish is made. There are also lots of people who have read about Scarpetta or have seen something about it online or on TV and who would love to try our polenta with mushrooms (see page 74), but who don't live near one of the restaurants. For that reason, these recipes reflect almost exactly what it is we do every day in the Scarpetta kitchen. They have been edited for the home cook, but we have not skipped an element on the plate for the sake of simplifying the recipe or left out an ingredient just because it's super seasonal or not available at all supermarkets. (You can get just about anything online these days.) That said, some of the recipes are drop-dead simple, and all of them should be doable for enthusiastic home cooks, with a few tips to keep in mind:

READ THE RECIPE START TO FINISH BEFORE YOU BEGIN COOKING. I know this is a truism for any recipe, but for these perhaps more so. Look closely at how much time the recipe will require. In the case of, say, marinating or brining, this is hands-off time, but you will need to figure out what needs to be done when and how much time you will need—some recipes require a day or more—before serving.

DO MOST OF THE WORK AHEAD OF TIME. Because we are a professional kitchen making hundreds of dishes a night, we *have* to be prepared. That means anything and everything that does not have to be cooked *à la minute* (French for "right now!") is prepped earlier in the day. Some of these recipes include many components, but the beauty is that they can be made one day, two days, or even weeks before you have to pull the dish together. (Look for detailed make-ahead information within the recipe itself.) This actually makes entertaining easy, as you have done most of the time-consuming work ahead and can enjoy that glass of wine while you pull the meal together. You'll find many of these make-ahead recipe components in The Scarpetta Pantry (see page 308).

USE THE BEST INGREDIENTS YOU CAN AFFORD. High quality can cost more, but for a special occasion, it's worth it.

INVEST IN A COUPLE OF KEY PIECES OF KITCHEN EQUIPMENT. We're not all crazy modernist cooks in the Scarpetta kitchen, but there are a few items we can't work without. They include a high-quality blender (we like Vitamix blenders) for making purées (a food processor just can't do the job as well), an immersion (handheld) blender for froths, and a pasta machine for rolling fresh pasta dough. A spice grinder (you can use a coffee grinder dedicated to spices) will also come in handy. I also highly recommend investing in a stand mixer if you don't already have one. Same with a mandoline; while you can use a chef's knife for some of the recipes requiring vegetables sliced paper-thin, a mandoline makes the job so much easier. (And you don't need a big, $200 stainless steel one, either. In our kitchen, we use the inexpensive Japanese ones that fold flat and can fit into a kitchen drawer.) One or two recipes call for a whipped cream canister, which may sound out there but is really easy to use and doesn't cost a lot to purchase. That's about it for anything specialized, but to make cooking more enjoyable, you will also want sharp knives, high-quality cookware, rimmed baking sheets, and a mix of good music in the background.

CONSIDER THE WINE. At Scarpetta, we take pride in helping our customers choose a wine that will go well with their dish. Many of the recipes included in this book include a wine pairing selected by Paolo Barbieri, master wine sommelier at Scarpetta Las Vegas. Not only is Paolo from Italy and an exceptional sommelier, but he also makes his own wine. He is good to have around.

Whether I am hosting an event (often), or having friends and family to my home for a get-together (not as often as I would like), I know that what people want right away is a drink and a little something to nibble on. That's what the recipes here are all about. These are the nuts, olives, dips, canapés, and hors d'oeuvres that set the tone for the rest of the night. At home, these are the bites you put out before dinner, while guests are gathering, catching up, getting acquainted.

When we do events, we'll often set a long table against one wall and center a dramatic bouquet of flowers on it, which helps draw attention to the table. Wine and wineglasses go at one end and, at the other, some cheeses, a bowl of Herbed Potato Chips (page 8), Spiced Almonds (page 2), and Warm Olives (page 3). This setup not only lets guests nosh on something immediately, but it also creates a natural meeting place.

All of these *assaggini* ("small tastes") pack loads of flavor and texture into a single balanced bite. Some are easy to make. Others take more time and effort but, like most good things in life, are worth it.

ASSAGGINI & APERITIVI

GATHERING

SPICED ALMONDS

These almonds, which pack a little more heat than most people expect in a bar nut, pair well with cocktails. We make them in 20-pound batches; you may never have a need for that many nuts in your life, but know that you can easily multiply this recipe. The egg white helps the spices adhere to the nuts. You want to use just enough to make that happen but not so much that the spices clump.

MAKES ABOUT 4 CUPS

Grapeseed or canola oil, for the baking sheet

¾ cup granulated sugar

3 tablespoons kosher salt

3 tablespoons sweet paprika

1½ tablespoons cayenne pepper

1½ tablespoons whole star anise, broken into pieces

1 large egg white

1 pound (3 cups) whole almonds

Heat a convection oven to 350°F or a conventional oven to 375°F. Very lightly oil a large rimmed baking sheet.

In a small bowl, combine the sugar, salt, paprika, cayenne, and star anise.

In a large bowl, whisk the egg white until frothy. Add the almonds and toss well to coat. Sprinkle the spices over the almonds and toss well to coat evenly. Transfer the almonds to a colander set in a clean sink and shake gently to remove excess spices.

Spread the nuts out on the baking sheet in a single layer and bake, stirring about halfway through, until nicely toasted, about 25 minutes. Remove the almonds from the oven and let cool on the baking sheet.

Remove the pieces of star anise and discard. Use your hands to lightly separate clusters of the almonds, then return the almonds to the cleaned colander and gently shake to remove any excess spice. Serve right away, or store airtight for up to 2 days.

WARM OLIVES WITH GARLIC AND HERBS

Sure, you can put out just a plain bowl of olives, but why would you do that when you can easily boost their flavor by infusing them with garlic, rosemary, thyme, and crushed red pepper? Not only that, but a bowl of these olives contributes a wonderful aroma to the table. People always comment on it.

MAKES 3 CUPS

¼ cup extra-virgin olive oil

4 cloves garlic, lightly smashed

⅛ teaspoon crushed red pepper

2 sprigs fresh rosemary

2 sprigs fresh thyme

3 cups mixed olives, such as Cerignola, Taggiasca, Gaeta, and Picholine

In a medium saucepan over medium heat, heat the olive oil, garlic, and crushed red pepper until the garlic starts to sizzle. Add the rosemary and thyme and cook, stirring occasionally, until fragrant, about 2 minutes. Stir in the olives, lower the heat, and cook, stirring occasionally, until the olives are warmed through and have absorbed the flavors, 8 to 10 minutes. Serve warm.

CRISPY FRIED ARTICHOKES WITH LEMON YOGURT AND BASIL

If you've ever been to Italy, then you know all about fried artichokes. I can't get enough of them when I am in Rome, but I sometimes find that the ones I'm served are too brown, with a flavor that's bitter from spending too much time in the oil and a texture that's not as supple as I would like. This recipe keeps intact the essence of the dish but elevates it for a better overall experience. The secret is frying the artichokes twice: first at a lower temperature and then at a higher temperature. The first fry makes the artichokes tender without overcooking the exterior. The second fry crisps and browns them to perfection. You can do the first fry (called a "blanch") several hours ahead of the second.

SERVES 6

Grapeseed or canola oil, for frying

30 baby artichokes, preferably purple

Kosher salt

12 fresh basil leaves, preferably a mix of opal and lemon

Lemon Yogurt (recipe follows)

Attach a candy/deep-fry thermometer to a deep, wide pot, and fill the pot with enough oil to come about halfway up the sides of the pot. Heat the oil to 275°F.

In batches, lower the artichokes into the oil and blanch until a metal cake tester or thin metal skewer can easily be inserted into the heart of the artichoke, 7 to 12 minutes. Using a wire skimmer or slotted spoon, transfer the artichokes to a rimmed baking sheet and let cool. Reserve the oil off the heat. Peel the outer leaves off, pulling downward to peel the stem. With the stem side up, flatten each artichoke, moving it in a circular motion on the baking sheet until the leaves open up. Refrigerate the artichokes until ready to fry the second time and serve. (The artichokes may be blanched 1 day ahead of serving; refrigerate until ready to use.)

To serve, heat the reserved oil to 350°F. Line a rimmed baking sheet with paper towels. In batches, gently lower the artichokes into the oil and fry until golden brown and crispy, about 1 minute. Transfer to the paper towels and season with salt. Drop the basil leaves into the hot oil for a few seconds to crisp them, and transfer to the paper towels.

Spread some of the Lemon Yogurt on each serving plate and divide the artichokes among the plates. Top with the fried basil and serve immediately.

LEMON YOGURT

Delicious with fried artichokes, this tangy yogurt would also go well with fried calamari or just about anything else deep-fried or panfried, for that matter.

1 cup plain full-fat yogurt, preferably sheep's milk

1 teaspoon fresh lemon juice

1 clove garlic, peeled and smashed with the side of a chef's knife

Pinch of crushed red pepper

1 teaspoon kosher salt

¼ cup extra-virgin olive oil

In a small bowl, combine the yogurt, lemon juice, garlic, crushed red pepper, and salt. Slowly whisk in the olive oil. Let sit for 20 minutes at room temperature, then remove the garlic so it doesn't overpower the other flavors. Cover and refrigerate if not using right away. (The yogurt may be made 2 days ahead; cover and refrigerate it, but let it warm a bit at room temperature before serving for the best flavor.)

BEEF CARPACCIO ON PARMESAN CRACKERS

Soft and supple slices of paper-thin raw beef drizzled with a little olive oil and served on a crisp cracker—the simplicity of this bite is part of its beauty. For the best results, buy the highest quality of beef you can afford. I recommend Australian Wagyu because its marbling means that the raw meat practically melts in the mouth when served at room temperature.

8 ounces high-quality, well-marbled sirloin strip

Parmesan Crackers (recipe follows), reheated in a low oven if necessary

Flaked sea salt and freshly ground black pepper

1 lemon, halved and seeded

1 to 2 ounces Parmigiano-Reggiano cheese

Microgreens

Extra-virgin olive oil, for finishing

Cut the sirloin into 8 equal pieces. Put one piece between two pieces of plastic wrap and pound with a meat mallet until paper-thin. Repeat with the other pieces, then cut each piece of carpaccio into 5 pieces. Place one piece of carpaccio on a Parmesan Cracker, allowing it to fall and fold naturally. Season with a tiny pinch of sea salt, a smidge of black pepper, and a couple of drops of lemon juice. Using a vegetable peeler, shave a thin slice of Parmigiano-Reggiano onto the beef. Top with a pinch of microgreens and a light drizzle of olive oil. Repeat until you have used up all the beef; you may have extra crackers. Serve immediately.

PARMESAN CRACKERS

MAKES ABOUT 50 CRACKERS

1¼ cup all-purpose flour

1 teaspoon kosher salt

½ teaspoon freshly ground black pepper

8 tablespoons (4 ounces) cold, unsalted butter, cut into pieces

½ cup plus 2 tablespoons finely freshly grated Parmigiano-Reggiano cheese

3 tablespoons ice water

3 tablespoons finely chopped fresh chives (optional)

Heat a convection oven to 325°F or a conventional oven to 350°F. Put the flour, salt, and black pepper in a food processor and pulse until combined. Add the butter and ½ cup of the Parmigiano-Reggiano and pulse until the dough looks sandy. Add the ice water and pulse until the dough just comes together. Remove the dough from the food processor and, if using the chives, knead them in by hand.

Put the dough on a piece of parchment paper, put another piece of parchment over it, and roll the dough ⅛ inch thick. Remove the top sheet, trim any jagged edges, and transfer the dough on the parchment to a rimmed baking sheet. With a pizza cutter, divide the dough into 1 x 2-inch rectangles (press just hard enough to cut the dough and not the paper). With a fork, prick each rectangle a few times. Bake for 10 minutes, then take the pan out of the oven and sprinkle the crackers with the remaining 2 tablespoons Parmigiano-Reggiano. Return the pan to the oven and bake for 5 minutes.

The crackers are best served warm, but they can be made 1 day ahead. Let them cool completely on the baking sheet before storing airtight. Reheat in a warm oven before serving.

HERBED POTATO CHIPS

Homemade potato chips are so easy to make and so much better than bagged, especially when they're fried with garlic and fragrant herbs like rosemary and sage. It's hard to say what I like better: the crisp chips or the fried herbs, which, though they hardly look different when fried, will shatter in your mouth in the most pleasant way. Make these chips for friends, and you will be regarded as a hero. While I prefer my chips skin on—I think they look sexier that way—you can peel the potatoes, if you prefer.

MAKES 1 BIG BOWL OF CHIPS

2 large russet potatoes, skin on, well washed

Grapeseed or canola oil, for frying

¼ cup fresh sage leaves

¼ cup fresh rosemary leaves

¼ cup fresh flat-leaf parsley leaves

2 cloves garlic, sliced paper-thin

Kosher salt

Crushed red pepper

Fill a medium bowl with cold water. Using a mandoline, slice the potatoes into very thin (1/16-inch) rounds. As you slice, transfer the potatoes to the water and refrigerate for at least 2 hours and up to 24 hours.

Attach a candy/deep-fry thermometer to a deep, wide pot, and fill the pot about halfway with oil. Heat the oil to between 300°F and 325°F. Meanwhile, drain the potatoes and spread them out on paper towels to absorb excess water.

Line a rimmed baking sheet with dry paper towels. Carefully add a handful of the potatoes to the oil; the oil will bubble furiously. Fry, turning the potatoes occasionally, until the oil stops bubbling and the potatoes are golden brown, about 5 minutes. Add a portion of the sage, rosemary, and parsley and a portion of the garlic and fry for another 10 to 15 seconds. Using a wire skimmer or slotted spoon, transfer everything from the oil to the baking sheet. Immediately season with salt and a tiny pinch of crushed red pepper.

Repeat with the remaining potatoes, herbs, and garlic, kosher salt, and crushed red pepper. Let the chips cool to room temperature, then transfer to a large bowl and serve.

THE APERITIVO

An *aperitivo* is a pre-meal drink crafted to whet your appetite. Campari, that iconic Italian red spirit, on the rocks, is the most basic and classic *aperitivo*. And it's an ingredient in one of Scarpetta's signature cocktails, the San Remo, a stimulating blend of citrus, bitter, and bourbon. To make it, combine the following in a mixing glass: 2 ounces Carpano Antica, 1 ounce Campari, ¼ ounce St-Germain, ¼ ounce Maker's Mark, 1 ounce orange juice, and the juice from ½ lemon and ½ lime. Top the mixing glass with ice, shake, strain, and pour into a rocks glass. Garnish with an orange twist. Easy enough, but do as we do and pay attention to the details: Make sure to use fresh ice, not the stuff that's been in the freezer for years. And serve the drink in a good glass, one that feels balanced in your hand and holds the right amount of liquid. We serve the San Remo in an Schott Zwiesel Iceberg Double Old Fashioned glass, which has a straight side and a thick base that makes drinking out of it a pleasure. It's the little things.

GOUGÈRES WITH PARMIGIANO-REGGIANO

Gougères, savory little cheese puffs, may come from France, but I give my bite-size ones an Italian accent by flavoring them with Parmigiano-Reggiano and filling the profiterole-like ball with a basil purée. When we serve these at a party, we layer the serving tray with grated Parmigiano-Reggiano and grate even more of it over the gougères. It not only looks cool, but the texture of the grated cheese against the warm gougères is really great.

MAKES ABOUT 50 BITE-SIZE GOUGÈRES

1 cup whole milk

2 sticks (8 ounces) unsalted butter, cut into pieces

1 tablespoon granulated sugar

1 tablespoon kosher salt

2¼ cups all-purpose flour

6 large eggs

¼ cup finely freshly grated Parmigiano-Reggiano cheese, plus more for sprinkling

Basil Purée (page 12)

Heat a convection oven with the fan on low to 350°F (if the fan does not have low speed, don't use it) or heat a conventional oven to 375°F. Line two rimmed baking sheets with parchment.

In a large saucepan over medium-high heat, combine 1 cup water, the milk, butter, sugar, and salt. Cook, stirring, until the butter has melted and the mixture has just come to a boil. Immediately add the flour all at once while stirring constantly until a dough forms and pulls cleanly from the sides of the pot.

Transfer the dough to a stand mixer fitted with the paddle attachment. Mix on low speed until the dough is cool enough to combine with the eggs without cooking them, about 1 minute. Add 1 egg and mix on low speed until it's well blended and the dough is smooth again. Repeat with the rest of the eggs until all are incorporated. Add the Parmigiano-Reggiano and mix until incorporated.

Using a pastry bag with a plain tip, pipe the dough into cherry tomato–size mounds on the baking sheets about 1 inch apart. Alternatively, use a mini ice-cream scoop or 2 tablespoons to drop small mounds of dough onto the sheets. (The gougères can be frozen at this point. Freeze them on the baking sheet until rock-hard, then store airtight in a freezer bag. Before baking, space frozen gougères out on a parchment-lined baking sheet and thaw for 1 hour at room temperature before baking as directed.)

Bake the gougères, turning the sheets about halfway through, until light golden brown, about 15 minutes. Remove the pan from the oven and sprinkle the gougères with grated Parmigiano-Reggiano. Return to the oven to finish baking, about 5 minutes. Let the gougères cool slightly before filling them. (The gougères can be made 1 day ahead; let them cool completely before storing airtight.)

To serve, transfer the Basil Purée to a squeeze bottle and the gougères to a low oven to warm, if necessary. Using the tip of the squeeze bottle, poke a hole in the bottom of the warm gougères and fill completely with the purée. Place on a serving tray and garnish with additional grated Parmigiano-Reggiano.

VARIATIONS: *These flavorings—use 1½ cups of whichever you choose—may be added to the dough along with the Parmigiano-Reggiano. Serve these flavored gougères with or without the filling.*

SPECK: *Cut into julienne.*

PANCETTA: *Cut into cubes, cooked in oil until crisp, drained, and finely chopped.*

SPICY SAUSAGE: *Removed from casings, cooked, cooled, and crumbled.*

BASIL PURÉE

MAKES 1½ CUPS

I just love the way the bright green of this purée looks against the light-colored gougères on the previous page, but it's also delicious drizzled on pasta or grilled meats or added to a vinaigrette, especially one destined for a salad that includes ripe summer tomatoes. Blanching the basil before puréeing it softens the leaves, which makes them emulsify easier for a more supple result. Blanching also gives the sauce a brighter green color that will stay vibrant for a couple of days.

8 cups loosely packed fresh basil leaves

½ teaspoon kosher salt

¼ cup grapeseed or canola oil

¼ cup extra-virgin olive oil

Bring a large saucepan of water to a boil and have ready a bowl of ice water. Boil the basil, pressing on it gently to submerge it, for 1 minute. Immediately transfer it to the ice water and let cool completely.

Remove the basil from the water (reserve the ice water) and squeeze it to remove excess water. Wrap the basil in a clean kitchen towel and wring it out. (It's important to remove as much moisture as possible.) Coarsely chop the basil and transfer it to a blender. Add the salt, grapeseed oil, and olive oil and purée until completely smooth. Transfer the purée to a bowl, set it over the ice water (add ice to the water if needed), and stir until cold. Season to taste with additional salt. (The purée may be made 2 days ahead and kept covered and refrigerated. You can also freeze it for up to 2 months.)

CHICKEN LIVER AND FOIE GRAS PÂTÉ

This is our take on a traditional Tuscan chicken liver pâté. I love the touch of brine the capers add, and the depth of flavor from the anchovy, but it's the addition of a little foie gras that takes this humble pâté to new heights. It melts into the chicken liver, making for an ultrasmooth texture. It's simply the best pâté I have ever had, and it makes me very happy. Note that the foie gras needs to "cure" in the Vin Santo for at least 24 hours before being added to the pâté, and that the pâté itself will taste better, and have a better texture, after about 8 hours in the refrigerator, so plan accordingly.

SERVES 6 TO 10

⅓ cup Vin Santo

Kosher salt

9 ounces foie gras, cut into ½-inch cubes

3 tablespoons extra-virgin olive oil

2 cups thinly sliced red onion (about 2 medium onions)

¼ cup capers, well rinsed if salt packed

4 cloves garlic, thinly sliced

3 anchovy fillets, well rinsed and patted dry

1 sprig fresh sage

½ teaspoon crushed red pepper

1 pound chicken livers, trimmed, rinsed, and spread out on paper towel to dry

½ cup Chicken Stock (page 310)

½ cup puréed canned tomatoes

Combine the Vin Santo and 1½ teaspoons salt in a heavy-duty storage bag or bowl. Add the foie gras and turn to coat it with the liquid and salt. Refrigerate, turning the foie gras occasionally, for 24 hours.

Drain the foie gras over a bowl to collect the soaking liquid. Heat a medium saucepan over medium-high heat. Add the olive oil, onions, capers, garlic, anchovy, sage, crushed red pepper, and ½ teaspoon salt. Cook, stirring occasionally, until the onions are soft, 7 to 8 minutes. Add the chicken livers, Chicken Stock, and tomatoes and stir. Lower the heat to medium, cover, and cook for 10 minutes.

Remove the lid, increase the heat to medium-high, and bring the mixture a boil. Cook, stirring occasionally, for 2 minutes. Add the foie gras and immediately take the pan off the heat; the residual heat will melt the foie gras. Transfer to a blender, add the reserved soaking liquid, and purée until smooth. Taste and season with additional salt, if necessary. Transfer to a serving dish, cover, and refrigerate for 8 hours. Serve at room temperature.

HERBED POTATO CHIPS, PG. 8

GOUGÈRES, PG. 10

SPICED ALMONDS, PG. 2

WARM OLIVES, PG. 3

BALSAMIC GLAZED PORK RIBS, PG. 20

GRISSINI, PG. 36

CHICKEN LIVER AND FOIE GRAS PÂTÉ, PG. 13

OLIVES ASCOLANE, PG. 16

OLIVES ASCOLANE (SAUSAGE-STUFFED FRIED OLIVES)

I love serving something and watching people swoon. These breaded, tangy, meaty, cheesy, fried—fried!—olives do just that, making them totally worth the time and effort that goes into preparing them. I remember the first time I ever had one of these beauties. I was young and in Le Marche and we were hanging out at a friend-of-a-friend's apartment when suddenly, the guy who lived there pulled a few of these out of his freezer and just fried them up for us. They were crazy good.

MAKES 40 TO 50 DEPENDING ON THE SIZE OF THE OLIVES

FOR THE STUFFING

10 ounces ground veal

8 ounces sweet Italian sausage, casings removed

½ cup panko bread crumbs

½ cup finely freshly grated Parmigiano-Reggiano cheese

1½ tablespoons chopped fresh flat-leaf parsley

1½ teaspoons chopped fresh basil

½ large egg, beaten

2 cloves garlic, coarsely chopped

1 tablespoon fennel seeds, finely ground using a mortar and pestle

½ teaspoon kosher salt

¼ teaspoon crushed red pepper, plus more to taste

Freshly ground black pepper (about 15 grinds)

FOR THE OLIVES

4 cups large green olives, such as Cerignola or Castelvetrano, pitted, soaked for 5 minutes in water to remove excess briny flavor, and drained

Grapeseed or canola oil, for frying

3 cups panko bread crumbs, very finely ground in a food processor

1½ cups all-purpose flour

Kosher salt

4 large eggs

20 small fresh basil leaves

20 fresh flat-leaf parsley leaves

20 fresh sage leaves

FOR THE STUFFING: In a large bowl, gently combine all of the stuffing ingredients. Using a meat grinder or a food processor, grind the stuffing to make it finer, which makes stuffing the olives easier. If using a food processor, pulse the ingredients, being careful not to overprocess. (The stuffing may be made 1 day ahead and kept covered and refrigerated.)

FOR THE OLIVES: Fit a pastry bag with a tip small enough to fit into the pitted olive (or cut a small hole in the tip of the pastry bag). Fill the bag with the stuffing, then pipe each olive full of the stuffing.

Attach a candy/deep-fry thermometer to a large heavy-duty saucepan and fill the pan about halfway with oil. Heat the oil to 350°F.

Meanwhile, line a rimmed baking sheet with parchment paper. Put the panko on a plate or in a shallow dish. Put the flour on another plate or shallow dish and season with a little salt. In a medium bowl, whisk the eggs with $1/3$ cup water. Coat the olives in the flour, then the egg, then the panko, then back into the egg, and then back into the panko. (Only coat with flour one time.) Transfer the olives to the baking sheet as you bread them. (The olives may be made up to this point and frozen; when rock-hard, transfer to freezer bags. They can go right from the freezer into the hot oil, but they will take a little longer to cook.)

Line a rimmed baking sheet with paper towels. In batches of about 10, fry the olives until well browned, about 3 minutes (the time will vary depending on the size of your olives). Just before removing the olives from the oil, add a few leaves of each herb to the oil and fry briefly. Using a wire skimmer or slotted spoon, retrieve the olives and herbs from the oil and transfer them to the lined baking sheet. Let the olives cool a little before serving, but serve, with the herbs, while still hot.

MINI SCALLION AND SPINACH PANCAKES WITH STRACCIATELLA AND TROUT ROE

Flavored and colored with spinach and scallion, these tasty little pancakes make the perfect base for some creamy *stracciatella* and briny trout roe. The variety of textures and colors (green pancakes, white cheese, and bright orange roe) in this one small bite is amazing.

Kosher salt

3 medium Yukon gold potatoes

1 cup chopped scallions (dark green part only; about 2 bunches)

1 cup lightly packed baby spinach

⅔ cup whole milk

1 large egg, lightly beaten

1 teaspoon packed fresh yeast (see page 31)

⅓ cup plus 1 tablespoon all-purpose flour

Grapeseed or canola oil, for the griddle

⅔ cup stracciatella (see Note)

⅓ cup trout roe

Bring a medium saucepan of salted water to a boil. Add the potatoes, lower the heat to a simmer, and cook until the potatoes are easily pierced with a cake tester or thin metal skewer, 20 to 30 minutes. Drain the potatoes and, when cool enough to handle, pass them through a ricer. Reserve ½ cup of the riced potato for the pancakes and save the rest for another use.

Bring a small saucepan of salted water to a boil and have ready a bowl of ice water. Cook the scallions until tender yet still bright green, 4 minutes. During the last 30 seconds, add the spinach to wilt it. Drain the spinach and scallions and transfer to the ice water. Once cool, squeeze out the excess liquid well and transfer to a blender. Add the milk and 1 teaspoon salt and purée until smooth. Transfer to a medium bowl and, with a fork, stir in the egg and the yeast until well combined. Add the flour and the ½ cup riced potato and stir well. Cover the bowl and leave at room temperature for 1 hour.

Lightly coat a nonstick griddle with oil. In batches, drop the batter by the tablespoonful to make rounds about the size of a 50-cent piece. Let cook undisturbed until bubbles begin to form on one

side, about 1 minute. Flip and cook the other side. The pancakes should be mostly green, with a beautiful light gold crust. Repeat with the remaining batter.

Top each pancake with 1 teaspoon of the *stracciatella* and ½ teaspoon of the trout roe and serve immediately.

NOTE: Stracciatella, *while worth tracking down, is not so easy to find. However,* burrata *(see Note, page 97), which is becoming more readily available, makes a good substitute because* stracciatella *is actually the creamy mixture inside the ball of* burrata. *For best results, scoop/squeeze out the* stracciatella *(and save the outside of the ball— the mozzarella—for grating on your next pizza).*

BALSAMIC-GLAZED PORK RIBS

Because I love barbecued ribs so much, I wanted to have a version made in the Scarpetta spirit. So we created this recipe using many of my favorite Italian ingredients: lots of garlic, thyme, crushed red pepper, and, obviously, balsamic vinegar. To make the glaze, we begin with a large quantity of good-tasting but inexpensive vinegar and cook it until it's reduced to a thick, syrupy, intensely flavored sauce, which we slather on the ribs as one might barbecue sauce. You can serve the ribs on the bone or, if you are feeling fancy, you can pull out the bones (before glazing) and cut the meat into neat, easy-to-eat-squares, which is what we do for events. Do note that because

SERVES 10 TO 12

FOR THE BRINE AND RIBS

1 cup kosher salt

½ cup granulated sugar

10 cloves garlic

8 sprigs fresh thyme

4 dried bay leaves

1 tablespoon whole black peppercorns

4 to 5 pounds pork spareribs (about 1 rack), trimmed of fat, flap, and tough membrane

FOR THE MARINADE

1 cup extra-virgin olive oil

10 cloves garlic, thinly sliced

Leaves from 4 sprigs fresh rosemary

1½ teaspoons crushed red pepper

FOR THE GLAZE

4 cups balsamic vinegar

1 teaspoon extra-virgin olive oil

1 small onion, quartered

2 ounces thick-cut bacon (about 2 slices), cut into large dice

2 cups Chicken Reduction (page 315)

2 sprigs fresh thyme

Pinch of crushed red pepper

FOR SERVING

1 cup Spicy Tomato-Apricot Jam (page 22)

Chopped fresh chives (optional)

Flaked sea salt

FOR THE BRINE: In a large pot, combine 4 quarts water with the kosher salt, sugar, garlic, thyme, bay leaves, and peppercorns. Bring to a gentle boil over medium-high heat and cook, stirring occasionally, until the sugar is dissolved, about 8 minutes. Remove from the heat, let cool to room temperature, then refrigerate until cold. Cover the spareribs with the brine and refrigerate for 3 hours.

these ribs are brined as well as marinated to give them a deep flavor and an exceedingly tender texture, they need some hands-off brining and marinating time, so plan to start at least 1 day ahead of serving them.

FOR THE MARINADE: Remove the ribs from the brine, pat dry with paper towels, and put them on a rimmed baking sheet or dish. In a bowl, combine the olive oil, garlic, rosemary, and crushed red pepper. Pour the marinade over the ribs, and turn the ribs to coat them. Cover with plastic wrap and refrigerate for at least 4 hours and up to 24 hours.

FOR THE GLAZE: In a medium saucepan, bring the vinegar to a boil over medium-high heat and cook until reduced to about ¾ cup. In another medium saucepan, heat the olive oil over medium heat. Add the onion and bacon and cook, stirring, until the onion is tender, about 5 minutes. Add the vinegar, Chicken Reduction, thyme, and crushed red pepper. Bring to a boil and cook until thick with big bubbles forming on the surface, 15 to 20 minutes. Strain and reserve. (The glaze will keep for 1 week covered and refrigerated; warm to room temperature before using.)

TO SERVE: Heat a convection oven to 300°F or a conventional oven to 325°F. Wrap the ribs in aluminum foil, place on a baking sheet, and roast until very tender but not falling off the bone, 2½ to 3 hours. Remove the ribs from the oven, unwrap the foil, and wipe off as much of the rosemary and garlic as possible. (You can make the ribs ahead up to this point. Let cool to room temperature, then wrap in plastic wrap and refrigerate for up to 2 days. Reheat the ribs wrapped loosely in aluminum foil in a low oven until hot throughout.) Brush the ribs with the glaze and return to the oven on the baking sheet, unwrapped, periodically brushing with more glaze to get a nice shine.

Cut the racks into individual ribs and top each rib with a spoonful of spicy jam. Finish with a sprinkle of chives if you like and a tiny pinch of sea salt.

SPICY TOMATO-APRICOT JAM

MAKES ABOUT 4 CUPS

This makes more than you need for the ribs, but no worries: It's also delicious served with pork tenderloin or barbecued chicken, and it will keep for at least 1 week covered and refrigerated.

1 cup apricot preserves

½ cup red wine vinegar

2 tablespoons yellow mustard seeds

2 teaspoons crushed red pepper

8 plum tomatoes, peeled (see below), seeded, and diced

Kosher salt

In a medium saucepan, heat the preserves with 3 tablespoons of water and bring to a boil. Cook until the preserves are a deeper color, 3 to 4 minutes. Stir in the vinegar, mustard seeds, and crushed red pepper and cook for 3 minutes. Add the tomatoes and cook, stirring occasionally, until the tomatoes release their pectin, about 5 minutes. Season lightly with salt and reserve. (The preserves will keep, covered and refrigerated, for about 1 week. Allow to come to room temperature before serving.)

HOW TO PEEL A TOMATO

We almost always peel tomatoes. It may seem fussy, but I really don't like those bits of skin in a sauce or on the plate. To peel tomatoes, use a paring knife to cut a small x on the tomato. Bring a saucepan of water to a boil, and have ready a bowl of ice water. Boil the tomatoes for about 10 seconds, then plunge them into the ice bath. The shock of going from hot to cold should cause the skin to contract, making it easier to peel. Use your fingers or a small paring knife to pull the skin off. If the skin is stubborn, try boiling and shocking the tomato again.

MUSHROOM ARANCINI

Arancini are little balls of rice, usually made with leftover risotto, that are breaded and fried. Our version begins with a deeply flavored mushroom risotto made specifically for the *arancini*.

FOR THE RISOTTO

¼ cup dried porcini mushrooms

4 cups Chicken Stock (page 310)

¼ cup plus 1 tablespoon extra-virgin olive oil

2 cloves garlic, very finely chopped

1 shallot, very finely chopped

Kosher salt

1 cup finely chopped button mushrooms

1 cup finely chopped shiitake mushrooms

1 cup Vialone Nano rice (see Note, page 183)

¼ cup dry white wine

2 cups freshly grated Parmigiano-Reggiano cheese

3 tablespoons (1½ ounces) unsalted butter

1½ teaspoons chopped fresh thyme

FOR SERVING

Grapeseed or canola oil, for frying

2 cups panko bread crumbs, very finely ground in a spice grinder or food processor

1½ cups all-purpose flour

Kosher salt

3 large eggs

FOR THE RISOTTO: Soak the porcini in 1 cup hot water until softened, about 20 minutes. Lift the mushrooms out of the liquid and reserve the soaking liquid. Gently squeeze the mushrooms to remove excess liquid. Chop the porcinis finely and reserve.

In a medium saucepan over medium-low heat, combine the chicken broth and the reserved porcini liquid.

In a large saucepan, heat ¼ cup olive oil over medium heat. Add the garlic and shallot, season lightly with salt, and cook, stirring occasionally, until tender, 2 to 3 minutes. Add the button mushrooms, shiitakes, porcinis, and 1 tablespoon olive oil and cook, stirring occasionally, until the mushrooms have released all their liquid and the pan is almost dry, about 9 minutes.

Add the rice and stir to coat. Add 2 teaspoons salt and cook, stirring, to toast the rice lightly, 2 to 3 minutes. Add the wine and cook, stirring, until most of the wine is gone. Add 1 cup of the warm stock and cook, stirring, until the liquid is absorbed. Add another cup and increase the heat until there is a fair amount of bubbles on the surface (the agitation helps release the starch). Continue to cook, stirring and adding more stock as needed, until the rice is creamy but al dente and flows when poured from a large spoon, about 18 minutes.

Take the risotto off the heat and stir in the Parmigiano-Reggiano, butter, and thyme. Taste—the rice needs to be well seasoned—and add additional salt if necessary. Spread the risotto out on a rimmed baking sheet to cool quickly. (The risotto may be made 1 day ahead. When completely cooled, cover with plastic wrap and refrigerate.)

TO SERVE: Attach a candy/deep-fry thermometer to a large, heavy-duty saucepan, add enough oil to come halfway up the sides of the pan, and heat the oil to 350°F.

Meanwhile, put the panko on a plate or shallow dish. Put the flour on another plate or shallow dish and season with salt. In a medium bowl, whisk the eggs with 1/3 cup water.

Using your hands, roll the cooled risotto into balls about the size of a large marble.

Coat the balls in the flour, then the egg, and then the panko, and transfer to a rimmed baking sheet as you bread them. (The *arancini* may be made up to this point and frozen on the baking sheet; when rock-hard, transfer to freezer bags. They can go right from the freezer into the hot oil, but will take a little longer to cook.)

In batches of about 10, fry the rice balls until golden brown, 3 to 4 minutes. Using a slotted spoon, retrieve them from the oil and let drain briefly on paper towels. Season lightly with kosher salt and serve immediately.

ROASTED POTATOES WITH FONDUTA

I'm always a little surprised by how much people love these. It seems like such a small thing, a tiny roasted potato topped with a creamy cheese. It's true comfort food made elegant but not fussy. To keep the potatoes from rolling or toppling over when serving, fill a tray with rock salt; the uneven surface will support the rounded potatoes. The potatoes are also just wonderful filled with whisked crème fraîche and topped with a generous amount of caviar. I love that.

FOR THE POTATOES

1 pound baby potatoes

2 tablespoons extra-virgin olive oil, plus more if needed

5 sprigs fresh thyme

5 sprigs fresh rosemary

5 sprigs fresh oregano

3 cloves garlic, crushed

Kosher salt

FOR SERVING

1 cup heavy cream

1 cup freshly grated Fontina cheese

Extra-virgin olive oil

Finely chopped fresh chives or grated fresh truffles

Flaked sea salt

FOR THE POTATOES: Heat a convection oven to 350°F or a conventional oven to 375°F. On a rimmed baking sheet, toss the potatoes with the olive oil, herb sprigs, and garlic, and season lightly with kosher salt. Roast until the potatoes are tender, about 25 minutes.

Let the potatoes cool. Cut a tiny bit off the top and bottom of each potato to make a more stable base, then cut the potatoes in half. Using a small melon baller, scoop out the center of each potato half. Spread out the potatoes on a rimmed baking sheet, scooped-out side up, and reserve. (The potatoes can be roasted and scooped earlier in the day; cover and refrigerate if not using them within a couple of hours.)

TO SERVE: Heat a convection oven to 350°F or a conventional oven to 375°F. In a small saucepan, heat the cream over medium-high heat until reduced by half, about 5 minutes. Lower the heat to low, and whisk the Fontina, a little at a time, into the cream. Keep the fonduta warm, preferably over a pot of simmering water, to avoid overheating.

Drizzle a little olive oil over the potatoes and reheat in the oven if not warm. Spoon some of the warm fonduta into each potato. Sprinkle each with some chives and finish with a tiny pinch of sea salt.

PANE & CONDIMENTI

BREAD

When we opened Scarpetta, its name meaning what it does (see page X), we knew that serving excellent bread was going to be vital. People expect bread when they go to a fine restaurant, but we were going to take that experience to the next level and only make and serve the very best. We have been getting accolades for our bread service ever since. The basket itself contains a variety of breads and is served with a trio of house-made condiments, including an eggplant caponata (see page 42), a citrus- and herb-infused olive oil (see page 43), and butter whipped with mascarpone (see page 41). As soon as our customers see that bread basket, they get a sense that they will be well taken care of. Yes, they are paying for their meal, but an abundant and well-crafted bread basket demonstrates an inherent generosity on our side.

Though we buy some of the bread, we make most of it, including our stromboli, which has become a phenomenon in and of itself. The bread basket, especially the meat-filled stromboli, is expensive for us to produce. In fact, I only planned to include the stromboli during Scarpetta's early days and then switch it out. But people loved it so much that we just couldn't replace it. Would it have been more practical to do so? Yes. But the decision to keep it reflects our overriding desire to please. The goodwill it generates (as well as the good press) does help justify what it costs us to produce.

If you ever bake bread for family and friends, you know how much it's appreciated. The bread recipes that follow are not difficult and would make a big impact the next time you entertain. But even if you don't bake your own bread (and there is increasingly more and more great bread to buy at the market), consider making the condiments to offer along with whatever bread you serve. Two of them, the Citrus-Herb Oil and the Mascarpone Butter, take just minutes to make yet can transform the whole bread-basket experience.

FOCACCIA

This dimpled bread, topped with olive oil, rosemary, and sea salt, is a staff—as well as a customer—favorite. When it comes out of the oven, all fresh and warm and filling the air with its fragrance, it's almost impossible for us to resist.

MAKES 1 LARGE LOAF

FOR THE STARTER

2 cups (8 ounces) all-purpose flour

¼ ounce fresh (cake) yeast (see Note, page 31)

FOR THE FOCACCIA

Extra-virgin olive oil

1 tablespoon unsulfured molasses

1 tablespoon granulated sugar

½ ounce fresh (cake) yeast (see Note, page 31)

2½ cups (10 ounces) all-purpose flour

2½ cups (10 ounces) bread flour

1 cup (4 ounces) whole-wheat flour

1 tablespoon plus 1½ teaspoons kosher salt

1 tablespoon finely chopped fresh rosemary plus 1 tablespoon coarsely chopped

1½ teaspoons flaked sea salt

FOR THE STARTER: Combine the flour, yeast, and ¾ cup water in a medium bowl. Leave at room temperature until doubled in size, 2 to 3 hours, then cover and refrigerate. Use within 2 days.

FOR THE FOCACCIA: In a stand mixer fitted with the dough hook, combine 1 tablespoon olive oil, the molasses, sugar, and yeast. Mix on low speed until well combined. Add 1½ cups water; the all-purpose, bread, and wheat flours; and 4 ounces by weight of the starter. Mix on low speed for 5 minutes, then increase the speed slightly and mix for another 5 minutes. Add the kosher salt and finely chopped rosemary, and mix until well combined, then mix in 1 tablespoon olive oil.

Oil a large (13 x 18-inch) rimmed baking sheet. Transfer the dough to the baking sheet, drizzle a little oil on top, cover the baking sheet with plastic wrap, and leave at room temperature until doubled in size, about 1 hour. Drizzle the dough with oil and flip it over on the baking sheet. Punch the dough down with your fingers and stretch it to fit the baking sheet. Dimple the dough all over with your fingertips. Cover with plastic wrap and let rise until doubled in size again, about 1 hour.

Meanwhile, heat a convection oven to 375°F or a conventional oven to 400°F.

Sprinkle the coarsely chopped rosemary and the sea salt over the dough and bake for 8 minutes. Rotate the baking sheet and bake until golden brown on top and bottom, about another 8 minutes. Transfer to a cooling rack and brush with additional oil.

CIABATTINI

There's almost nothing better than these square little ciabatta rolls served warm, especially if they're paired with some Mascarpone Butter (page 41).

FOR THE POOLISH

⅛ teaspoon fresh (cake) yeast (see Note, page 31)

2¼ cups (9 ounces) bread flour

FOR THE CIABATTINI

1 teaspoon fresh (cake) yeast (see Note, page 31)

2 cups (8 ounces) bread flour

¼ teaspoon unsulfured molasses

1 tablespoon plus 1 teaspoon kosher salt

FOR THE POOLISH: In a large bowl or container, mix the yeast with 1½ cups water. Add the flour and mix by hand to get rid of any lumps. Cover with plastic wrap and refrigerate for at least 8 hours; use within 48 hours.

FOR THE CIABATTINI: In a stand mixer fitted with the dough hook, mix together the yeast and ½ cup water. Add the flour, molasses, and the poolish, and mix on medium-low speed for 10 minutes. Cover with plastic wrap and let rest for 20 minutes. Sprinkle the salt on top and mix on medium-low speed for 5 minutes.

Oil a rimmed baking sheet and flatten the dough onto the pan. Cover with plastic wrap and let rest for 15 minutes. Fold the dough in thirds, like a letter. Cover and let rest for another 15 minutes, then fold in thirds again.

Meanwhile, lightly flour a clean work surface and line a rimmed baking sheet with parchment paper. Transfer the dough to the floured surface and pat it down to make a 1-inch-thick square measuring about 9 x 9 inches. Using a bench scraper, cut the dough into 5 even rows across and 5 even rows down to make 25 squares, each about 1¾ inches. Transfer to the prepared baking sheet, spacing them evenly, and let sit at room temperature for 10 to 15 minutes.

Meanwhile, heat a convection oven, preferably with the fan on high, to 350°F or heat a conventional oven to 375°F. Bake the ciabattini until light golden, rotating the pan about halfway through baking, about 18 minutes. Transfer to a cooling rack. For best flavor, reheat in a warm oven before serving.

FRESH YEAST

Our bread bakers tend to bake with fresh yeast (also called compressed yeast or cake yeast) rather than instant yeast. Fresh yeast is sold refrigerated in foil-wrapped blocks or cubes. Not all supermarkets carry it, but a well-stocked specialty food store should have it. Fresh yeast has a short shelf life, which is not a problem in a professional kitchen. You can experiment with substituting active dry yeast for fresh, but use half the amount called for; that is, for every ounce of fresh yeast, use ½ ounce of active dry. To substitute instant dry yeast for fresh, use about 40 percent as much instant as fresh.

POTATO AND CARAMELIZED SHALLOT FOCACCIA

While we do serve this bread in our bread basket, its hearty topping—thinly sliced potato coated with melted butter and herbs and sweet, beautifully browned shallots—also makes it a satisfying bite as an hors d'oeuvre. For events, we'll cut the focaccia into small squares and top each piece with a dollop of crème fraîche and generous spoonful of caviar.

MAKES 1 LARGE LOAF

FOR THE STARTER

1 teaspoon fresh (cake) yeast (see Note, page 31)

1½ cups (7 ounces) all-purpose flour

FOR THE FOCACCIA

Extra-virgin olive oil

1½ teaspoons unsulfured molasses

1 tablespoon fresh (cake) yeast (see Note, page 31)

1 teaspoon granulated sugar

1 cup plus 3 tablespoons (4¾ ounces) all-purpose flour

1 cup plus 3 tablespoons (4¾ ounces) bread flour

½ cup (2 ounces) whole-wheat flour

1 tablespoon kosher salt

FOR THE TOPPING

8 tablespoons (4 ounces) unsalted butter

6 cloves garlic

6 sprigs fresh thyme

4 sprigs fresh rosemary, plus 1 tablespoon coarsely chopped

Crushed red pepper

Kosher salt

4 cups paper-thin slices small potatoes, preferably a mix of colors

2 tablespoons extra-virgin olive oil

5 shallots, halved and thinly sliced lengthwise

1 teaspoon flaked sea salt

FOR THE STARTER: In a large bowl or container, mix the yeast with ¾ cup water, then add the flour and mix by hand until smooth. Cover with plastic wrap and let sit at room temperature for 2 to 3 hours. Refrigerate for longer storage (the starter will keep for 2 days refrigerated).

FOR THE FOCACCIA: In a stand mixer fitted with the dough hook, combine 1½ teaspoons olive oil, the molasses, yeast, and sugar on low speed for 5 minutes. Add ¾ cup water; the all-purpose, bread, and wheat flours; and 2 ounces of the starter. Mix on

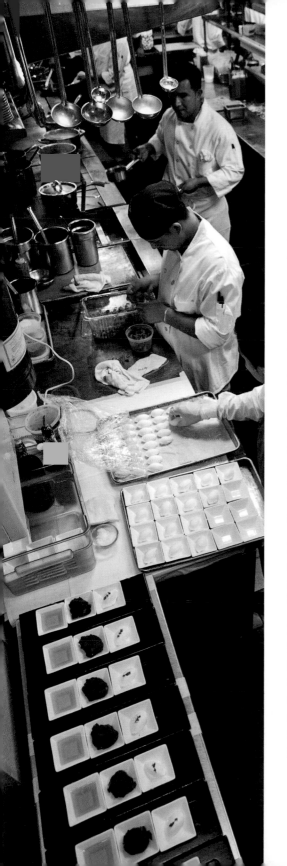

low speed for 5 minutes, then increase the speed for a few minutes, until well kneaded. Add the kosher salt and 1½ teaspoons olive oil and mix to combine.

Oil a large (13 x 18-inch) rimmed baking sheet. Transfer the dough to the baking sheet, drizzle a little oil on top, cover the baking sheet with plastic wrap, and leave at room temperature until doubled in size, about 1 hour. Drizzle the dough with oil and flip it over. Punch down the dough with your fingers and stretch it to fit the baking sheet. Dimple the dough all over with your fingers, then cover with plastic wrap and let rise until doubled in size again, about 1 hour.

FOR THE TOPPING: In a medium saucepan over low heat, melt the butter. Add the garlic, thyme, rosemary sprigs, and a pinch of crushed red pepper. Increase the heat to medium and cook, stirring occasionally, until the butter just starts to bubble. Remove from the heat and let sit for 5 minutes. Strain into a large saucepan and season with 1 teaspoon kosher salt. Add the potatoes, toss to coat, and heat over medium heat until the potatoes are warm. Take the pan off the heat and let sit until the potatoes are pliable but not cooked through, about 10 minutes.

Heat the olive oil in a sauté pan over medium-low heat. Add the shallots, season lightly with kosher salt and a pinch of crushed red pepper, and cook, stirring occasionally, until the shallots have browned, about 15 minutes.

Heat a convection oven to 375°F or a conventional oven to 400°F. Sprinkle half of the chopped rosemary over the proofed focaccia. Spread the caramelized shallots over, then top with the potatoes (use all of them; they should not be in a single layer). Sprinkle with the remaining chopped rosemary, a pinch of crushed red pepper, and the sea salt. Bake for 10 minutes, rotate the baking sheet in the oven, and bake until golden brown on the bottom, another 10 minutes. Serve warm or at room temperature.

CAPONATA, PG. 42

FOCACCIA, PG. 28

MASCARPONE BUTTER, PG. 41

CIABATTINI, PG. 30

CITRUS-HERB OIL, PG. 43

STROMBOLI, PG. 39

GRISSINI WITH HERBS AND PARMIGIANO-REGGIANO

Crispy, cheesy, and full of fresh herb flavor, these skinny, rustic-looking breadsticks are a hit at events. We usually stand them up in a vase for serving. The recipe makes a lot, but it's easy to eat a bunch of these, so they will likely all go if you are having a party. The breadsticks will keep for about a week stored airtight.

MAKES ABOUT 150 BREADSTICKS

½ ounce fresh (cake) yeast (see Note, page 31)

2 tablespoons extra-virgin olive oil

2 tablespoons whole milk

1 tablespoon unsulfured molasses

3 large eggs

5½ cups (22 ounces) bread flour

1 cup finely freshly grated Parmigiano-Reggiano cheese, plus more for sprinkling

2 tablespoons finely chopped fresh chives

1½ tablespoons kosher salt

1 tablespoon finely chopped fresh flat-leaf parsley

1 tablespoon finely chopped fresh thyme

½ tablespoon finely chopped fresh rosemary

⅛ teaspoon sweet paprika

Semolina flour, for dusting

In a stand mixer fitted with the dough hook, stir the yeast with 1¼ cups warm water and let sit until bubbly, about 5 minutes. Add the olive oil, milk, molasses, and 1 of the eggs, and mix well. Add half the flour and mix for 8 minutes, making sure there are no lumps. Add the remaining flour, the Parmigiano-Reggiano, chives, salt, parsley, thyme, rosemary, and paprika and mix/knead for 10 minutes.

Refrigerate the dough in the bowl until doubled in size, about 1 hour.

Heat a convection oven to 300°F or a regular oven to 325°F. Line two rimmed baking sheets with parchment paper. Sprinkle semolina flour on your work surface. In a small bowl, beat the remaining 2 eggs well.

Remove the dough from the bowl and fold it over to get rid of the large air pockets. Divide the dough in half and, working with one piece and using a pasta rolling machine, roll the dough from thickest to thinnest setting until the dough is $1/16$ inch thick (the last or second-to-last setting on the machine). Cut the dough into 10-inch lengths. By hand or using the linguine attachment, cut the dough into thin ($1/16$-inch) strands and dust them with semolina flour to keep them separate. Repeat with the remaining piece of dough.

Transfer the strands to a baking sheet, leaving about $1/2$ inch between each. With a small pastry brush, brush the strands with the beaten eggs, then sprinkle lightly with additional Parmigiano-Reggiano. (You may need to bake the breadsticks in batches.)

Bake until golden brown, 12 to 15 minutes. Let cool completely, then store airtight. They will keep for 1 week.

LET YOUR DOUGH RISE IN A "LEXAN"

In the Scarpetta kitchen, we put bread dough in a clear, square plastic container to rise. (You may hear chefs refer to this as a "Lexan," which is actually just a reference to the plastic it's made with.) It's handy because you can see exactly how much your bread has risen. Look for these containers at professional kitchen supply shops and online.

STROMBOLI

I grew up eating stromboli. Slices of the stuffed and rolled bread made an appearance at every family gathering. So when we opened Scarpetta, I thought it would be fun to include some slices of it in the bread basket. But not your typical, heavy, overstuffed pepperoni-filled roll. Our stromboli starts with a light and supple home-made dough that gets rolled around imported paper-thin salami and grated smoked mozzarella. Fresh basil and rosemary, strewn over the dough, add their beguiling fragrance, which helps counter the richness. We slice the loaf thinly and then warm the slices before serving. It's good stuff.

MAKES 1 LARGE LOAF

1 tablespoon active dry yeast

Extra-virgin olive oil

5 cups (20 ounces) bread flour

Kosher salt and freshly ground black pepper

8 ounces smoked mozzarella cheese, shredded (2 cups)

2 ounces fresh mozzarella cheese, shredded (½ cup)

1 clove garlic, finely chopped

4 ounces thinly sliced salami (we use sweet salami at the restaurant, but hot is good, too)

½ cup coarsely chopped fresh basil

4 cherry tomatoes, halved

2 teaspoons coarsely chopped fresh rosemary

Flaked sea salt

In a stand mixer fitted with the dough hook, combine the yeast and 1 tablespoon olive oil with 1⅓ cups cool water using the lowest speed. Add the flour and mix on the lowest speed to combine the ingredients well and begin kneading, about 6 minutes. Increase the speed to level 2 and continue to knead for about 4 minutes. Add 1 tablespoon kosher salt and continue to knead for another 2 minutes.

Oil a bowl or other container large enough to hold the dough. Transfer the dough to the bowl, cover with plastic wrap, and let rise until doubled in size, about 1 hour.

Oil a clean work surface and oil your hands. Transfer the dough to the work surface and pat it into a rectangle ⅛ inch to ¼ inch thick. Sprinkle the smoked and fresh mozzarella over the dough, leaving just a little space around all edges. Season the dough lightly with kosher salt and black pepper and sprinkle the garlic over it. Lay the sliced salami over the cheese, overlapping slightly, to cover the entire area. (You may not need it all.) Sprinkle the basil over the salami.

To roll the dough, begin by folding over a small lip of dough along one long side. Then using both hands, fold the dough over twice, until there is just another small lip of dough left unrolled. Seal the sides of the roll by pulling some of the dough from the top and bottom of one rolled edge and pressing them together with the heel of your hand. Do the same to the other side. Now take the little lip of dough on the bottom and stretch it up and over the roll as far as it will go. Finally, stretch both sealed sides up onto the roll.

Line a rimmed baking sheet with parchment paper, or oil it. Gently lift the stromboli and place it seam side down on the baking sheet. Rub some olive oil on top and let it rest for 20 minutes.

Meanwhile, heat a convection oven to 400°F or a conventional oven to 425°F.

Press the tomatoes into the top of the dough, spacing them evenly. Sprinkle the dough with the rosemary and a little bit of sea salt and bake for 15 minutes. Rotate the stromboli and bake until golden brown, another 15 to 20 minutes. Let cool a bit before slicing. If you have made the bread well ahead of serving, reheat slices in a 375°F oven for a few minutes before serving.

MASCARPONE BUTTER

It's funny how something so simple can resonate with so many people. This butter is an example of that.

2 sticks (8 ounces) good-quality unsalted butter

⅓ cup (3 ounces) mascarpone cheese

Flaked sea salt

Small thyme sprig or pinch of fresh thyme leaves

Let the butter and mascarpone warm to room temperature. In a stand mixer fitted with the paddle attachment, combine the butter and cheese on medium speed until light and fluffy, about 5 minutes. At this point you can pack the butter into serving vessels, such as small ramekins, then cover with plastic wrap and refrigerate. Alternatively, refrigerate all of it in one storage container then use warm spoons to shape quenelles (see page 79). Allow to soften a bit at room temperature before serving. Top the butter with a few flakes of salt and the thyme just before serving.

CAPONATA

Serving this refined version of caponata along with bread makes us a lot of friends. People just love the stuff, and the kitchen often gets requests for some jarred to go.

MAKES ABOUT 2½ CUPS

Extra-virgin olive oil

1 medium onion, cut into small dice

1 anchovy fillet, rinsed well, patted dry, and chopped (optional)

Pinch of crushed red pepper

1 tablespoon capers, chopped, plus 1 tablespoon caper brine

2 (28-ounce) cans puréed San Marzano tomatoes

1 large Italian (globe) eggplant (about 1 pound)

Kosher salt

1 tablespoon chopped fresh basil

1½ teaspoons chopped fresh flat-leaf parsley

Heat 2 tablespoons olive oil in a medium, wide, shallow pot (called a rondeau) or Dutch oven over medium heat. Add the onions and cook, stirring occasionally, until they just begin to color, then add the anchovy, if using, and the crushed red pepper. Cook, stirring and adjusting the heat as needed, until the onions are soft and sweet, about 5 minutes. Add the capers, caper brine, and tomatoes. Bring to just under a boil, then lower the heat to a simmer and cook until thick, about 1½ hours.

Meanwhile, peel most of the eggplant (a little skin is okay) and cut it into ½-inch dice. Put the eggplant in a colander, generously season with salt, and allow the eggplant to drain for 1½ hours. (Put the colander on a rimmed baking sheet or in a clean sink to catch the liquid.) Rinse the eggplant, squeeze out excess water, and lay it on paper towels to dry.

Heat about 2 inches of olive oil in a large saucepan over medium-high heat. In batches, fry the eggplant, turning it occasionally, until tender and browned, 3 to 5 minutes. Drain briefly on paper towels, then add to the tomato sauce and toss to coat. Stir in the basil and the parsley and season to taste with salt. Let cool to room temperature before serving. (The caponata will keep for 3 days, covered in plastic wrap and refrigerated. Allow it to come to room temperature before serving.)

CITRUS-HERB OIL

Putting oil in a bowl on the table for people to dip their bread into is not such a big deal anymore. Tons of restaurants do it. So I wanted to take that notion a step further, which is how I came up with this citrus-infused oil. Steeped with aromatic zest and fresh herbs, it's easy to prepare, yet it makes a big impact.

MAKES ABOUT 2 CUPS

1 orange

1 lemon

1 lime

1 cup grapeseed or canola oil

1 cup extra-virgin olive oil

2 sprigs fresh rosemary

2 sprigs fresh thyme

1 clove garlic

Pinch of crushed red pepper

Using a vegetable peeler, peel off 2 wide strips of zest from the orange, the lemon, and the lime, avoiding the white pith. (Reserve the fruit for another use.) In a small saucepan, combine the grapeseed oil and olive oil with the zest, rosemary, thyme, garlic, and crushed red pepper. Heat over low heat until warm, about 10 minutes. Take off the heat, cover, and let steep until cooled to room temperature, about 20 minutes. Strain into a storage container, cover, and refrigerate for up to 2 weeks.

ANTIPASTI, INSALATE, ZUPPE

———

TO BEGIN

THERE ARE A FEW DIFFERENT OCCASIONS in the course of a diner's experience with our restaurant when we get to make an impression. The very first may come when a call is made for a reservation. Next is clearly when the customer walks into the restaurant for the first time. The waiter will certainly make an impression, as will the bread basket we send out to the table. And this is all a very important part of the overall experience. But the first real impression of the meal, of the food, of the level of the skill in the kitchen, comes with the appetizer. This is such an important opportunity, which is why these plates are thoughtfully composed so that they deliver to as many senses as possible in a way that feels seamless. Since we initially feast with our eyes, the plate has to look appealing. There should be an aroma that entices. And that first bite must pop with flavor.

All of the recipes in this chapter are offered as first courses. However, if I were to do a tasting menu, I would serve *crudo* first. These bites of raw fish are just so colorful and exciting and fresh—they're the perfect way to start a meal. That might be followed by a warm starter, then a salad, and then a soup. I don't expect anyone to do all that at home, but you can certainly present friends with a *crudo* plate and then a warm appetizer, like the Mushroom Fricassee (page 74), or a salad or a soup, which are also included in this chapter, before the main course.

One of my favorite things to overhear when I am on the floor of the restaurant is a group of people who, sharing bites of their appetizers, can't decide which of the plates before them is best. While the dishes may vary tremendously, from a soulful braised short rib and farro risotto starter (see page 81) to a cold pea soup topped with smoked trout and trout roe (see page 109), they are all put together with the same goal of hitting your palate with a variety of flavors that come together in a harmonious whole. As important are the varied textures on each plate, which add to the excitement. Enjoy.

ANTIPASTI

Literally translated, antipasto means "before the pasta." In a formal Italian meal, the antipasto course is the first course, and is served only after everyone is seated at the table. These are some of my favorite dishes, each bite bursting with flavors that wake up the palate and stimulate the appetite. Most are seafood, such as bright bites of *crudo,* perfectly seared scallops, and tender octopus. I like to start with seafood because it feels fresh and light and doesn't overwhelm in its heft. If I do serve something rich, such as the braised short ribs on page 81 or the mushrooms with creamy polenta on page 74, it's in a tantalizing amount, enough for people to fully appreciate their rich, deep flavors but not so much that it leaves them feeling satiated. After all, there are more courses left to savor.

TUNA SUSCI

This stunning dish began as a tuna carpaccio featuring the same flavors. It evolved into a roll when I was trying to figure out how I could serve tuna carpaccio at an event in bite-size pieces. I think the tuna roll actually delivers a better bite. People never want to share this appetizer, and I don't blame them. The trick to making it taste as good as it looks is to use best-quality ingredients and to take the utmost care with each step. If you happen to have a fresh truffle, you can make this dish even more amazing with a flourish of truffle shaved over the roll just before serving.

SERVES 4

Extra-virgin olive oil

4 ounces (about 2 cups) white hon-shimeji mushrooms (see page 48), cleaned and trimmed, or shiitake mushrooms, stemmed, cleaned, and cut into thin slices

Kosher salt

3 tablespoons red wine vinegar

2 or 3 carrots

2 sprigs fresh thyme

1½ teaspoons finely minced preserved truffles, plus a little of the oil from the jar

10 ounces best-quality tuna (see Note), cut into 4 equal portions, ideally in a rectangle shape

3 tablespoons very finely chopped fresh chives

Flaked sea salt

4 ounces (4 small handfuls) microgreens

Heat 2 teaspoons olive oil in a small sauté pan over medium-low heat. Add the hon-shimeji, season lightly with kosher salt, and cook, stirring, until the mushrooms are soft but not colored, about 5 minutes. Add the vinegar and cook, stirring, for another 30 seconds. Transfer the mushrooms and any liquid to a small bowl.

Peel a carrot and cut it into the tiniest cubes you can muster. Take your time here and make nice cuts, as the dice of the carrots will affect the texture of the whole roll. Continue cutting until you have 1 cup.

Heat 2 teaspoons olive oil in a small sauté pan over medium-low heat. Add the carrots and thyme and season lightly with kosher salt. Cook, stirring occasionally, until tender but not colored. Transfer to a bowl, let cool a bit, then stir in the preserved truffles. Taste and season with additional kosher salt if necessary.

Lay a 10-inch piece of plastic wrap down on your work surface. Position a piece of the tuna near the center and place another piece of plastic wrap over the tuna. With a meat mallet, gently pound the tuna until it is ⅛ inch thick, being careful not to rip the flesh. (I tell my staff, "No windows.") Strive for a rectangle shape similar to the nori used in Japanese sushi. Remove the top layer of plastic wrap.

With your fingers, evenly spread a light coating of olive oil over the tuna. Sprinkle about 2 teaspoons of the chives over the top half of the tuna, leaving room at the top, and sprinkle with a little sea salt. Spread about one-quarter of the carrots and preserved truffles over all of the tuna, leaving a little room at the edges. Spread a tiny handful of the microgreens over the carrots.

Using the plastic wrap to help lift the tuna, roll it into a sushi-like spiral. Make sure to pull back on the tuna in the plastic wrap, using all your fingers to form a tight, but not too tight, spiral. Remove the plastic wrap and put the roll on a cutting board. Repeat the process with the remaining pieces of tuna. (The rolls can be assembled a few hours ahead and refrigerated. Let them warm slightly at room temperature before serving so the chill can fade and the flavors can emerge.)

HON-SHIMEJI MUSHROOMS

Also known as beech mushrooms and white beech mushrooms, these tiny mushrooms are usually sold in tight clusters, and to use them, you cut them off at their common base. That's about all the preparation they need, however, since they lack the dust and dirt you find on many mushrooms. When raw, hon-shimeji mushrooms can have a somewhat bitter flavor, which is why I always cook them. Even after cooking, they stay pleasantly firm. Look for them at Asian food markets (they were originally cultivated in Japan) and gourmet food markets. If you can't find them, you can substitute thinly sliced shiitake mushrooms. They won't have the same flavor or add the same whimsy, but they will contribute the umami flavor that mushrooms bring to the party.

which wine? This appetizer demands a wine with refreshing acidity and minerality, medium body, and not too much fruit, so perhaps a Vermentino blend like Angelo Gaja Ca' Marcanda Vistamare, from Tuscany.

Drizzle a little olive oil over the rolls and sprinkle each with another pinch of chives and a bit of sea salt. With a very sharp knife and a sawing motion, trim the raggedy ends off the rolls. (Consider these bites your treat.) Cut each roll into 4 or 5 equal pieces. Use the tip of the knife to transfer the pieces to small serving plates. Place a few hon-shimeji on the plate between the pieces (at the restaurant, we use tweezers to do this). Drizzle a little olive oil over all, and serve immediately.

NOTE: *Be sure to buy what would be considered sashimi-grade tuna, and let your fishmonger know that you will be serving the tuna raw.*

TUNA AND AVOCADO

This dish is so simple, but when it's done 100 percent right, it just sings. What that means is the tuna must be pristine and the avocado must be at that perfect point of ripeness, when it gives a little and has a creamy texture but is still fully green and able to be diced without mashing under the knife. If you don't have an avocado at its peak, don't consider making this.

which wine? For a refreshingly different pairing, try a Gewürztraminer from Friuli. Its tropical core of chalky minerality, woven into a medium-bodied frame with persistent spices, lime, and rose petals, brings harmony to the incredible purity of the fish.

SERVES 4

8 ounces best-quality tuna (see Note)

1 lemon

½ cup extra-virgin olive oil, plus more for drizzling

Flaked sea salt

1 ripe Hass avocado, pitted, peeled, and diced

1 tablespoon finely chopped fresh chives

Microgreens

Chill serving plates.

Cut the tuna into medium dice and put it in a medium bowl. Using a rasp-style grater, finely zest half of the lemon, letting the zest fall into the bowl. Add the olive oil and a pinch of salt, and gently toss with the tuna. Fill a slightly larger bowl with ice and place the bowl of tuna in it for 1 to 2 minutes to chill it.

Very gently toss the avocado and the chives with the tuna. Divide among serving plates; drizzle with a little extra-virgin olive oil and top with a few microgreens. Serve immediately.

NOTE: *Be sure to buy what would be considered sashimi-grade tuna, and let your fishmonger know that you will be serving the tuna raw.*

YELLOWTAIL CRUDO WITH CHILE AND GINGER OILS

This is my favorite *crudo*. Its looks are so deceiving; it's just a few slices of fish on a plate. But the way the two different infused oils conspire along with a pinch of pickled minced onion and a few flakes of sea salt is just astonishing.

which wine? For this interpretation of raw fish, a clean, mineral-style white with a slight touch of the exotic plus layers of stone fruits would work with terrific harmony. Look for a Falanghina from Campania like one from Feudi di San Gregorio or Terredora.

SERVES 4

10 ounces best-quality yellowtail (see Note)

4 teaspoons Ginger Oil (page 342)

1 teaspoon Chile Oil (page 341)

2 teaspoons minced Pickled Red Onions (page 331)

1 teaspoon Hawaiian sea salt

Microgreens

With a sharp knife, slice the yellowtail into neat pieces each about ¼ inch thick. Divide the slices among serving plates in a single layer and in a row. Drizzle the Ginger Oil and the Chile Oil over the slices, and use your fingers to spread the oils over the fish. Sprinkle the Pickled Red Onions over the slices and top each slice with a few flakes of salt and just a few microgreens. Serve immediately.

NOTE: *Be sure to buy what would be considered sashimi-grade yellowtail, and let your fishmonger know that you will be serving the fish raw.*

SNAPPER CRUDO

What I love about this dish is that it pushes the edge. Just when you think you're getting too much of one flavor, another cuts in. It also looks like a work of art on the plate.

10 to 12 radishes

1 lemon

1 lime

1 navel orange

8 ounces best-quality red snapper fillet (see Note)

Flaked sea salt

2 teaspoons Chile Oil (page 341)

40 (¼-inch) cubes Balsamic Gelée (page 56)

1 ripe Hass avocado

2 tablespoons extra-virgin olive oil

4 whole almonds

Microgreens

Chill serving plates. Slice the radishes paper-thin, preferably using a mandoline. You'll need about 32 slices total. Keep the slices in ice water until ready to use.

SEGMENT THE LEMON, LIME, AND ORANGE IN THE FOL-LOWING WAY: Cut both ends off of the fruit. With cut side up and using a sharp, flexible knife, cut the skin and white membrane away; use a sawing motion and cut from top to bottom, following the contours of the fruit. Free the segments (also called suprêmes) from each fruit by cutting along the seams that separate one segment from the other. You will need 8 suprêmes from each fruit (save the rest for another use). Cut each suprême into 3 pieces and reserve.

With a very sharp knife, slice the snapper as thinly as possible. Divide the slices among the chilled plates, spreading them out in a single layer in a random-looking way. Very lightly sprinkle each fish slice with a few flakes of salt and drizzle with the Chile Oil. Place 10 cubes of Balsamic Gelée on each plate, on and around the snapper. Evenly divide the suprême pieces among the plates, placing them on and around the snapper as well.

which wine? Choose
a light, aromatic wine like
a dry Malvasia Bianca from
Venica or Bastianich.

With a sharp knife, pit the unpeeled avocado by cutting it in half lengthwise and removing the pit. Cut one half lengthwise into quarters. (Reserve the remaining half for another use.) Carefully peel the skin off the 2 avocado quarters, then cut each lengthwise into 8 ribbon-like pieces. Divide the avocado ribbons among the plates, carefully placing them over the fish.

Drain the radish slices and scatter them over the plates. Drizzle a little olive oil over everything. Using a rasp-style grater, grate an almond over each plate, letting the wispy flakes cover everything as though it were grated cheese. Finish by placing a smattering of microgreens on top. Serve immediately.

NOTE: *Be sure to buy what would be considered sashimi-grade red snapper, and let your fishmonger know that you will be serving the fish raw.*

BALSAMIC GELÉE

MAKES 1 CUP CUBED GELÉE

This makes more than you need for the snapper *crudo* but is delicious eaten with extra avocado or tossed into a green salad for a burst of flavor.

5 gelatin sheets

⅔ cup balsamic vinegar

2 tablespoons saba (optional; see Note)

Fill a medium bowl with ice water. Soak the gelatin sheets in the water for 5 to 10 minutes.

Meanwhile, in a medium saucepan over medium heat, combine the vinegar and saba, if using, with ⅓ cup water and bring to a simmer. Remove the gelatin sheets from the ice water and squeeze to wring out excess water. Add the gelatin to the saucepan and stir to dissolve. Remove the pot from the heat and pour the mixture into an 8-inch square pan or similar size container. Refrigerate until set, about 2 hours. Cut into cubes for serving.

NOTE: *Saba is a condiment with which most Italians are familiar, but not so most Americans. It's made by reducing grape must, the unfermented juice and residue leftover from winemaking; in Italy it goes by the name* mosto cotto, *which means "cooked wine." Mildly sweet and fruity, it's often served with roasted meats and used in desserts. In this preparation, it softens the vinegar flavor while complementing the grape notes.*

CURED SALMON SALAD WITH NEW POTATOES, CUCUMBERS, AND HORSERADISH CRÈME FRAÎCHE

I have to tell you, I really like this dish. There's something about the potatoes and horseradish paired with the salmon that just feels so right. And then you get a bite that includes the crisp and jaggedy croutons, it's just the perfect texture.

SERVES 6

30 small creamer or red bliss potatoes

Extra-virgin olive oil

3 sprigs fresh rosemary

3 sprigs fresh thyme

Kosher salt and freshly ground black pepper

1 clove garlic, lightly smashed

½ loaf filone or ciabatta, torn into ¾- to 1-inch pieces (about 36 pieces total)

Herb Oil (page 342)

½ small cucumber, peeled, seeded, and cut into ½-inch pieces, preferably oblique cut (see page 58; about 36 pieces total)

1 teaspoon red wine vinegar

1 cup crème fraîche

¼ cup prepared horseradish

3 cups mixed tender greens

6 ounces (about 24 slices) Citrus-Cured Salmon (page 58)

Fresh horseradish, for grating

which wine? A dry Pinot Gris or a rich but mid-weight Chardonnay from northern Italy would bring textural complexity to the salmon. Look for producers like Les Crêtes from Val d'Aosta or Lis Neris from Friuli.

Heat a convection oven to 350°F or a conventional oven to 375°F. On a rimmed baking sheet, toss the potatoes with just enough oil to coat well. Add the rosemary and thyme, season with salt and pepper, and toss again. Roast until tender when poked with a skewer, about 25 minutes.

Meanwhile, in a large sauté pan, heat 3 tablespoons olive oil over medium-high heat. Add the garlic and torn bread and cook, tossing occasionally, until golden, 4 to 5 minutes. Season with salt and set aside.

When the potatoes are just cool enough to handle but still quite warm, squeeze them to open up the top as you would a baked potato, and toss them with ⅓ cup Herb Oil.

OBLIQUE CUTTING

Oblique or roll cutting is used for long vegetables to create attractive pieces with lots of area exposed for fast and even cooking. To do it, make an initial cut on a diagonal. Then roll the vegetable a quarter turn, and cut again at the same diagonal angle. Continue rolling and cutting in this way all along the length of the vegetable.

In a large bowl, combine the potatoes, croutons, and cucumber. Gently toss with 2 teaspoons of Herb Oil and the red wine vinegar, and season with salt and black pepper. Let sit for a few minutes to allow the flavors to meld.

In a small bowl and with a whisk, lightly whisk the crème fraîche, horseradish, and ½ teaspoon salt. Very slowly whisk in 2 tablespoons olive oil.

To serve, spread each serving plate with 1 heaping tablespoon of the horseradish crème fraîche. Add the greens to the bowl with the potatoes and toss lightly. Divide the salad among the plates and top each salad with 4 slices of the Citrus-Cured Salmon. Drizzle with a little of the remaining Herb Oil, and grate some fresh horseradish over each plate.

CITRUS-CURED SALMON

SERVES 15 TO 20

1 whole side fresh salmon, filleted and skin on (2½ to 3 pounds)

1¼ cups kosher salt

1 cup lightly packed dark brown sugar

1 tablespoon yellow mustard seeds

1 teaspoon coarsely ground black pepper

1 bunch fresh dill

1 bunch fresh flat-leaf parsley

1 small shallot, thinly sliced

1 lemon, thinly sliced

1 lime, thinly sliced

1 orange, thinly sliced

¼ cup extra-virgin olive oil

¼ cup grappa

This is really simple to make, but it requires the best-quality salmon you can get and needs to cure for 3 days before it's ready to be served. You will make more salmon than you need for the salmon salad on the previous page, but it will keep for at least a week well wrapped in plastic wrap and refrigerated. Use it as you would lox or gravlax.

Remove any pin bones from the salmon, if necessary. Trim the stomach flaps if necessary for a neater presentation. On a rimmed platter or baking sheet large enough to hold the fish, gently rub the kosher salt onto both sides of the salmon. Lay the salmon skin side down and cover with plastic wrap. Place another baking sheet, platter, or cutting board on top of the length of the fish and weight it lightly. Refrigerate for 12 to 24 hours.

Remove the weights, unwrap the salmon, and gently wipe off the excess salt and moisture. Lay the salmon skin side down on the platter. Sprinkle the brown sugar, mustard seeds, and black pepper over the salmon, then cover the fish with the dill, parsley, shallot, lemon, lime, and orange, distributing and layering the ingredients as evenly as you can along the length of the fish. Drizzle the olive oil and the grappa over everything. Cover the salmon with plastic wrap, weight it again as before, and refrigerate it for 24 hours.

Unwrap the salmon and spoon any accumulated juices onto it. Carefully turn the salmon over (don't worry about rearranging the marinade ingredients; just let them fall onto the platter and rest the fish on top of everything). Cover the fish with plastic wrap, weight it, and refrigerate it for 24 to 36 hours.

Unwrap the fish, gently scrape any remaining marinade mixture off the salmon, and pat it dry. (The salmon will keep, wrapped in plastic wrap and refrigerated, for 1 week.)

TO SLICE THE SALMON: Using a long, thin, very sharp knife and beginning at the tapered tail end, cut thin slices in the direction of the tail end at a slight angle.

TO DICE THE SALMON: Remove larger "blocks" of flesh and dice those.

LARDO-WRAPPED PRAWNS

Lardo is cured pig fat, but that hardly describes the beauty of this artisanal product. It has the texture of butter and imparts a flavor much more subtle than bacon or pancetta. Wrapped around prawns (or very large shrimp), it makes them silky and supple. I like to serve this with stewed lentils infused with a stock made from the prawn shells. If you would like to do that, use the shells from the prawns to make the quick and easy broth on page 312. Head-on prawns not only look cool, but they are also packed with flavor from the heads. Feel free to forego them, however, if that's not your thing.

SERVES 4

½ cup extra-virgin olive oil

1 sprig fresh rosemary

1 clove garlic, thinly sliced

Pinch of crushed red pepper

8 prawns or very large shrimp (12 to 15 per pound), head on if you like, peeled and tail removed (save the shells for making the stock on page 312, if you like)

4 ounces lardo, very thinly sliced

1 cup Braised Rosemary Lentils (optional; page 62)

¼ cup Prawn/Shrimp Stock (optional; page 312)

Basil Oil (page 345)

In a medium bowl, combine the olive oil, rosemary, garlic, and crushed red pepper. Add the shrimp and toss to coat. Refrigerate for at least 4 hours and up to 24 hours.

Remove the shrimp from the marinade and pat the excess off with paper towels. Line a rimmed baking sheet with parchment paper. Fill a second baking sheet with crushed ice and nestle the parchment-lined one on top of the ice. (This is to keep the *lardo* cold while working with it.) Put 3 or 4 strips of *lardo* (depending on the size) on the baking sheet, overlapping them slightly. Position a shrimp at one end and roll the *lardo* up around the shrimp. Continue with the rest of the shrimp and *lardo*. (The shrimp may be wrapped earlier in the day and kept covered and refrigerated.)

Heat a convection oven to 400°F or a conventional oven to 425°F.

If serving the shrimp with the Braised Rosemary Lentils, add the stock to the lentils, if you like, and heat the lentils, if necessary, over medium heat.

Heat a large sauté pan over medium heat. In batches if necessary, cook the shrimp until the *lardo* is crispy and the shrimp are just which wine? Kerner from Alto Adige, with its saline and fresh aromatics, would be a good choice. Try Kerner Aristos Cantina Valle Isarco from Alto Adige.

We like to serve these fragrant, tender lentils with lardo-wrapped prawns, but they're also a great side dish and can make a vegetarian entrée when served with sautéed broccoli rabe and some Concentrated Tomatoes (page 324).

cooked through, about 2 minutes per side. (If the shrimp are very thick, finish cooking them in the oven.)

To serve, divide the lentils among serving plates and top with 2 shrimp. Drizzle with some Basil Oil to finish.

BRAISED ROSEMARY LENTILS

MAKES 3 CUPS

1 cup lentils du Puy

Kosher salt

Extra-virgin olive oil

1 medium shallot, diced (¼ cup)

2 tablespoons chopped fresh rosemary

Pinch of crushed red pepper

4 cloves garlic, finely chopped

1 (14-ounce) can puréed plum tomatoes

1 tablespoon chopped fresh chives

In a medium saucepan, cover the lentils with 2 inches cold water. Season with 1 teaspoon salt and bring to a simmer over medium heat. Cook, adding more water if needed, until al dente, 20 to 25 minutes. Drain the lentils over a bowl to collect the cooking liquid, and reserve.

Meanwhile, in a large saucepan, combine ¼ cup olive oil, the shallot, rosemary, and crushed red pepper. Season lightly with salt and cook over medium-low heat until the shallot is tender and well browned, 10 to 15 minutes. Add the garlic and cook until tender and starting to color. Add the tomatoes and cook until thickened and darkened slightly, about 5 minutes. Add the lentils and ½ cup of the reserved cooking liquid. Continue cooking, adding more liquid in ¼-cup increments to build flavor, until the lentils are very tender, 45 to 60 minutes. Stir in the chives and season to taste with salt.

STRACCIATELLA WITH PICKLED EGGPLANT, CONCENTRATED TOMATOES, AND BASIL

If you have a southern Italian background, it's almost impossible not to think of your heritage when enjoying this dish. It's a perfect summer starter.

SERVES 4

2 tablespoons pitted oil-cured olives

6 ounces stracciatella (see Note)

16 Concentrated Tomatoes (page 324), plus about 1 tablespoon of their oil for drizzling

¼ cup Pickled Eggplant (page 333), drained

24 small fresh basil leaves

Flaked sea salt

Halve the olives and slice them into thin strips.

Using a large spoon, divide the *stracciatella* among serving plates, centering it. Divide the Concentrated Tomatoes among the plates, placing them on top of the cheese. Divide the Pickled Eggplant and the olives among the plates, scattering them on and around the tomatoes. Top with the basil leaves and drizzle a little of the oil from the Concentrated Tomatoes over the plate. Finish with a tiny pinch of salt.

NOTE: Stracciatella, *while worth tracking down, is not so easy to find. However,* burrata *(see Note, page 97), which is becoming more readily available, makes a good substitute because* stracciatella *is actually the creamy filling inside the ball of* burrata. *For best results, scoop/squeeze out the* stracciatella *(and save the outside of the ball— the mozzarella—for grating on your next pizza).*

which wine? This dish reflects both freshness and creaminess, so serve a white with similar characteristics. A Pinot Bianco, with its rich expression of ripe fruits and sweet expansive aromatics, would be perfect. Look for Alto Adige producers like Colterenzio or Franz Haas.

DIVER SCALLOPS WITH SUNCHOKES AND PORCINI

The combination of scallop and sunchokes is a favorite of mine. There's a deep sweetness to a perfectly cooked scallop, and when it meets up with the mild sunchoke flavor, it does a little dance in your head. I often use this combination in a soup, but I also love it in this appetizer.

SERVES 4

8 large (10 per pound) sea scallops, preferably diver-caught

Extra-virgin olive oil

2 teaspoons chopped fresh thyme

Pinch of crushed red pepper

1 cup thinly sliced shallot

Kosher salt

1 cup peeled and thinly sliced sunchoke

8 ounces fresh porcini mushrooms, cut into ½-inch pieces (about 2 cups)

Freshly ground black pepper

2 teaspoons chopped fresh chives

½ lemon

¾ cup Sunchoke Purée (page 327)

Flaked sea salt

Pull off the muscle on the side of the scallops and discard.

In a small bowl, combine 2 tablespoons olive oil, 1 teaspoon of the thyme, and the crushed red pepper. Add the scallops and toss gently to coat. Cover and refrigerate for at least 1 hour and up to 4 hours.

Heat 1 tablespoon olive oil in a medium sauté pan over medium heat. Add the shallot, season lightly with kosher salt, and cook, stirring occasionally, until tender, about 5 minutes. Take off the heat and reserve.

In a large sauté pan, heat 1 tablespoon olive oil over medium-high heat. Add the sunchokes and cook, stirring occasionally, until golden brown, 2 to 3 minutes. Add the porcinis, season with kosher salt and black pepper, and cook for 3 minutes. Stir in the shallots and the remaining 1 teaspoon thyme, and take the pan off the heat. Stir in the chives and keep warm.

which wine? A rich and expansive white should work here, bringing depth to the dish. Considering the combination of the ingredients and the texture of the scallops and porcini, a more complex wine makes the most sense. What comes to mind is Paolo Bea Santa Chiara, which is a blended wine full of personality.

Heat a large sauté pan over high heat. When hot, add 1 tablespoon olive oil to the pan and swirl to coat. Season the scallops lightly with kosher salt. Add the scallops to the pan and cook, undisturbed, for 1½ minutes. Turn the scallops over and cook for another 1½ minutes. Take off the heat and squeeze a few drops of lemon juice over each scallop.

Divide the Sunchoke Purée among serving plates. Divide the porcini and sunchokes among the plates, placing them on top of the purée. Top with the scallops and finish with a few flakes of sea salt.

MEDITERRANEAN OCTOPUS WITH SMOKED POTATO CREMA

This octopus recipe was developed at Scarpetta in Miami, and when I first tried it I was absolutely blown away by it. It's just got every flavor covered—smoky, sweet, briny, tangy, earthy, and creamy, but in such a balanced and thoughtful way. The octopus tentacles look wild on the plate, but their flavor is gentle and their texture supple.

SERVES 4

FOR THE OCTOPUS

Extra-virgin olive oil

2 medium onions, sliced (about 2 cups)

4 sprigs fresh rosemary

¼ cup red wine vinegar

Kosher salt

24 ounces octopus tentacles, cleaned (see Note)

FOR SERVING

Extra-virgin olive oil

1 clove garlic, thinly sliced

1 anchovy fillet

6 tiny potatoes, such as marble potatoes, boiled until tender and halved

1 tablespoon plus 1 teaspoon salted capers, rinsed well

6 Gaeta olives, pitted and halved

Crushed red pepper

Roasted Cherry Tomatoes (page 323)

½ teaspoon red wine vinegar

Kosher salt

2 tablespoons chopped fresh flat-leaf parsley

2 teaspoons coarsely chopped fresh oregano

Flaked sea salt

Smoked Potato Crema (page 69), warmed if necessary

2 tablespoons fresh micro basil (or fresh basil chiffonade; see page 68)

which wine? Because octopus calls to mind southern Italy, a flinty and floral Inzolia from Cusumano or even a Falanghina from I Feudi di San Gregorio makes perfect sense.

FOR THE OCTOPUS: Heat ¼ cup olive oil in a 4-quart saucepan over medium-high heat. Add the onions and cook, stirring occasionally, until just tender and lightly browned, about 8 minutes. Add 2 sprigs of the rosemary and cook, stirring occasionally, until fragrant, about 1 minute. Add 2 quarts water, the red wine vinegar, and ¼ cup kosher salt and bring to a boil. Lower the heat to a simmer and dip the tentacles in and out of the liquid 3 times. (I'm not sure why this is done, but we do get better results when we do it.) Lower the tentacles into the liquid and simmer gently until tender; the time will vary depending on the size of the tentacles. (The

CUTTING FRESH BASIL INTO A CHIFFONADE

I always say it's the little things that are important to get right. Cutting basil into a chiffonade (as opposed to chopping it) doesn't seem like a big deal, but doing so creates a better texture and doesn't bruise the leaves as much. To do it, stack some fresh basil leaves no more than 10 high. Roll the pile fairly tightly lengthwise, like a cigar. Using a very sharp chef's knife, slice crosswise. The closer together you make the slices, the finer the chiffonade will be. Fluff the strands of basil and use them immediately, as the cut edges darken fast. This technique also works for other fresh herbs, such as mint and sage.

tentacles are tender when you can cut them with a spoon.) Large tentacles can take 45 minutes, but start checking after 20 minutes for smaller tentacles. Take the pan off the heat, cover, and let the octopus cool in the liquid. Once cool, remove from the liquid and toss with ¼ cup olive oil and the remaining 2 sprigs rosemary.

TO SERVE: Heat 1 tablespoon olive oil in a small saucepan over medium heat. Add the garlic and anchovy and cook, stirring, breaking up the anchovy and adjusting the heat so the garlic does not take on any color, until the anchovy dissolves, about 2 minutes. Add the potatoes, capers, olives, and a pinch of crushed red pepper and cook, stirring, until heated through, about 2 minutes. Lower the heat and cook, stirring occasionally, until warm, about 5 minutes. Take the pan off the heat and gently fold in the Roasted Cherry Tomatoes and the vinegar. Taste and season with kosher salt if needed. (It may not be, as there are salty ingredients in the dish.)

Heat a grill or grill pan until hot. Season the octopus with salt, then place on the hottest part of the grill. Let cook undisturbed until lightly charred, 2 to 3 minutes. Flip and char the other side. Take the octopus off the grill, sprinkle with the parsley and oregano, drizzle with olive oil, and season with a little flaked sea salt.

Spread about 3 tablespoons of the Smoked Potato Crema on each serving plate. Divide the tentacles among the plates, placing them on top of the crema, and arrange the tomatoes and potatoes around them. Finish with the micro basil.

NOTE: *Octopus tentacles vary tremendously in size. We have served this appetizer with one large tentacle on the plate, and it looks striking. However, a tangle of 3 or 4 smaller tentacles also looks good.*

SMOKED POTATO CREMA

MAKES ABOUT 3 CUPS

This smoked potato sauce is what really makes the octopus so special.

Extra-virgin olive oil

3 medium shallots, thinly sliced

1 sprig fresh thyme

Kosher salt

1½ cups diced (½-inch) Yukon gold potato

Pinch of crushed red pepper

2 cups applewood chips, soaked in water for 4 hours for smoking

1 cup Chicken Stock (page 310)

2 tablespoons whole milk

⅓ cup crème fraîche

⅓ cup mayonnaise

Heat 2 tablespoons olive oil in a medium saucepan over medium heat. Add the shallots and thyme, season with salt, and cook, stirring occasionally, until the shallots are tender but not colored, about 5 minutes. Add the potato, 1 teaspoon salt, and the crushed red pepper and cook, stirring occasionally, for 5 minutes; the potatoes will still be slightly undercooked. Transfer to a rimmed plate or shallow container and cold-smoke for 10 minutes (see following page).

Transfer to a blender. Add the stock and milk and purée. With the machine running, add 2 tablespoons olive oil and blend until emulsified. Pass the purée through a fine-mesh strainer, then whisk in the crème fraîche and mayonnaise. Taste and season with additional salt if necessary. (The crema can be made 2 days ahead and kept covered and refrigerated. Reheat gently to warm it before serving.)

HOW TO COLD-SMOKE INDOORS

You don't need any special equipment to cold-smoke indoors. What you will need is 2 cups of wood chips (we use applewood) soaked in water for at least 4 hours, a roasting pan, and heavy-duty aluminum foil.

Begin by making a foil holder for the wood chips: Measure out a 38-inch piece of heavy-duty foil. Fold it in half like a book to make an 18 x 19-inch sheet. Fold in half again to make it 9½ x 18 inches. Fold the 18-inch side up to create almost a square. Fold in half one more time to create a 4½ x 9-inch rectangle. Fold all four sides of the rectangle in to make a lip; the final size should be 4 x 6 inches.

Place about 1 cup of the wood chips on the bed of foil and place on the stove over high heat. As the chips begin to smoke, gently poke with tongs to allow the heat to distribute.

Meanwhile, place the item to be smoked on a plate and put the plate in the roasting pan. When the chips start smoking, use tongs and a spatula to carefully transfer the chips and foil to the roasting pan, placing next to the plate. (Be very careful, as the aluminum foil is extremely hot.) Immediately cover the roasting pan with foil, crimping all of the edges to prevent any smoke from escaping. Allow the smoke to permeate the item for 10 to 15 minutes. Repeat the smoking process with fresh chips if the recipe directs.

FRIED WHITEBAIT WITH PICKLED MUSTARD SAUCE

When I was a kid, my mother would fry white-bait for us. We loved it. You can't go wrong serving these tiny fried fish with Pickled Mustard Sauce, as the combination of flavors hits all sides of the palate.

SERVES 4

12 ounces whole whitebait

3 cups whole milk

Grapeseed or canola oil, for frying

2 cups all-purpose flour

Kosher salt

3 tablespoons fresh rosemary leaves

20 fresh flat-leaf parsley leaves

20 fresh sage leaves

3 cloves garlic, thinly sliced

12 very thin slices lemon, plus 4 lemon wedges for serving

Freshly ground black pepper

Crushed red pepper

¼ cup Pickled Mustard Sauce (page 73)

which wine? This is a delicate fish, but the mustard sauce adds spiciness, so a Gewürztraminer, with its core of exotic sweet spices and layers of citrus peel, should possess enough acidity and freshness to balance the dish. Try one from Köfererhof or Abbazia di Novacella.

In a medium bowl, cover the fish with the milk and refrigerate for 2 hours.

Attach a candy/deep-fry thermometer to a large, heavy-duty saucepan and fill the pan no more than halfway with grapeseed oil. Heat the oil to 350°F. Line a rimmed baking sheet with paper towels.

Meanwhile, put the flour on a rimmed plate and season with 1 teaspoon salt.

Put the rosemary, parsley, sage, and garlic in the oil and fry for 10 seconds. Using a wire skimmer, remove the herbs and garlic and drain on the paper towels.

Transfer the fish from the milk to the flour without draining. Add the lemon slices to the flour, too, and toss to coat. Lift a small handful of the fish and lemon out of the flour and shake off any excess. Carefully lower it into the oil and fry for 1 minute. Drain on the paper towels. Repeat with the remaining fish and lemon. Transfer the fried herbs and fish to a metal bowl and season to taste with salt, black pepper, and crushed red pepper. Serve immediately with Pickled Mustard Sauce and lemon wedges.

PICKLED MUSTARD SAUCE

MAKES ABOUT 1 CUP

I'd have some of this sauce with just about anything fried. The tangy mustard and capers and the fresh herbs counter the oily nature of deep-fried fare.

2 large egg yolks

Juice of 1 lemon

1 cup grapeseed or canola oil

¼ cup Pickled Mustard Seeds (page 331)

2½ tablespoons chopped capers, plus 1 tablespoon caper brine

2 tablespoons chopped fresh chives

2 tablespoons chopped fresh tarragon

Pinch of cayenne pepper

In a blender, combine the yolks, lemon juice, and 2 tablespoons water until emulsified. With the machine running, slowly drizzle in the oil until emulsified; it should become as thick as mayonnaise. (If too thick, add another 1 tablespoon water.) Transfer to a bowl and mix in the Pickled Mustard Seeds, capers and brine, chives, tarragon, and cayenne. (The sauce can be made 2 days ahead and kept covered and refrigerated; let warm to room temperature before serving.)

MUSHROOM FRICASSEE WITH CREAMY POLENTA

This is a quintessential Scarpetta dish that has not lost its popularity over the years. At the restaurant, waiters bring these mushrooms to the table in tiny saucepans. The lid to the pan is ceremoniously lifted, and you first experience the dish with what I call "the breathe," that initial aromatic hit that puts the dish right in your head. The mushrooms and their cooking juices are then spooned over a waiting bowl of our creamy polenta.

which wine? This rich dish needs a wine with intensity and weight to match the richness of the polenta and the woody nature of the mushrooms. A red from Umbria, like Caprai Montefalco Riserva or Sagrantino from Fattoria Scacciadiavoli, would fit the bill.

SERVES 4

6 tablespoons plus 1 teaspoon extra-virgin olive oil

4 medium shallots, halved and thinly sliced lengthwise

Kosher salt

10 ounces mixed domestic and wild mushrooms, sliced or cut into bite-size pieces (about 4 cups)

2 sprigs fresh thyme

2 cups Chicken Reduction (page 315), plus more as needed

1 tablespoon preserved black truffles

1 tablespoon chopped fresh chives

Pinch of crushed red pepper

3 cups Creamy Polenta (page 77)

In a medium saucepan, heat the 6 tablespoons olive oil over medium heat. Add the shallots, season lightly with salt, and cook, stirring, until the shallots just begin to color, about 4 minutes. Add the mushrooms, thyme, and the remaining 1 teaspoon olive oil, and cook, stirring occasionally, until the mushrooms release their liquid, about 2 minutes. Add the Chicken Reduction, bring to a boil, then reduce to a simmer. Cook, stirring occasionally, until the liquid is reduced by half and has a saucy consistency, 2 to 3 minutes. Stir in the preserved truffles. If the mixture thickens too much—you want the mushrooms to be swimming in the sauce but there should be a mushroom in every bite—add 2 tablespoons of the Chicken Reduction to thin it out a bit. Stir in the chives and crushed red pepper.

Divide the Creamy Polenta among serving bowls. Top with the mushrooms and their cooking liquid and serve immediately.

CREAMY POLENTA

SERVES 8 TO 10

Rich, soft, and creamy, this polenta offsets the deep, earthy flavors of the mushroom fricassee. This recipe makes more than you need for the fricassee, but having leftover polenta is rarely a problem; serve it reheated with roasted or braised meats or use it to make the Polenta Dumplings on page 266. (It will keep, covered and refrigerated, for up to 2 days. Reheat it over low heat, adding a little more milk if necessary.) When making the polenta, it's very important to use coarsely ground cornmeal, which stays more savory and does not get as sweet as the more finely ground variety. I use an imported Italian polenta called *bramata*, a word that refers to the coarse grind of the grain.

4 cups heavy cream

4 cups whole milk

1 tablespoon kosher salt

1 cup coarse polenta

4 tablespoons (2 ounces) unsalted butter

⅓ cup freshly grated Parmigiano-Reggiano cheese

In a large, heavy-based saucepan over medium-high heat, heat the cream and milk until warm, about 5 minutes. Whisk in the salt and keep whisking until the liquid is very frothy (like a cappuccino) and hot. While still whisking, slowly rain the polenta into the pot. Continue to whisk until the granules swell, about 8 minutes. At this point, switch to a wooden spoon to stir the polenta. (It will get too thick for the whisk.) Keep stirring until the polenta has begun to thicken, about 5 minutes. Turn the heat down to medium and cook until it evenly begins to bubble. Reduce the heat to low, cover with a tight-fitting lid, and cook, stirring every 10 to 15 minutes, until cooked through and the liquid has reduced, about 1½ hours. The polenta might look "done" sooner, but it does continue to soften, so be patient. During this time, a skin might form on the bottom of the pan, which is fine.

Just before serving, raise the heat to medium-high, stir in the butter and the cheese, and cook, stirring, until the butter is melted, then take the pot off the heat. If the polenta looks thin, don't worry, as it will thicken as it cools.

CARNE CRUDA ALBESE

Carne cruda, like tartare, is raw beef, but it's not ground as in many tartare recipes. Instead the meat—in Piedmont, they make this with Fassone, a rare breed of cattle—is finely diced. *Albese* refers to the addition of truffles from Alba. I use preserved truffles because I like to make this year-round. But if you have fresh truffles, grate some over the beef for an even more amazing bite. *Carne cruda* is utterly simple to prepare but requires best-quality ingredients. Setting the mixing bowl over ice keeps everything cool as you mix.

SERVES 4

10 ounces trimmed, best-quality beef sirloin, very finely diced

½ teaspoon kosher salt

1 tablespoon finely chopped fresh chives

2 teaspoons chopped preserved black truffles

2 teaspoons extra-virgin olive oil, plus more for drizzling

Shaved Parmigiano-Reggiano cheese

Baby greens

In a bowl set over ice, gently toss the beef and salt. Add the chives, preserved truffles, and olive oil, and mix gently but well.

To serve, use large spoons to shape 4 quenelles (see opposite). Place a quenelle on each serving plate, drizzle with olive oil, and top with Parmigiano-Reggiano shavings and a small amount of baby greens.

which wine? Because this is a dish from Piedmont, and because it includes truffles, try a lovely white, like an Arneis or even a juicy Dolcetto Bianco, if you can find one. Look for producers like Giacosa or Enaudi.

SHAPING QUENELLES

Quenelles are small, oval-shaped dumplings. To create a quenelle, you'll need two spoons of the same size, which will determine the size of your quenelle. With a spoon in each hand, scoop a generous amount of the mixture into one spoon. Gently press the bowl of the second spoon against the mixture, scooping the contents from the first spoon into the second. Transfer the mixture back to the first spoon in the same manner. This begins to create a smooth, rounded surface where the mixture has molded to the spoon. Keep scooping back and forth until you have a nice, smooth oval shape.

SHORT RIBS WITH FARRO AND VEGETABLE RISOTTO

This is one of our most popular starters, and it's easy to understand why. Slices of tender, meaty braised short ribs are paired with farro cooked in the risotto style. It's comfort food taken to a whole new level.

FOR THE RISOTTO

Kosher salt

¾ cup farro

Extra-virgin olive oil

½ cup diced (¼-inch) carrot

Crushed red pepper

½ cup diced (¼-inch) yellow squash

½ cup diced (¼-inch) zucchini

1½ cups Chicken Stock (page 310), warmed

2 tablespoons (1 ounce) unsalted butter

1 to 2 tablespoons freshly grated Grana Padano or Parmigiano-Reggiano cheese

Freshly ground black pepper

2 cups small tomatoes, such as pear, grape, or currant tomatoes (any larger ones cut in half)

¼ cup sliced scallions

FOR SERVING

18 to 24 slices Braised Short Ribs (page 320), reheated in their braising liquid

Shaved Grana Padano or Parmigiano-Reggiano cheese

Microgreens (optional)

FOR THE RISOTTO: Bring a medium saucepan of salted water to a boil. Add the farro, lower the heat to a gentle boil, and cook until chewy but no longer hard, about 15 minutes. Drain and spread the farro out on a rimmed baking sheet to cool evenly.

Heat 1 tablespoon olive oil in a medium sauté pan over medium-high heat. Add the carrots and season with salt and a pinch of crushed red pepper. Cook, stirring, for 1 minute, then add the yellow squash and zucchini. Season again and cook, adding additional oil if needed and stirring, until the vegetables are just tender, about 2 minutes. Remove from the heat and reserve.

In a medium saucepan, heat 2 tablespoons olive oil over medium-high heat. Add the farro and ½ cup of the stock and bring to a boil,

Serve a full-bodied wine with some earthiness, depth, and ripe dark fruits, like a Montepulciano from either Abruzzo or Le Marche, such as Poderi San Lazzaro Grifola or Emidio Pepe. These richly flavored reds should have all the right elements to meld with the short ribs.

stirring, until the broth is almost completely absorbed, about 4 minutes. (Do not let the pot become completely dry.) Add another ½ cup stock and cook, stirring, until the pan is almost dry. Season with a little salt, then add the remaining ½ cup stock and the sautéed vegetables. Cook, stirring, for 2 minutes. Take the pan off the heat and stir in the butter. Add the grated Grana Padano and stir, shaking the pan to help release the starch. Season with salt, a tiny pinch of crushed red pepper, and a few grinds of black pepper. Cover the pot and let sit for 5 minutes. Stir in the tomatoes and scallions and season to taste.

TO SERVE: Divide the risotto among shallow serving bowls. Gently place 3 or 4 slices of Braised Short Ribs on top of the risotto. Drizzle a little reduced braising liquid over the beef, top with a few shavings of Grana Padano, and finish with a tiny handful of microgreens if you like.

NOTE: *Farro is an ancient cousin of wheat cultivated in Italy. It has a firm, nutty texture and is available at Italian groceries and gourmet markets and through mail order.*

SWEETBREADS WITH PAN-ROASTED FALL VEGETABLES AND DRUNKEN PRUNES

I just love the autumnal feel of this dish and look forward to it coming on the menu as the leaves begin to change color. For the best flavor, the prunes need to soak in the wine and brandy for at least 8 hours, so plan accordingly.

SERVES 4 TO 6

FOR THE PRUNES

½ cup quartered prunes

½ cup red wine

¼ cup brandy

FOR THE SWEETBREADS

1 pound sweetbreads

½ onion, sliced

1 carrot, chopped

1 tablespoon black peppercorns

2 dried bay leaves

1 cup white wine

2 tablespoons kosher salt

FOR THE PAN-ROASTED VEGETABLES

Extra-virgin olive oil

5 cloves garlic, lightly smashed and peeled

5 sprigs fresh thyme

½ cup diced (½-inch) butternut squash

Kosher salt

½ cup diced (½-inch) parsnips

½ cup diced (½-inch) carrots

½ cup coarsely chopped shiitake mushrooms

½ cup white pearl onions, peeled

FOR SERVING

Kosher salt

Extra-virgin olive oil

½ cup thinly sliced shallots

3 sprigs fresh thyme

2 tablespoons red wine vinegar

¾ cup Chicken Reduction (page 315)

2 tablespoons chopped fresh chives

1 tablespoon coarsely chopped toasted hazelnuts (see page 89)

1 tablespoon toasted pumpkin seeds (see page 89)

2 tablespoons whole-grain mustard

Thinly sliced Parmigiano-Reggiano cheese

1 handful young hearty greens, such as escarole or kale

which wine?

Sweetbreads are a chef's favorite ingredient because they possess an unparalleled texture and tenderness. To go along with its delicate nature as well as the caramelized flavors of the winter vegetables, choose a mid-weight red wine like a Valtellina Superiore. Chiavennasca (the local name for Nebbiolo), with its spices, herbs, and earthiness wrapped around a core of sweet dark fruits, definitely creates an extra layer of complexity.

FOR THE PRUNES: Put the prunes in a small heatproof bowl. In a small saucepan over medium heat, bring the wine and brandy to a simmer. Pour over the prunes and refrigerate for at least 8 hours and up to 24 hours.

FOR THE SWEETBREADS: Trim the sweetbreads and remove the outer membrane. Soak them in cold water in the refrigerator for 2 hours.

Remove the sweetbreads from the cold water, rinse, and pat dry. In a large saucepan, bring 6 cups water, the onion, carrot, peppercorns, bay leaves, wine, and salt to a boil. Reduce to a gentle simmer and let the ingredients steep for 25 minutes. Add the sweetbreads and simmer until medium-rare, 12 to 15 minutes. (The inside of the sweetbreads will still be pinkish.)

Remove the sweetbreads from the poaching liquid and let cool slightly. When cool enough to handle, gently tear the sweetbreads into 1- to 2-inch lobes, removing and discarding any membranes or blood vessels as you tear. (You can prepare the sweetbreads to this point a few hours before assembling the final dish; keep them covered and refrigerated.)

FOR THE PAN-ROASTED VEGETABLES: In a small sauté pan over medium-high heat, heat 1 tablespoon olive oil. Add 1 garlic clove, 1 thyme sprig, and the butternut squash. Season lightly with salt and cook, stirring occasionally, until the squash is tender and nicely browned in spots. Repeat with the other vegetables, wiping out the pan between roasting and using 1 tablespoon olive oil, 1 garlic clove, and 1 thyme sprig for each. (The vegetables may be roasted a few hours before serving and kept at room temperature.)

TO SERVE: Season the sweetbreads lightly with salt. Heat 2 tablespoons olive oil in a large sauté pan over high heat. Drop the sweetbreads into the pan and cook on both sides until well browned. Remove from the pan, drain off most of the oil, and keep the sweetbreads warm.

Return the pan to medium-high heat and add 2 teaspoons olive oil. Add the shallots and thyme, season lightly with salt, and cook, stirring, until the shallots are tender and browned, about 5 minutes. Drain the prunes and add them and all of the roasted vegetables to the pan. Cook, stirring occasionally, until heated through. Add the vinegar and cook until there is no more liquid in the pan, 1 to 2 minutes. Add the Chicken Reduction and cook until there is no more liquid left in the pan, 3 to 5 minutes. Stir in the chives, hazelnuts, and pumpkin seeds and season to taste with salt.

Divide the sweetbreads and vegetables among serving plates. Place dots of mustard on each plate. Crumble a few slices of Parmigiano-Reggiano over the sweetbreads and top with the greens.

INSALATE

AT SCARPETTA, WE TAKE AS MUCH CARE WITH OUR SALADS as we do our other first courses, and maybe more, as they use mainly raw ingredients that have to be at their best. Although a salad can be quick to prepare, a good salad benefits from forethought and a lot of care. For example, we're always thinking about how to maximize flavors and textures: toasting nuts, adding cheese, roasting vegetables. We also use only the best seasonal ingredients—our ever-changing Farmers' Market Salad (see page 91) is the perfect example of that—as flaws and age are especially apparent when food is raw. Then we treat these ingredients with the utmost care, washing and drying well where needed. When it comes time to dressing a salad, we often assemble the elements on the salad plate and drizzle a little dressing over each layer, which allows for better control. As you come upon the various elements of the salad, the flavors get more—not less—interesting with every bite.

Because salads tend to be dressed with an acidic ingredient, the process of pairing wine with them has taken on some mystique. Many types of wines can match many types of salads, and there is considerable room for experimentation in terms of finding one that will work almost like a condiment. Try serving the salads that follow with a crisp Sauvignon Blanc from Friuli, a floral and rich Inzolia from Sicily, or a creamy and succulent Vermentino from Sardinia. And off-dry Rieslings or Gewürztraminers can be matched with salads that have sweet notes, such as roasted beets (see page 98).

RADISH CRUDO WITH TOASTED PINE NUTS AND BROWN BUTTER VINAIGRETTE

When we tested this recipe for the book, none of us could get enough of it. Refreshing, with a crisp texture, it's also got a warm nuttiness from the toasted pine nuts and the browned butter and lemon vinaigrette. A perfect start to a summertime meal, this salad is especially striking if made with radishes of different sizes, shapes, and colors. The actual number of radishes you will need will depend on their size, but each serving should contain a good handful of thinly sliced radishes. Feel free to substitute sunflower seeds for the pine nuts. In fact, when we first had this on the menu, that's what we used. But during testing, we were out of sunflower seeds and so subbed pine nuts

SERVES 4

8 ounces radishes, preferably a mix of shapes, sizes, and colors

8 tablespoons (4 ounces) unsalted butter

¼ cup fresh lemon juice

Kosher salt

3 ounces (4 small handfuls) sunflower greens or other sturdy sprout-like greens

¼ cup pine nuts, toasted (see opposite)

Flaked sea salt

Have a bowl of cold water ready. Slice the radishes paper-thin, preferably with a mandoline, adding them to the water as you go to keep them crisp and fresh.

Melt the butter in a small saucepan over medium heat. Continue cooking the butter, whisking it occasionally, until the butter turns golden brown, 4 to 6 minutes. (The whisking breaks up the milk solids, helping them to brown evenly, which gives the butter a deeper flavor.) Take the butter off the heat and carefully add the lemon juice; the juice will cause the hot butter to bubble. Season with a good pinch of kosher salt. Let cool a bit, but don't let it get cold or the dressing will taste greasy.

Drain the radishes well and lightly pat them dry with paper towels. In a medium bowl, toss the radishes and the sunflower greens. Whisk the vinaigrette well and add just enough to lightly coat the radishes and the greens.

Divide the greens and radishes among large serving plates. Sprinkle the pine nuts over all and finish with a drizzle of the vinaigrette and a pinch of sea salt.

and actually liked them better. You will likely have leftover vinaigrette. If you do, consider it a gift. It will keep for a couple of days in the refrigerator and is delicious drizzled over grilled or sautéed fish as well as asparagus and artichokes. Reheat it gently before serving and whisk it well to recombine.

Almost all the nuts we use are toasted first to intensify their flavor and maximize their crunch. The easiest way to toast nuts is in an oven set around 350°F. Spread the nuts in a single layer on a rimmed baking sheet or in an ovenproof skillet and toast in the oven, stirring the nuts once or twice, until the nuts are golden and fragrant, 5 to 10 minutes. The time will vary depending on the nut and whether whole or in pieces. Stay close and check often; pine nuts especially can burn quickly.

You can toast small amounts of nuts in a skillet on the stove. This method is quick since you don't have to wait for the oven to heat up, but you will need to shake the pan often to avoid burnt spots.

If the nuts have a skin on them that you want off (such as with hazelnuts) wrap the nuts in a clean dish towel while still hot and rub vigorously until most of the skin has come off.

FARMERS' MARKET SALAD WITH TRUFFLED PECORINO

Freddy Vargas, chef de cuisine at Scarpetta Beverly Hills, had been cooking for me for a very long time in New York when we opened Scarpetta in Los Angeles. A born and bred New Yorker, he did not want to make the move west and did so only reluctantly. In no time at all, he just took to the place. He couldn't get enough of all the seasonal, year-round vegetables available there. So every day, Freddy would go to the market and pick what looked best that day for this salad made with vegetables and greens that are so fresh they never even see the refrigerator. There is a list here of suggested vegetables, but you should be like Freddy and just grab whatever looks best the day you're making this salad.

SERVES 4 TO 6

FOR THE VINAIGRETTE

2 teaspoons Dijon mustard

2 tablespoons red wine vinegar

⅓ cup extra-virgin olive oil

3 tablespoons grapeseed or canola oil

Kosher salt

FOR SERVING

½ cup thinly sliced (on the bias) asparagus

½ cup peeled and thinly sliced baby beets

½ cup thinly sliced (on the bias) carrots, preferably a mix of colors

½ cup thinly sliced cucumbers

½ cup thinly sliced fennel

½ cup thinly sliced radishes

½ cup sugar snap peas, sliced in half lengthwise

½ cup thinly sliced zucchini

1 cup hearty or tender greens torn into bite-size pieces, such as kale or mizuna, depending on the season

¼ cup coarsely freshly grated truffled pecorino cheese (see Note), plus more for finishing

2 tablespoons whole hazelnuts, toasted (see page 89) and crushed

Kosher salt and freshly ground black pepper

Crispy Shallots (page 92)

FOR THE VINAIGRETTE: In a small bowl, combine the mustard and vinegar and whisk vigorously. A little at a time, whisk in the olive oil and grapeseed oil until emulsified. Season lightly with salt.

TO SERVE: In a large bowl, toss the asparagus, beets, carrots, cucumbers, fennel, radishes, peas, and zucchini with just enough vinaigrette to coat them well, about ¼ cup. Toss the greens, pecorino, and hazelnuts with the vegetables. Season to taste with salt and pepper. Divide among large serving plates and top with the Crispy Shallots. Drizzle with a little additional vinaigrette and sprinkle with more grated pecorino.

NOTE: *You can find truffled pecorino at a good cheese shop or Italian market.*

CRISPY SHALLOTS

MAKES ⅓ CUP

These shallots add a bit of crunch and flavor to any dish. Delicious in salad, they're also a great garnish for soup.

2 to 3 tablespoons grapeseed or canola oil	1 large shallot, thinly sliced

Heat the grapeseed oil in a small sauté pan over medium heat. Add the shallot and cook, stirring occasionally, until well browned all over and crisp, about 10 minutes. Be patient. If you rush them, they won't be as sweet or crispy. Drain on paper towels.

ROASTED FALL VEGETABLE SALAD WITH STRACCIATELLA

Growing up in the Northeast, I have always loved the changing of the seasons, but even more so as a chef. I get excited about interpreting new flavors and ingredients for the plate. This salad, with its mix of pickled and roasted root vegetables, is the perfect salad for fall. *Stracciatella*, made from thin strands of mozzarella combined with cream, is rich, creamy, and sweet, and it perfectly balances the tang of the quickly pickled vegetables.

SERVES 6

FOR THE PICKLED VEGETABLES

Kosher salt

½ small acorn squash, peeled and sliced paper-thin

½ small celery root, peeled and sliced paper-thin

1½ cups distilled white vinegar

1½ cups granulated sugar, preferably superfine

FOR THE ROASTED VEGETABLES AND TOASTED NUTS

12 baby carrots

1 medium yam or sweet potato, cut into ¾-inch squares

½ small head cauliflower, cut into florets

Extra-virgin olive oil

3 sprigs fresh thyme

Crushed red pepper

Kosher salt

¼ cup whole hazelnuts

FOR SERVING

⅓ cup extra-virgin olive oil

2 tablespoons balsamic vinegar

8 ounces stracciatella, at room temperature

½ cup Butternut Squash Purée (page 329)

12 tatsoi leaves (or substitute watercress)

FOR THE PICKLED VEGETABLES: Have ready a bowl of ice water. Bring a small saucepan of salted water to a boil. Cook the acorn squash and celery root in the boiling water until just crisp-tender, then transfer to the ice water. Drain and transfer to a bowl or other small container.

In a small saucepan, bring the vinegar and sugar to a boil. Pour over the squash and celery root and refrigerate for at least 2 hours. (The pickles will keep for 1 week, covered and refrigerated.)

FOR THE ROASTED VEGETABLES AND TOASTED NUTS:
Heat a convection oven to 425°F or a conventional oven to 450°F.
On a rimmed baking sheet and keeping the vegetables separate,
toss the carrots, yam, and cauliflower with enough oil to coat, the
thyme sprigs, and a pinch of crushed red pepper. Season lightly
with salt and roast until well browned in spots, then lower the
heat to 350°F (375° for a conventional oven) and cook until tender,
about 30 minutes; you may need to take one vegetable out sooner
than the rest. (You can roast the vegetables ahead and keep them
refrigerated; let them warm at room temperature for 30 minutes
to take the chill off before serving.)

Meanwhile, in a small sauté pan, toast the hazelnuts at 350°F (375°
for a conventional oven) until fragrant and golden brown, about 8
minutes. Transfer the nuts onto a clean kitchen towel, gather the
towel around the nuts, and rub aggressively until most of the skins
come off, then coarsely chop the nuts.

TO SERVE: In a small bowl, whisk the olive oil into the vinegar.
Divide the *stracciatella* among serving plates. Spoon about 2 tablespoons of the Butternut Squash Purée onto the center of each
plate. Put 2 or 3 pieces of each of the roasted vegetables on the
plates. Divide the strands of pickled vegetables among the plates
as well, scattering them randomly. Whisk the vinaigrette and
spoon a little onto each plate in little pools. (You won't use all of
it.) Sprinkle with the hazelnuts and finish with the tatsoi leaves.

NOTE: Stracciatella, *while worth tracking down, is not so easy to
find. However,* burrata *(see Note, page 97), which is becoming more
readily available, makes a good substitute because* stracciatella *is
actually the creamy filling inside the ball of* burrata. *For best results,
scoop/squeeze out the* stracciatella *(and save the outside of the ball—
the mozzarella—for grating on your next pizza).*

LOBSTER SALAD WITH BURRATA AND PEACHES

Sweet, tender lobster; creamy *burrata* cheese; fresh, juicy peaches; ripe, just-picked tomatoes: On their own, these ingredients are amazing. Combined, they make the best summer salad you can imagine.

SERVES 4

2 lobsters, each about 1½ pounds

Extra-virgin olive oil

2 teaspoons red wine vinegar

1½ pounds heirloom tomatoes, preferably a mix of sizes and colors, cut into ½-inch pieces

1 pound ripe peaches (2 large), peeled, pitted, and cut into ½-inch pieces

2 tablespoons fresh basil chiffonade (see page 68)

Kosher salt and freshly ground black pepper

1 teaspoon fresh lemon juice

Pinch of crushed red pepper

8 ounces burrata (see Note)

Flaked sea salt

A few torn leaves of young spicy greens, such as baby mustard greens or arugula

---

Bring a large pot of water to a boil over high heat. Add the lobsters and cook uncovered for about 8 minutes. Check for doneness by twisting a tail off; the meat should be opaque throughout. If it's still translucent, continue cooking for another 1 to 2 minutes. Drain and let cool. Remove the meat from the tails and claws and slice it into 1-inch pieces. (If not using right away, cover and refrigerate for up to 1 day.)

Meanwhile, in a medium bowl, whisk 2 tablespoons olive oil into the vinegar. Add the tomatoes, peaches, and basil, and toss gently to coat. Season with kosher salt and black pepper and let sit for at least 30 minutes and up to 2 hours.

Put the lobster pieces in a medium saucepan. Add ¼ cup olive oil, the lemon juice, and crushed red pepper, and season lightly with kosher salt. Heat over very low heat, gently tossing the lobster occasionally, until warmed through; be careful not to overcook the lobster.

TO SERVE: Slice the *burrata* in half. With the cut side up, slice each half lengthwise and then crosswise to create 1-inch pieces.

Carefully transfer the *burrata* to serving plates, leaving space in between each piece. Season each piece of *burrata* with flaked sea salt and a little black pepper. Toss the tomatoes and peaches together, then distribute evenly on the plates, next to and on top of the *burrata*. Drizzle a little of the juices from the tomatoes and peaches over the plate. Divide the lobster evenly among the plates and drizzle some of the juices from the saucepan over the plates. Finish with a few leaves of greens.

NOTE: Burrata *is a fresh Italian cheese made from mozzarella and cream. The outer shell is solid, supple, fresh mozzarella, while the inside contains both mozzarella and cream, giving it an exceedingly soft texture.*

BEET AND LA TUR CHEESE SALAD

Hidden beneath the greens of this salad is one of my favorite cheeses: La Tur. Hailing from Piedmont, this is a dense, creamy cheese with a full, earthy flavor that pairs beautifully with the from-the-earth flavor of roasted beets. If your beets vary in size and color, put them in separate packets so that you can customize their cooking time and keep their colors intact. Any leftover beet purée will keep, refrigerated, for a few days; use it to dress bitter greens, or add a small amount to risotto to finish.

SERVES 4

12 ounces baby beets, preferably a mix of colors, trimmed

1 large red beet (or 2 or 3 additional baby beets)

3 sprigs fresh thyme

Extra-virgin olive oil

Kosher salt and freshly ground black pepper

1 tablespoon red wine vinegar

1 tablespoon fresh lemon juice

1 endive, sliced ½ inch wide on the bias

1 small head frisée, trimmed, yellow leaves only

1 small head radicchio, sliced ½ inch wide on the bias

1 wheel (6 ounces) La Tur cheese

¼ cup whole hazelnuts, toasted (see page 89) and cut in half

Heat a convection oven to 350°F or a conventional oven to 375°F. Toss the beets with the thyme and enough olive oil to coat lightly. Season with salt and pepper. Keeping yellow and red beets separate, wrap the beets tightly in aluminum foil; put the large beet in its own foil packet. Bake until a cake tester or knife can be easily inserted and removed, 30 to 40 minutes for baby beets and up to 1½ hours for the large beet. While still warm, peel the beets using a paper towel so you don't stain your fingers. Let cool.

Chop the large roasted red beet (or 3 red baby beets) and quarter the remaining beets. Combine the chopped beets with the vinegar in a blender and purée. With the machine running, slowly add ½ cup olive oil, blend until emulsified, and let cool.

In a small bowl, whisk ¼ cup olive oil into the lemon juice. Season lightly with salt and black pepper. In a medium bowl, combine the endive, frisée, and radicchio. Toss with just enough of the lemon vinaigrette to coat lightly, and season to taste with salt and pepper.

Divide the La Tur among serving plates. Divide the quartered beets among the plates, placing them on and around the cheese. Drizzle some of the lemon vinaigrette over the beets and place 4 or 5 penny-size dots of the puréed beet vinaigrette on the plate. Divide the greens among the plates and finish with the hazelnuts.

ENDIVE SALAD WITH CREAMY PINE NUT DRESSING AND SHAVED PARMESAN

Subtle and approachable, this is a salad that just about everyone loves.

SERVES 4

FOR THE DRESSING

¼ cup pine nuts, toasted (see page 89)

¼ cup fresh lemon juice

3 tablespoons honey, such as wildflower

Kosher salt

Pinch of crushed red pepper

½ cup extra-virgin olive oil

FOR SERVING

16 endive leaves, cut in half lengthwise

12 radicchio leaves, quartered

16 arugula leaves, preferably wild arugula, torn in half

28 strips shaved Parmigiano-Reggiano cheese

¼ cup pine nuts, toasted (see page 89)

FOR THE DRESSING: In a blender, purée the pine nuts, lemon juice, honey, 1½ teaspoons salt, and the crushed red pepper. With the machine running, slowly drizzle in the olive oil a little at a time; the dressing should be a thick, mayonnaise-like consistency. Transfer the dressing to a bowl and stir in 2 tablespoons water. Taste and season with additional salt, if needed. (The dressing can be made 2 days ahead and kept covered and refrigerated.)

TO SERVE: In a large bowl, gently toss the endive, radicchio, and arugula with ¼ cup of the dressing and half of the Parmigiano-Reggiano. Divide among serving plates and top with the remaining Parmigiano-Reggiano and the pine nuts. Drizzle with the remaining vinaigrette and serve.

ZUPPE

MOST OF THE SOUPS I MAKE ARE PURÉES. At Scarpetta, a waiter brings to the table a bowl that's empty save for a beautiful arrangement of vegetables or *crudo*. The server then pours the soup, which often is strikingly colored, into the bowl. This is not only good theater, but it also lets the person eating the soup catch a glimpse of what fun and flavor is in store.

A high-quality blender is crucial for giving these soups their silken texture. A little olive oil, added at the end of blending, adds body and rounds out the texture and flavor of the purée.

When pairing wine with these soups, the important thing to consider is the texture of the soups. The acidity of some white wines could be a wonderful refreshing counterpart for a creamy texture or even a spicy one, while soups that are based on meat stock or that have a tomato base would pair better with the full and earthy flavors of a red wine. A grassy, mineral-infused Sauvignon Blanc would pair nicely with the vegetable-based soups, such as the pea soup on page 109 and the asparagus soup on page 103, while the chestnut soup with short rib daube on page 115 could handle a soulful red or even a good dry Sherry or Marsala.

ASPARAGUS SOUP WITH GOAT CHEESE DUMPLINGS

The inherent grassiness of asparagus pairs perfectly with goat cheese in this whimsical salute to spring. Chilling the purée quickly locks in that beautiful green color and keeps the flavors bright.

SERVES 6

FOR THE SOUP

2 bunches asparagus (about 2 pounds)

Extra-virgin olive oil

¾ cup sliced shallots

Pinch of crushed red pepper

Kosher salt

5 cups Chicken Stock (page 310) or Vegetable Broth (page 314)

1 cup lightly packed baby spinach

2 tablespoons chopped fresh tarragon

FOR SERVING

Extra-virgin olive oil

3 white asparagus spears, cut on the bias ¼ inch thick

3 green asparagus spears, cut on the bias ¼ inch thick

2 tablespoons diced (¼-inch) carrot, boiled until just tender

2 tablespoons diced (¼-inch) blue potato, boiled until just tender

½ cup thawed frozen petite peas

Goat Cheese Dumplings (page 104)

1 teaspoon chopped fresh tarragon

Microgreens

FOR THE SOUP: Have ready a large bowl of ice water. Trim away just the very tough bottoms of the asparagus, then cut the spears into ¼-inch pieces.

Heat 2 tablespoons olive oil in a medium saucepan over medium heat. Add the shallots and crushed red pepper, and season lightly with salt. Cook, stirring occasionally, until the shallot is tender but not colored, about 5 minutes. Add the asparagus, increase the heat to medium-high, cover, and cook until just tender, about 2 minutes. Add the stock and bring to a boil. Take the pan off the heat and stir in the spinach and tarragon. Immediately transfer to a blender and purée. With the machine running, slowly add ¼ cup

olive oil and blend until well emulsified. Strain the soup through a fine-mesh strainer into a container set in the ice water. (The soup can be made 2 days ahead and kept covered and refrigerated.)

TO SERVE: Heat 1 tablespoon olive oil in a large sauté pan over medium heat. Add the white and green asparagus, carrot, potato, peas, and the Goat Cheese Dumplings and cook, stirring gently and occasionally, until warm. Add the tarragon and toss gently.

Carefully divide the dumplings and vegetables among wide soup bowls. Garnish with microgreens. Pour the cold soup over and around the ingredients in the bowl. Serve immediately.

GOAT CHEESE DUMPLINGS

MAKES 35 TO 40 DUMPLINGS

While you could simply add crumbled goat cheese to a soup, fashioning the cheese into these little dumplings is worth the effort.

8 ounces fresh goat cheese

¼ cup all-purpose flour

1 tablespoon panko bread crumbs

1 tablespoon finely chopped fresh chives

1 large egg yolk

Pinch of kosher salt

In a stand mixer fitted with the paddle attachment, combine all of the ingredients on low speed. Refrigerate for about 10 minutes to make shaping the dumplings easer.

Meanwhile, bring a medium saucepan of salted water to a boil and have ready a bowl of ice water. Form the cheese mixture into small (about ½-inch) quenelles (see page 79) using demitasse spoons. Boil for 1 minute, then transfer to the ice water to cool quickly. Drain and use as directed in your recipe, or use to garnish your favorite cold soup. (You can make the dumplings 1 day ahead; toss with a little olive oil and refrigerate on a small rimmed baking sheet.)

CHILLED GARDEN VEGETABLE SOUP WITH TUNA AND CLAM CRUDO

This soup is simply stunning and wonderfully refreshing on a hot day. There is no cooking involved in making it, either. The ingredients for the soup are marinated together and juiced. If raw fish is not your thing, you can garnish the soup with finely diced cucumber and tomato instead.

SERVES 4

FOR THE SOUP

7 beefsteak tomatoes (5 to 6 pounds total), chopped

1 English cucumber, peeled and chopped

1 red bell pepper, chopped

1 celery stalk, chopped

½ Vidalia onion, chopped

¼ cup extra-virgin olive oil

1 tablespoon sherry vinegar

1 tablespoon red wine vinegar, preferably Trucioleto brand

Pinch of crushed red pepper

3 tablespoons kosher salt

½ teaspoon freshly ground black pepper

FOR THE CRUDO

3½ ounces best-quality tuna (see Note), finely chopped

10 littleneck clams, shucked, juices reserved and clams finely chopped

1 tablespoon finely chopped scallions

1 tablespoon Chile Oil (page 341)

1 tablespoon extra-virgin olive oil

2 teaspoons finely chopped fresh chives

½ teaspoon flaked sea salt

FOR SERVING

1¼ cups clam juice (use the juice from shucking the clams plus bottled clam juice)

4 paper-thin slices English cucumber, cut in half

8 paper-thin slices radish, preferably breakfast radish

Microgreens

Seasonal edible flowers (optional)

Extra-virgin olive oil, for drizzling

FOR THE SOUP: In a large bowl, toss together all of the ingredients. Cover and refrigerate for at least 8 hours and up to 12 hours.

Purée the soup, ideally using a juicer. Pass through a fine-mesh strainer and keep the soup cold until ready to serve. (The soup may be made 1 day ahead and kept covered and refrigerated.)

FOR THE *CRUDO*: In a small bowl, combine the tuna, clams, scallions, Chile Oil, olive oil, chives, and sea salt. Toss gently.

TO SERVE: Chill the soup bowls. Add the clam juice to the soup, taste, and season with additional kosher salt if needed.

Divide the *crudo* among the bowls. Top with the cucumber and radish slices, a few microgreens, and the flowers, if using. Pour ¾ cup of the cold soup over the *crudo* and finish with a drizzle of olive oil.

NOTE: *Be sure to buy what would be considered sashimi-grade tuna, and let your fishmonger know that you will be serving the tuna raw.*

CHILLED PEA SOUP WITH SMOKED TROUT, TROUT ROE, AND PEAS

This soup has a lot going on, yet it all comes together beautifully. I just love the way the white smoked trout and the orange trout roe look against the green of the soup, but it's their flavor and texture that really make this soup sing. The briny pop of the roe and the subtle smokiness and silken texture of the trout are just amazing here. We cold-smoke our own trout, which is a fairly easy thing to do at home. You can substitute high-quality purchased smoked trout, but it may have a stronger smoked flavor, so you may want to use less of it.

SERVES 4

FOR THE SOUP

Extra-virgin olive oil

1½ cups thinly sliced shallots

¼ teaspoon crushed red pepper

Kosher salt

4 cups Vegetable Broth (page 314)

One 10-ounce package frozen petite peas (2 cups)

2 cups lightly packed baby spinach

¼ cup tightly packed fresh basil leaves

¼ cup chopped fresh mint

FOR SERVING

¼ cup Smoked Trout (page 110)

¼ cup trout roe

1 tablespoon peas, blanched (see page 194)

1 tablespoon thinly sliced blanched (see page 194) snow peas

1 tablespoon thinly sliced blanched (see page 194) sugar snap peas

Finely grated zest of 1 lemon

1 teaspoon fresh basil chiffonade (see page 68)

1 teaspoon fresh mint chiffonade (see page 68)

Extra-virgin olive oil

Kosher salt and freshly ground black pepper

2 tablespoons microgreens

FOR THE SOUP: Have ready a large bowl of ice water.

In a medium saucepan, heat 2 tablespoons olive oil over medium-low heat. Add the shallots and crushed red pepper and season lightly with salt. Cook, stirring occasionally, until tender and sweet, about 10 minutes. Add the broth, increase the heat to medium, and simmer for 10 minutes. Add the frozen peas and bring to a boil. Take the pan off the heat and add the spinach, basil, mint, and 1 tablespoon salt.

Transfer half of the broth and solids to a blender and purée. With the machine running, slowly add ¼ cup olive oil until well emulsified. Transfer to a bowl and set the bowl in the ice water to chill the soup quickly. Purée the rest of the soup, adding another ¼ cup olive oil, and combine it with the first batch to chill. (The soup can be made 2 days ahead and kept covered and refrigerated.)

TO SERVE: In a small bowl, gently mix together the Smoked Trout, half the trout roe, the blanched peas, snow peas, sugar snap peas, lemon zest, basil, mint, and 1 tablespoon olive oil. Season lightly with salt and black pepper. Divide the mixture among shallow soup bowls, mounding it in the center of the bowls. Top with the rest of the roe and the microgreens. Pour ½ cup soup in each bowl and finish with a drizzle of olive oil.

SMOKED TROUT

MAKES ABOUT ¾ CUP FLAKED TROUT

The trout is smoked raw and then cooked to just medium-rare, which makes it really supple. You will be making more than you need for the soup, but leftovers are excellent tossed with roasted potatoes or mixed with crème fraîche and chives for a topping for crostini. Feel free to smoke another fillet with the first if you want even more.

1 tablespoon kosher salt

1 tablespoon granulated sugar

1 trout fillet (about 6 ounces), pin bones removed

2 cups applewood chips, soaked in water for 4 hours

In a small saucepan, combine the salt and sugar with 1 cup water and heat just until the sugar is dissolved. Pour the solution over the trout fillet and let sit for 15 minutes. Remove the fish from the liquid and pat dry with paper towels. Transfer to a plate and refrigerate, uncovered and skin side up, for at least 4 hours and up to 12 hours.

Heat a convection oven to 300°F or a conventional oven to 325°F. Cold-smoke the trout two times, as directed on page 70. Transfer the trout to a small rimmed baking sheet or an ovenproof skillet, cover with aluminum foil, and bake until medium-rare, 10 to 12 minutes. Let the trout cool to room temperature, then flake the meat with a fork. (The trout can be made up to 3 days ahead and kept covered and refrigerated.)

SPICED BUTTERNUT SQUASH SOUP

Butternut squash with warm spices like cinnamon, star anise, and cloves makes a perfect fall soup. At the restaurant, we serve the soup with a *burrata* froth, which cuts through the spices to balance the flavor of the soup. If you don't have the whipped cream canister required to make the froth, you can simply cut the *burrata* into ½-inch pieces and use that instead.

SERVES 4

FOR THE SOUP

2 pounds butternut squash or pumpkin, peeled and cut into medium dice

6 cloves garlic (unpeeled)

Extra-virgin olive oil

12 sprigs fresh thyme

10 fresh sage leaves

¼ teaspoon crushed red pepper

Kosher salt and freshly ground black pepper

15 whole dried allspice berries

9 whole cloves

1½ whole star anise

1 stick cinnamon (2 to 3 inches)

4 cups Chicken Stock (page 310)

1 sprig fresh rosemary

2 cups thinly sliced shallots

FOR SERVING

Extra-virgin olive oil

4 fresh sage leaves

Kosher salt

1 cup diced (¼-inch) butternut squash or pumpkin

1 clove garlic, lightly smashed and peeled

Pinch of crushed red pepper

¼ cup cooked farro (cooked according to package directions)

¼ cup toasted pumpkin seeds (see page 89)

1 tablespoon finely chopped fresh chives

Burrata Froth (page 114), or 4 ounces burrata, cut into ½-inch pieces

FOR THE SOUP: Heat a convection oven to 375°F or a conventional oven to 400°F. On a large rimmed baking sheet, toss the squash and garlic cloves with 3 tablespoons olive oil, 10 sprigs of the thyme, the sage, crushed red pepper, ½ teaspoon salt, and a few grinds of black pepper. Roast, tossing once about halfway through, until tender and beautifully browned, 25 to 30 minutes. Let cool, then remove the peels from the garlic and discard the herbs.

Meanwhile, in a small sauté pan over medium heat, toast the all-spice, cloves, star anise, and cinnamon, stirring occasionally, until fragrant, 2 to 3 minutes.

In a medium saucepan, combine the toasted spices and the stock. Bring to a boil over medium-high heat, then remove from the heat. Add the remaining 2 sprigs thyme and the rosemary and let steep for 5 minutes. Strain the stock into a bowl and discard the herbs and spices left behind.

In a large pot over medium heat, heat 2 tablespoons olive oil. Add the shallots and cook, stirring, until soft, well browned, and very sweet, 15 to 20 minutes. Add the roasted squash and garlic and cook, stirring occasionally, for 4 minutes. Add the stock, increase the heat, and bring to a boil. Lower the heat to medium-low and let the soup simmer for 15 minutes.

Transfer the soup to a blender and purée, in batches, until smooth. With the machine running, slowly add 2 tablespoons olive oil and blend to emulsify.

TO SERVE: In a small sauté pan, heat 3 tablespoons olive oil over medium-high heat. Add the sage leaves and fry until the oil stops bubbling, about 5 seconds. Use a fork to remove the leaves from the pan, leaving the oil behind. Drain on paper towels, season lightly with salt, and reserve.

Pour off all but 1 tablespoon of the oil from the sauté pan and heat the pan over medium heat. Add the diced squash, garlic, and crushed red pepper, and season lightly with salt. Cook, stirring occasionally, until the squash is tender and browned in spots, 3 to 4 minutes. Add the farro, 3 tablespoons of the pumpkin seeds, and the chives, and cook, stirring gently, until heated through, 2 to 3 minutes.

Divide the squash and farro among 4 soup bowls, centering it in the middle. Top with about ¼ cup Burrata Froth or diced *burrata*. Pour ¾ cup soup in each bowl. Top with the remaining 1 table-spoon pumpkin seeds and the fried sage leaves.

BURRATA FROTH

SERVES 8 TO 10

To make this froth, you will need a whipped cream canister. Store any leftover froth in the canister in the refrigerator, where it will keep for a day. It's delicious on grilled bread along with some olive oil.

8 ounces burrata

2 tablespoons whole milk, plus more as needed

1 tablespoon extra-virgin olive oil

½ teaspoon kosher salt

Put the *burrata*, milk, olive oil, and salt in a blender and purée until it is the consistency of yogurt; add more milk a little at a time to thin if necessary. Transfer to a whipped cream canister with two chargers and keep refrigerated until ready to use.

CHESTNUT SOUP WITH SHORT RIB DAUBE

I love to get chestnuts on the menu in the wintertime. In this soup, I pair their deep, intense flavor with an equally intense short rib daube. This is really good stuff.

SERVES 8

FOR THE SOUP

Extra-virgin olive oil

1 cup thinly sliced shallots

Kosher salt

1 pound (about 3 cups) thawed frozen Italian chestnuts

1 sprig fresh thyme

1 cup diced celery root

6 cups Chicken Stock (page 310)

1½ teaspoons preserved black truffles

FOR SERVING

Extra-virgin olive oil

1 cup diced (¼-inch) thawed frozen chestnuts

2 cups diced (¼-inch) celery root

1 clove garlic, lightly crushed

1 sprig fresh thyme

1 tablespoon finely chopped fresh chives

½ cup Short Rib Daube (page 117)

Microgreens

FOR THE SOUP: In a medium saucepan, heat 2 tablespoons olive oil over medium heat. Add the shallots, season with a little salt, and cook, stirring occasionally, until tender, 3 to 4 minutes. Add the chestnuts and thyme, and cook, stirring, until lightly browned, 3 to 4 minutes. Add the celery root, and cook, stirring occasionally, for 1 minute. Add the stock, increase the heat to high, and bring to a boil. Lower the heat to a simmer and cook until the celery root is tender, about 20 minutes.

Remove the thyme sprig, transfer the soup to a blender, and purée, in batches, until smooth. With the machine running, slowly add 3 tablespoons olive oil and the preserved truffles, and blend until emulsified. (If not using right away, let the soup cool to room temperature, then cover and refrigerate for up to 2 days. Reheat gently before serving.)

TO SERVE: Heat 1 tablespoon olive oil in a medium sauté pan over medium heat. Add the chestnuts and cook, stirring occasionally, until the chestnuts are lightly browned, 3 to 4 minutes. Add the celery root, and cook, stirring occasionally, until tender and browned, about 5 minutes. Add the garlic and thyme and cook, stirring, until fragrant, about 1 minute. Take the pan off the heat and stir in the chives.

Gently reheat the soup and the Short Rib Daube if necessary. Divide the daube among shallow soup bowls, ideally shaping it into quenelles (see page 79). Remove the thyme and garlic from the chestnuts and celery root and discard. Divide the vegetables among the soup bowls, placing them on the daube. Pour about ½ cup soup into each bowl. Finish each bowl with a drizzle of olive oil and a smattering of microgreens.

SHORT RIB DAUBE

MAKES ABOUT 2 CUPS

This makes more than you need for the soup, but it is delicious tossed with pasta, spooned over polenta, or spread on grilled bread. It also freezes really well.

Extra-virgin olive oil

1 cup diced (¼-inch) onion

1 clove garlic, thinly sliced

2 cups diced Braised Short Ribs (page 320), plus 1¼ cups of the reduced braising liquid or 1¼ cups Chicken Reduction (page 315) or a combination

1 sprig fresh rosemary

1 sprig fresh thyme

Kosher salt

½ cup red wine

2 teaspoons red wine vinegar

In a medium saucepan, heat 2 tablespoons olive oil over medium heat. Add the onions and cook, stirring occasionally, until the onions are tender and lightly browned, 6 to 8 minutes. Add the garlic and cook, stirring, for another 1 minute. Add the short ribs and cook, stirring occasionally, for 2 minutes. Add the rosemary and thyme, season with salt, and cook for another 1 minute. Add the red wine and the vinegar and cook, stirring occasionally, until the liquid has been absorbed and evaporated. Add ¼ cup of the reduced short rib braising liquid and cook, stirring occasionally, until the pan looks almost dry. Add another ¼ cup liquid and cook, stirring occasionally, until the pan looks mostly dry. Do this three more times. After the final addition, remove the pan from the heat while the meat still looks moist. Remove and discard the rosemary and thyme. (The daube may be made up to 2 days ahead and kept covered and refrigerated; reheat gently before serving.)

PRIMI PIATTI

PASTA

HOW MANY CHEFS OF ITALIAN RESTAURANTS have memories of their Italian grandmothers making pasta? I sure do, though she would have called it *maccheroni* and not "pasta." For many of us, it's why we got into this business. Not so much to make pasta, though that's great fun, too, but because of the way our grandmothers made food and shared it with others. As she sat at the table rolling dough for the Sunday supper, family and friends would be coming and going, in and out of the house throughout the day. And she would *always* have some food and drink—some espresso, some bread, fruit, cheese, and, of course, homemade wine—to offer. You were always welcome there. If you are going to go into the restaurant business, you need to have that same sensibility, that desire to take care of people and even if they are not part of the family, to make them feel like they are.

But back to pasta. Almost all of the pasta dishes that we make at Scarpetta start with fresh pasta. There are a few reasons for that. Customers come to our restaurants expecting that their pasta is going to be handmade, and I get that. Also, on a practical level, fresh pasta cooks so much more quickly than dried that we are able to get out more orders faster using it. And perhaps more important, with some sauces, you are really looking for that full integration of pasta and sauce, something you can't truly get with a dried pasta. But dried pasta, especially artisanal imported ones, can be outstanding, too. I love the pasta made in Gragnano, a small town near Naples famous for its dried pasta; several brands make their pasta there (including one called Pasta di Gragnano), so read labels to find them. Such high quality is pricey, but even at its most expensive it is still a bargain. Barilla is another good, and more widely available, choice.

While I truly think making your own fresh pasta is something everyone should try—it's easier than most people think, and the results are better than most people expect—you can, for some of the stuffed pastas that follow, buy sheets of pasta dough from an Italian market and experiment with using those.

SCARPETTA SPAGHETTI WITH TOMATO SAUCE

This spaghetti is among the first recipes of mine that got a lot of attention, and I love that fact because it exemplifies everything I believe in as a chef: treating ingredients with respect, paying attention to detail, and elevating simplicity.

which wine? A red wine with low acidity will counter the intense tomato sauce. Barbera or Dolcetto should work well. Choose a classic with medium body and dark red fruits, like Enaudi or Marcarini.

SERVES 4

Kosher salt

Scarpetta Tomato Sauce (page 322)

1 pound Fresh Spaghetti (page 122)

½ cup freshly grated Parmigiano-Reggiano cheese

2 tablespoons (1 ounce) unsalted butter, cut into pieces

16 whole fresh basil leaves, cut into chiffonade (see page 68)

Extra-virgin olive oil, for drizzling

Bring a large pot of well-salted water to a boil.

Meanwhile, put the tomato sauce in a large sauté pan and cook over medium heat to further concentrate the sauce's flavors.

Cook the spaghetti until just shy of tender. Reserve some of the pasta cooking water and gently drain the spaghetti. Add the spaghetti and a little of the pasta cooking water to the pan with the sauce; the starch and salt in that water will help the sauce adhere to the pasta. Give the pan a good shake, increase the heat to medium-high, and let the pasta finish cooking in the sauce. The sauce should coat the pasta and look cohesive, and when you shake the pan, the sauce and pasta should move together.

Take the pan off the heat and add the Parmigiano-Reggiano, butter, and basil. Using two wooden spoons (tongs can tear the fresh pasta), toss everything together well.

Divide the pasta among serving bowls. Finish with a drizzle of extra-virgin olive oil and serve.

FRESH SPAGHETTI

This is the dough we use for our signature spaghetti. Purists comment that this is not a true spaghetti because the strands are not extruded and are squared off and not round. But this pasta shape (which is actually *tonnarelli*) is about as thick as spaghetti and has a similar mouthfeel, and it's that feel of spaghetti that really matters to me. What it comes down to is accessibility. If people see *tonnarelli* on the menu, they hesitate. But when it's called "spaghetti," they get excited. The addition of semolina gives this fresh pasta a somewhat sturdier texture while keeping the suppleness.

MAKES ABOUT 2 POUNDS

5 cups "00" flour (see opposite), plus more as needed

⅓ cup semolina flour, plus more as needed

1½ teaspoons kosher salt

13 large egg yolks

2 tablespoons extra-virgin olive oil

In a stand mixer fitted with the dough hook, combine the "00" flour, semolina flour, and salt on low speed. Add the egg yolks, olive oil, and ⅓ cup water and continue to mix on low speed. Once the flour is incorporated, increase the speed to medium-low and mix/knead the dough for 5 minutes.

Lightly dust a work surface with a mix of "00" flour and semolina.

Dump the dough out onto the work surface and knead by hand for a few minutes. Shape the dough into a rectangle, wrap it in plastic wrap, and let it rest for 1 hour.

To roll and shape the dough, set the pasta machine on its widest setting. Lightly flour a rimmed baking sheet. Cut the pasta dough into 4 pieces. Work with one piece at a time and wrap the others in plastic wrap to prevent them from drying out. Very lightly flour the dough and run it through the pasta machine twice. Fold it in half and run it through again. Do that a couple more times; this serves as a final kneading.

Set the machine to the next level of thickness and run the piece of dough through again. Keep running the dough through the machine, adjusting the rollers to a thinner setting each time, until the sheet is ⅛ inch thick; on most machines this means stopping at the 3.5 or 4 setting. Cut the sheet to lengths of about 12 inches. Then, using the linguine cutter, cut the sheet into strands. Repeat with the remaining dough pieces.

Dust the strands with a little flour (preferably a mix of the "00" and the semolina), and gather the strands into nests by wrapping them around your hand. (At the restaurant, we portion the spaghetti into 4-ounce nests.) Dust the nests with a little more flour, place on the baking sheet, and freeze until hard. (Once the spaghetti is rock-hard, it can be transferred to a freezer bag or other airtight container and kept frozen for up to 1 month.)

"00" FLOUR

In Italy and the rest of Europe, flours are labeled as "1," "0," or "00," depending on how finely they're ground. "00" (*doppio zero*) flour is one of the finest. It's light and soft and makes the most tender pasta. Your supermarket may carry it, but you can definitely find it in Italian markets and specialty food shops.

TAGLIATELLE WITH SPRING VEGETABLES AND TRUFFLE ZABAGLIONE

Tagliatelle tossed with fresh seasonal vegetables is a great dish, but what makes this one special is the "zabaglione" that gets added to it just before serving. Note the quote marks. This is not as thick as the famous dessert custard, but it has a similar mouthfeel and the same richness thanks to the eggs. At the restaurant, we present the pasta and then serve the zabaglione tableside.

SERVES 4

3 large egg yolks

¼ cup freshly grated Parmigiano-Reggiano cheese

1 teaspoon preserved black truffles, chopped

Kosher salt

Extra-virgin olive oil

4 ounces guanciale, cut into matchstick-size strips

8 ounces wild mushrooms, such as chanterelles or blue foots, cut into 1-inch pieces

8 ounces (4 to 6 spears) asparagus, peeled, tips cut off and cut in half lengthwise, and spears cut on a sharp bias ⅛ inch thick

½ cup fresh peas, blanched (see page 194)

12 ounces Fresh Pasta (page 129), cut into tagliatelle

½ cup freshly grated Grana Padano cheese

6 tablespoons (3 ounces) unsalted butter, cut into pieces

In a double boiler (off the heat) or a bowl that can fit over a simmering saucepan of water, whisk together the egg yolks, Parmigiano-Reggiano, and preserved truffles. Heat the water for the double boiler or heat water in the saucepan over medium heat, but keep the eggs off the heat for now.

Meanwhile, bring a large pot of well-salted water to a boil.

Heat 3 tablespoons olive oil in a large sauté pan over medium-high heat. Add the guanciale and cook, stirring occasionally, until lightly crisped, about 2 minutes. Add the mushrooms and cook, stirring occasionally, until tender, 3 to 5 minutes. Add the asparagus and peas, and cook to heat through, 2 to 3 minutes. Take the pan off the heat.

Cook the pasta until pliable but still firm to the bite. Transfer the pasta to the sauté pan (a spider or a large wire skimmer works well for this) along with 1½ cups of the pasta cooking water (reserve another 1 cup of the pasta cooking water) and cook, tossing occasionally, until the pasta is tender.

which wine? Most Romans would drink what's called "popular wine" with this dish, like a Cesanese del Piglio from Corte dei Papi, which has a unique aromatic nature, earthy flavors, and velvety tannins.

Meanwhile, put the egg yolk mixture over the simmering water in the double boiler or saucepan. Add ½ cup of the reserved pasta cooking water and whisk until the mixture thickens to the thickness of melted ice cream.

Add the Grana Padano and butter to the sauté pan and toss gently but well. Divide the pasta among wide, shallow serving bowls. Use an immersion blender to froth the egg mixture; pour 2 to 3 tablespoons of it—you want about three-quarters of it to be foamy and the rest to be liquid—over each bowl of pasta. Serve immediately.

TRUFFLE LOVE

It's kind of trendy these days for chefs to claim that truffles are overrated. I use them, often preserved, in a lot of my dishes. So much so I have been asked. "You really love truffles, eh?" (You can tell this was in Toronto.) To which my reply was: "What's not to love?" What's not to love indeed? When I talk about the experience of eating great food, I bring up something I call "the breathe." It's that moment when a dish is put down before you and you inhale, and then suddenly your whole head is filled with the aroma. Truffles offer "the breathe" in spades. I remember when I first got hooked: I was about 18 years old and working at a restaurant that was having a party to celebrate truffle season. We were offering six courses for about 150 people and running an auction to raise money for City Meals on Wheels, a New York City charity. The chef purchased about $30,000 of the most fabulous and fragrant white truffles. I have never seen better since. The aroma from these huge piles of truffles, which were stacked in the downstairs kitchen, permeated the *entire* restaurant. You could even smell the truffles out on the sidewalk. These days, when white truffles are available, we celebrate (though not to that extent) with dishes like the ricotta and white truffle ravioli on page 153, which gets finished with a heap of shaved fresh truffle. But I incorporate that singular flavor throughout the year by using high-quality preserved truffles. Usually used in small amounts, they don't make the dish necessarily scream "truffle." They just make it taste delicious.

MACCHERONI WITH BABY TOMATO RAGÙ AND RICOTTA SALATA

This pasta reminds of me of the pasta I ate growing up. Not so much the dish itself, which is far more refined than what we used to eat, but the comforting flavors in it. Baking the ricotta cheese dries it out and rounds out the flavor. It's actually a pretty amazing transformation.

SERVES 2 OR 3

4 ounces ricotta salata cheese

Extra-virgin olive oil

2 cloves garlic, very thinly sliced

¼ teaspoon crushed red pepper

Kosher salt

1 small shallot, thinly sliced lengthwise

4 cups cherry tomatoes, preferably a mix of yellow and red, cut in half lengthwise

1 teaspoon chopped fresh oregano

3 tablespoons Scarpetta Tomato Sauce (page 322)

12 ounces Fresh Pasta (page 129), cut into maccheroni

1½ tablespoons fresh basil chiffonade (see page 68)

1½ tablespoons freshly grated Parmigiano-Reggiano cheese

Heat a convection oven to 350°F or a conventional oven to 375°F. Put the ricotta salata in a small baking dish and bake until well browned, 25 to 30 minutes.

In a large sauté pan, heat 1 tablespoon olive oil over medium-high heat. Add the garlic, crushed red pepper, and 1 teaspoon salt. When the garlic begins to sizzle, add the shallot, reduce the heat to medium-low, and cook, stirring occasionally, until the shallot is tender, 3 to 4 minutes. Increase the heat to medium-high, add the tomatoes, and cook, stirring occasionally, until the tomatoes release their pectin and begin to look cooked, about 5 minutes. Add the oregano and the Scarpetta Tomato Sauce, stir to combine, and bring to a boil. Remove from the heat.

Look
for a more complex
Chianti Classico Riserva,
like Castellare. This classic Tuscan expression of
Sangiovese is loaded with
personality and has enough
concentration to match the
opulent sauce.

Bring a large pot of well-salted water to a boil. Cook the pasta until not quite al dente. Meanwhile, reheat the sauce, adding ¼ cup of the pasta cooking water. Reserve some of the pasta cooking water, then drain the pasta. Take the sauce off the heat, add the pasta, and toss with the sauce. Add the basil, Parmigiano-Reggiano, and 1 tablespoon olive oil, and toss again, adding a little of the reserved pasta cooking water if the sauce looks dry. Divide the pasta among large shallow serving bowls and grate the baked ricotta salata over the pasta.

SPREZZATURA

There's a great Italian word that reflects what I am striving for on every plate: *sprezzatura*. Dating back to the Renaissance, *sprezzatura* is defined as "a certain nonchalance, so as to conceal all art and make whatever one does or says appear to be without effort." In modern times, Gianni Agnelli, the head of Fiat for many years beginning in the late 1960s, exemplified the spirit of *sprezzatura* like no one else. Though he was a scrupulous dresser, he accessorized in a way that made it look as if he really didn't care much at all about the way he looked: work boots with a bespoke suit, an artfully loosened tie, and most famously, the wristwatch he would wear over his shirtsleeve. That attitude, a certain effortless elegance, is what I am always after, whether it's in the way I present a plate of pasta, decorate my restaurant, or wear my jacket.

FRESH PASTA

I use this pasta for many of my fresh pasta dishes, including the *maccheroni* on page 127, the tagliatelle on page 125, the ravioli on page 156, and the *stracci* ("little rags") on page 138. Though exceedingly tender when cooked, it's easy to handle. I have just about always made fresh pasta using a stand mixer and a dough hook. But what about cracking eggs into a well of flour, as is the perceived "traditional" way? There is just no room in a professional kitchen for using that method for the amounts we need to make. Good news for home cooks is that the method here works really well, producing a consistent product with much less mess.

MAKES ABOUT 3 POUNDS

3 cups "00" flour, plus more as needed

1½ teaspoons kosher salt

11 large egg yolks

3 large eggs

2 tablespoons extra-virgin olive oil

In a stand mixer fitted with the dough hook, combine the flour and salt on low speed. Add the egg yolks, eggs, and olive oil and continue to mix on low speed. Once the flour is incorporated, increase the speed to medium-low and mix/knead the dough for 5 minutes.

Lightly flour your work surface. Dump the dough onto the surface and continue to knead for a few more minutes. At this point, the dough may look a little dry, which is fine. Wrap the dough well in plastic wrap and let it rest in the refrigerator for at least 1 hour before rolling it. This rest allows the flour to be fully absorbed by the wet ingredients for a smooth, tender dough. (You can make the dough up to 1 day ahead of rolling it; keep it refrigerated.)

To roll and shape the dough, set the pasta machine on its widest setting. Cut the pasta dough into 4 pieces. Work with one piece at a time and wrap the others in plastic wrap to prevent them from drying out. Very lightly flour the dough and run it through the pasta machine twice. Fold it in half and run it through again. Do that a couple more times; this serves as a final kneading. Set the machine to the next level of thickness and run the piece of dough through again. Keep running the dough through the machine, adjusting the rollers to a thinner setting each time, until the sheet is the thickness you want (see the following pages for specifications for our most commonly used shapes) or the recipe directs. Lightly flour the dough throughout the process if it is sticking; the

additional flour added at this point will not make it tough. (If the finished sheets of pasta have a lot of flour on them, brush it off using a brush with dark bristles so you can see any stray bristles should they come off on the pasta.)

FOR *MACCHERONI*: Lightly flour a rimmed baking sheet. Roll the dough into sheets about 1/8 inch thick; on most machines that means rolling to the 4 setting. Cut the sheets to lengths of about 5 inches. Using the linguine cutter, cut the sheets into strands. Dust the strands with a little flour, then gather into nests by wrapping them around your hand. Dust the nests with a little more flour, place on the baking sheet, and freeze until hard. (Once the *maccheroni* is rock-hard, it can be transferred to a freezer bag or other airtight container and kept frozen for up to 1 month.)

FOR *STRACCI*: Lightly flour a rimmed baking sheet. Roll the dough into sheets 1/16 inch thick (the last or second-to-last setting on most pasta machines). Using a fluted cutter, cut the strips of dough into 2-inch squares and place them in a single layer on the baking sheet. Freeze until hard. (Once the *stracci* is rock-hard, it can be transferred to a freezer bag or other airtight container and kept frozen for up to 1 month.)

FOR TAGLIATELLE: Lightly flour a rimmed baking sheet. Roll the dough into sheets about 1/16 inch thick (the last or second-to-last setting on most pasta machines). Trim the sheets until they measure 12 to 13 inches long. Tightly roll each sheet, from short end to short end, then use a sharp chef's knife to cut 3/8-inch-wide ribbons. Unroll and toss with a little flour, then gather into nests by wrapping portions of the ribbons of dough around your hand. Dust the nests with a little more flour, place on the baking sheet, and freeze until hard. (Once the tagliatelle is rock-hard, it can be transferred to a freezer bag or other an airtight container and kept frozen for up to 1 month.)

This makes a lot of pasta dough, but I figure, as long as you're making some pasta dough, why not make a lot? You can use the amount you need for whichever recipe you have in mind, and take what's left over and make some other kind of easily shaped pasta, such as linguine. Then portion it and freeze it for future good eating.

FOR FETTUCCINE AND LINGUINE: Lightly flour a rimmed baking sheet. Roll the dough into sheets about $1/16$ inch thick. Cut the sheets of pasta with the pasta roller designated for that shape. Gather the strands into nests by wrapping portions around your hand. Dust the nests with a little more flour, place on the baking sheet, and freeze until hard. (Once the pasta is rock-hard, it can be transferred to a freezer bag or other airtight container and kept frozen for up to 1 month.)

FOR PAPPARDELLE: Lightly flour a rimmed baking sheet. Roll the dough into sheets about $1/16$ inch thick. Use a plain or fluted ravioli cutter or a sharp chef's knife to cut long, $1/2$-inch-wide strips of pasta. Gather the strands into nests by wrapping portions around your hand. Dust the nests with a little more flour, place on the baking sheet, and freeze until hard. (Once the pappardelle is rock-hard, it can be transferred to a freezer bag or other airtight container and kept frozen for up to 1 month.)

TAGLIATELLE WITH PORCINI TRIFOLATI

Trifolati refers to sautéing something with garlic and parsley. In this case, we are sautéing beautiful fresh porcini mushrooms, which are such a special seasonal ingredient that I like to let it speak for itself during the few months we get them. This pasta is right up my alley because it's so simple and so good. Enjoy it with someone special.

which wine? The mushrooms create an earthy foundation, so seek out wines with similar characteristics, such as a full-bodied Montepulciano from either Le Marche or Abruzzo. Poderi San Lazzaro Grifola is a favorite.

SERVES 2

Kosher salt

6 ounces fresh porcini mushrooms

¼ cup extra-virgin olive oil

2 small cloves garlic, very thinly sliced

Pinch of crushed red pepper

10 ounces Fresh Pasta (page 129), cut into tagliatelle

2 tablespoons finely freshly grated Parmigiano-Reggiano cheese

1 tablespoon chopped fresh flat-leaf parsley

½ tablespoon (¼ ounce) unsalted butter

Bring a large pot of well-salted water to a boil.

Peel the stems of the mushrooms and wipe the caps clean with a damp paper towel. Slice the stems and caps very thinly; you should have about 2 cups.

Heat the olive oil in a 10-inch sauté pan over medium-high heat. Add the garlic, crushed red pepper, and a pinch of salt, and cook until the garlic begins to sizzle. Add the porcini mushrooms and cook, without stirring, until the mushrooms are golden brown on one side, 1½ minutes. Stir the mushrooms, season with a little more salt, and cook until tender, about 5 minutes.

Meanwhile, cook the pasta until just shy of tender. Reserve some of the pasta cooking water and gently drain the pasta. Add the pasta and ¼ cup of the reserved cooking water to the sauté pan and toss. Cook the pasta until al dente, adding a little more reserved cooking water if necessary. Take the pan off the heat and add the Parmigiano-Reggiano, parsley, and butter, and toss until the butter is melted.

BLACK FARFALLE WITH LOBSTER

This dish has become one of the most popular at Scarpetta Las Vegas. High rollers love to splurge on lobster, and the black pasta, flavored and colored by squid ink, is incredibly sexy. But it's the depth of flavor in this dish that keeps the regulars coming back for more. If you can buy good-quality black pasta, feel free to substitute that in place of the fresh.

which wine? Try something elegant and intense but with salinity and sweetness. A clean, mineral Alto Adige Chardonnay would harmonize well with this dramatic pasta. Cantina di Terlano Chardonnay has intense notes of minerality and offers great aromatics with a racy finish.

SERVES 4

3 lobsters, about 1¼ pounds each

Kosher salt

Extra-virgin olive oil

1 small clove garlic, sliced and blanched (see page 194)

½ teaspoon crushed red pepper

1 teaspoon chopped scallions

2 tablespoons peeled (see page 22), seeded, and finely diced tomato

½ cup Lobster Broth (page 311)

10 ounces Black Farfalle (page 136)

1 tablespoon fresh basil chiffonade (see page 68)

½ teaspoon chopped fresh flat-leaf parsley

Freshly ground black pepper

1 tablespoon plus 1 teaspoon Minted Bread Crumbs (page 355)

Bring a large pot of water to a boil and have ready a large bowl of ice water. Twist off the lobsters' large claws. Boil the bodies for 1½ minutes—you are not cooking the meat through—then transfer to the ice water. Boil the claws for 6 minutes, then transfer to the ice water. Remove the lobster meat, reserving the shells for the Lobster Broth, if you haven't already made it. Cut the meat into ½-inch pieces. (If not using the lobster meat right away, cover and refrigerate for up to 1 day.)

Bring another large pot of well-salted water to a boil.

Meanwhile, in a large sauté pan, combine 2 tablespoons olive oil, the garlic, the crushed red pepper, and a pinch of salt. Cook over medium-low heat, stirring occasionally, until the garlic is fragrant. Add the scallions, tomato, and Lobster Broth. Increase the heat to high and cook, stirring occasionally, until the sauce has reduced by half. Take the pan off the heat and reserve.

Cook the Black Farfalle until al dente. Using a slotted spoon, transfer the pasta to the sauté pan, and heat the pan over medium heat. Add the lobster, basil, parsley, and another 1 tablespoon olive oil and cook over medium heat, stirring gently just to combine, until the lobster is just cooked through, about 8 minutes. Taste and season with salt, if needed, and a few grinds of pepper. Divide the pasta among serving plates and top each with about 1 teaspoon of the Minted Bread Crumbs.

BLACK FARFALLE

MAKES ABOUT 3 POUNDS

5 large egg yolks

2 large eggs

3 tablespoons squid ink

1 tablespoon extra-virgin olive oil

½ teaspoon kosher salt

3½ cups plus 1 tablespoon "OO" flour (see page 123), plus more as needed

In a stand mixer fitted with the dough hook, combine the egg yolks, eggs, squid ink, olive oil, and salt. Add the flour and mix on medium-low speed until well combined. If dough seems very dry, add water, a little at a time, up to ¼ cup.

Lightly flour your work surface. Dump the dough onto the surface and continue to knead for a couple more minutes. Wrap the dough well in plastic wrap and let it rest in the refrigerator for at least 1 hour before rolling it. This rest allows the flour to be fully absorbed by the wet ingredients for a smooth, tender dough. (You can make the dough up to 1 day ahead of rolling it and keep it refrigerated.)

To roll the dough, lightly flour a baking sheet. Set the pasta machine on its widest setting. Cut the pasta dough into 4 pieces. Work with

The dramatic color of this pasta comes from the addition of squid ink, which you can find at some fish markets and specialty food markets.

one piece at a time and wrap the others in plastic wrap to prevent them from drying out. Very lightly flour this piece and run it through the pasta machine twice. Fold it in half and run it through again. Do that a couple more times; this serves as a final kneading.

Set the machine to the next level of thickness and run the piece of dough through again. Keep running it through the machine, adjusting the rollers to a thinner setting until the sheet is about $1/16$ inch thick. Using a large chef's knife or pastry wheel, cut the strips of dough into rectangles measuring 1 x 2 inches. Using your index finger and thumb, squeeze tightly in the middle of the rectangle to create a bow-tie shape. Transfer the farfalle to the baking sheet and freeze until hard. (Once the farfalle is rock-hard, it can be transferred to a freezer bag or other airtight container and kept frozen for up to 1 month.)

STRACCI WITH SHELLFISH AND LEEK SAUCE

Stracci translates to "rags," and that's kind of what these little pieces of pasta look like. I love how the leek sauce coats the small bites of pasta and how they easily toss together with the shrimp, mussels, and clams. The finished dish might look humble, but how it looks belies its amazing textures and flavors.

SERVES 4

FOR THE SHRIMP

20 rock shrimp (about 8 ounces), peeled (see Note)

1 teaspoon chopped fresh rosemary

1 teaspoon chopped fresh flat-leaf parsley

¼ teaspoon crushed red pepper

2 tablespoons extra-virgin olive oil

FOR THE LEEK SAUCE

4 tablespoons extra-virgin olive oil

1 medium shallot, sliced

1 clove garlic, chopped

Pinch of crushed red pepper

2 sprigs fresh thyme

1 cup sliced leeks (white and light green parts only), well rinsed (1 to 2 leeks)

1 medium zucchini, peeled, seeded, and chopped

½ teaspoon kosher salt

1 cup Vegetable Broth (page 314)

FOR THE MUSSELS AND CLAMS

1 tablespoon extra-virgin olive oil

1 clove garlic, sliced

3 sprigs fresh thyme

1 teaspoon kosher salt

Pinch of crushed red pepper

20 mussels, preferably P.E.I.

20 littleneck clams

FOR SERVING

Kosher salt

2 tablespoons extra-virgin olive oil

1 clove garlic, finely chopped

¼ cup finely diced leeks

¼ cup thinly sliced scallions

1 tablespoon chopped fresh flat-leaf parsley

Fresh Pasta (page 129), cut into stracci

Bottarga Bread Crumbs (page 354)

which wine? Try a dry and delicate white with pronounced acidity, like a Cortese di Gavi with its grapefruit overtones and refreshing flavors of green apple. It should be a perfect accompaniment to this pasta.

FOR THE SHRIMP: Toss the shrimp with the rosemary, parsley, crushed red pepper, and olive oil. Cover and refrigerate the shrimp for at least 3 hours and up to 24 hours.

FOR THE LEEK SAUCE: In a medium saucepan, heat 2 tablespoons of the olive oil over medium-low heat. Add the shallot, garlic, crushed red pepper, and thyme and cook, stirring occasionally, until the shallot is tender, 3 to 4 minutes. Add the leeks, zucchini, and ½ teaspoon salt and cook, stirring occasionally, until the leeks are tender and sweet, about 10 minutes. Add the broth, increase the heat, and bring to a gentle boil. Lower to a simmer and cook for 5 minutes. Transfer to a blender, add the remaining 2 tablespoons olive oil, and purée.

FOR THE MUSSELS AND CLAMS: Heat the oil over medium heat in a skillet large enough to hold the mussels and clams. Add the garlic slices and cook until they sizzle and you can smell that great aroma. Add the thyme, salt, crushed red pepper, mussels, and clams. Add ¼ cup of water and increase the heat to medium-high. Cover and cook until the clams and mussels open, about 5 minutes. Meanwhile, put a colander in a bowl. When most of the clams and mussels have opened, drain them in the colander, reserving the cooking liquid. When cool enough to handle, remove the clams and mussels from their shells. Decant the cooking liquid into a measuring cup, leaving any sediment behind in the bowl.

TO SERVE: Bring a large pot of well-salted water to a boil.

In a large sauté pan, heat the olive oil over medium heat. Add the garlic and cook, stirring, until tender but not browned, about 2 minutes. Add the leeks and scallions, and cook, stirring occasionally, until tender, about 5 minutes. Add 1 cup of the reserved cooking liquid from the mussels and clams (add additional water to make 1 cup if necessary). Increase the heat to medium-high, and cook until most of the liquid is gone, about 8 minutes. Add 1 cup of the leek sauce, the mussels, clams, shrimp, and parsley, stir to combine, and cook until everything is heated through, 1 to 2 minutes. Lower the heat and keep warm.

Meanwhile, cook the pasta until just shy of tender. Reserve some of the pasta cooking water and drain the pasta. Add the pasta to the sauté pan and gently toss to combine. Divide the pasta among warm serving bowls and sprinkle each with about 1½ teaspoons of the Bottarga Bread Crumbs.

NOTE: *Tiny rock shrimp are sweeter than most shrimp, with a lobster-like texture and taste, but if you can't get them, you can substitute conventional shrimp (cut them into thirds).*

CHEESE AND SEAFOOD

I've become known as the guy who doesn't like cheese with fish, but as the lobster recipe on page 197 shows, it's not *all* fish with *all* cheese. Anchovy and mozzarella, for example, is a classic combination, and one that makes sense; the mild cheese does not overwhelm the briny fish. But what sometimes gets me is when people, almost out of habit, automatically grate cheese over their pasta without any thought to the fact that a strong grating cheese can easily overwhelm the delicate flavor of most seafood. I don't always side with tradition when it comes to Italian cooking, but in this case I do: In the south of Italy, when people want that same kind of texture that grated cheese adds, they look to bread crumbs, and we do that in many of the seafood pastas in this chapter. I'm hoping more people will do the same.

SCIALATIELLI WITH CLAMS, ARUGULA, AND BASIL

This pasta reminds me of something my Italian grandmother would make. It's simple and comforting, but the crushed red pepper gives the clams some heat, too. I love how the milk that's used in place of water in the pasta gives it an inherent sweetness.

SERVES 4

¼ cup extra-virgin olive oil, plus more as needed

4 cloves garlic, sliced

¼ teaspoon crushed red pepper

24 littleneck clams

20 ounces Scialatielli (page 142)

8 ounces arugula, tough stems removed

¼ cup fresh basil chiffonade (see page 68)

1 tablespoon chopped fresh flat-leaf parsley

which wine?

Traditionally from Campania, this beautiful seafood pasta is delicate yet complex. The wine that comes to mind would be one from around the Amalfi Coast, like a Ravello Bianco with its pale straw color, racy green fruits, and savory aromatics. It's complex and polished, and the proximity of the ocean and the region's volcanic soils brings out the wine's salty minerality and firm structure.

Bring a large pot of well salted water to a boil.

In a large sauté pan, heat the ¼ cup olive over medium-low heat. Add the garlic and crushed red pepper and cook, stirring occasionally, until the garlic is tender, about 3 minutes. Add the clams and 1 cup water. Cover, increase the heat to medium-high, and cook, shaking the pan occasionally, until the clams have opened.

Meanwhile, cook the pasta until not quite tender, about 3 minutes. Reserve some of the pasta cooking water and gently drain the pasta. Add the pasta to the sauté pan with the clams and toss gently. Finish cooking the pasta in the sauté pan, adding a little pasta water if needed. When the pasta is al dente, add the arugula, basil, and parsley, and cook, tossing gently, until the arugula has wilted. Drizzle with a little olive oil if the pasta looks dry.

SCIALATIELLI

MAKES 2 POUNDS

The name of this pasta, which is typical in Sorrento, comes from the Neapolitan dialect word for "to tousle," as in hair. We add finely chopped herbs to the pasta, which adds a wonderfully fresh flavor. This has become one of my favorite pastas.

3 cups "00" flour (see page 123), plus more as needed

½ cup semolina flour

1 tablespoon kosher salt

½ teaspoon freshly ground black pepper, preferably medium grind

1 tablespoon very finely chopped fresh basil

1 tablespoon very finely chopped fresh flat-leaf parsley

1 cup whole milk, plus more as needed

In a stand mixer fitted with the paddle attachment, combine the flours, kosher salt, pepper, basil, and parsley on low speed. Add the milk a little at a time until the dough just comes together. Gather the dough, which may look cracked and dry, wrap it in plastic wrap, and refrigerate for at least 1 hour and up to 24 hours to hydrate. (If refrigerating the dough for more than 1 hour, wrap the dough in a towel to keep light out so that it doesn't oxidize and discolor.)

Lightly flour a rimmed baking sheet. Cut the dough into 3 pieces. Work with one piece at a time and keep the other pieces wrapped in plastic wrap and refrigerated. Flatten the piece into a square and run it through the widest setting on a pasta machine. Fold the dough and run it through again. Do this a few times to knead the dough. Adjust the machine to the next thinnest setting, flour the dough lightly, and roll it through. The herbs in the dough may make rolling a little tricky; if the dough tears, just gather it up and roll it through again.

Roll the dough into sheets ⅛ inch thick; on most machines that means rolling to the 4 setting. Cut the sheets into lengths of about 6 inches. Using the linguine cutter, cut the sheets into strands. Dust the strands with a little flour, then gather into nests by wrapping them around your hand (we gather them into 5-ounce nests). Dust the nests with a little more flour, place on the baking sheet, and freeze until hard. (Once the pasta is rock-hard, it can be transferred to freezer bags or other airtight containers and kept frozen for up to 1 month.)

SPAGHETTI WITH STEWED OCTOPUS

This pasta is all about the south of Italy and sunny but deep Mediterranean flavors like black olives, tomatoes, capers, garlic, and, of course, octopus, which is cooked long and low until it becomes beautifully tender.

SERVES 6

¼ cup extra-virgin olive oil

1 teaspoon crushed red pepper

2 cups thinly sliced onions (about 2 medium)

4 cloves garlic, very thinly sliced

2 tablespoons capers, rinsed if salted

2 anchovy fillets, well rinsed and chopped

2 fresh plum tomatoes, seeded and chopped

2 pounds cleaned octopus tentacles

Pinch of kosher salt

⅓ cup dry white wine

20 ounces whole canned tomatoes, with their juice

1 tablespoon plus 1 teaspoon chopped fresh oregano

3 tablespoons chopped black olives

½ cup chopped fresh flat-leaf parsley

2 tablespoons fresh basil chiffonade (see page 68)

1 pound best-quality dried spaghetti

Heat a convection oven to 350°F or a conventional oven to 375°F.

In a large saucepan, heat the olive oil over medium-high heat. Add the crushed red pepper, onions, garlic, capers, and anchovies. Cook, stirring occasionally and adjusting the heat as necessary, until the onions are browned, about 7 minutes. Add the fresh tomatoes and stir to combine. Add the tentacles and any residual liquid from the octopus. Season lightly with salt (remembering that the recipe contains salty ingredients), and stir to combine. Add the wine and cook, stirring occasionally, until the alcohol is cooked off, about 5 minutes.

Add the canned tomatoes and crush them coarsely with the back of a spoon to break them up. Add 1 tablespoon of the oregano and

which wine? A medium- to full-bodied white will work here because of the intense flavor of the octopus. Try a Vermentino di Gallura from Sardinia, like Capichera with its complex aromas of wild-flowers, herbs, and tangy minerals.

bring to a boil. Let bubble for 5 minutes, then cover the pan and transfer it to the oven. Cook, covered, for 35 minutes.

Remove the cover, and cook until the octopus is tender enough to be cut with the side of a spoon; the time this takes will vary considerably depending on the thickness of the octopus tentacles, from another 10 minutes to as long as 45 minutes; check about every 10 minutes.

Remove the octopus from the sauce, let it cool briefly at room temperature, then cover and refrigerate it; cold octopus is easier to slice and will be more tender after a rest. Pass the sauce through a food mill. (The octopus and the sauce can be cooked up to 2 days ahead and kept covered and refrigerated.)

When ready to serve, bring a large pot of well-salted water to a boil. Reheat the sauce in a large skillet over medium heat.

Slice the octopus at a slight angle about ¼ inch thick and add it to the sauce. Add the olives, the remaining 1 teaspoon oregano, the parsley, and the basil, and stir to combine.

Cook the pasta until not quite tender. Reserve about ½ cup of the pasta cooking water. Drain the pasta and add it to the sauce to finish cooking in the sauce. Add a little of the pasta cooking water to loosen the sauce if needed. Divide among warm, large, shallow serving bowls.

RICOTTA CAVATELLI WITH RABBIT RAGÙ AND ARUGULA

This is a great pasta dish, and I love it made with homemade cavatelli. But you can also substitute a high-quality frozen cavatelli and your results will be almost as good. Rabbit is such an under-appreciated meat in this country. I love its delicate flavor. But chicken thighs can substitute for it.

which wine? For this hearty southern Italian favorite, opt for a red wine with gamey characteristics, like Marisa Cuomo Ravello Rosso Riserva. With its savory and densely rich fruits and soft velvety character, this truly excellent red offers lip-smacking, chewy deliciousness.

SERVES 4

Kosher salt

Extra-virgin olive oil

1 cup sliced fresh porcini mushrooms

2 cloves garlic, thinly sliced

Pinch of crushed red pepper

2 cups Rabbit Ragù (page 148), plus 1 cup of the braising liquid

¼ cup Scarpetta Tomato Sauce (page 322)

12 ounces Ricotta Cavatelli (page 149)

1 tablespoon (½ ounce) unsalted butter

½ cup freshly grated Parmigiano-Reggiano cheese

2 packed cups arugula

Bring a large pot of well-salted water to a boil.

Meanwhile, heat ¼ cup olive oil in a large sauté pan over medium-high heat. Add the mushrooms and cook until browned, about 1 minute, then add the garlic and cook until it sizzles, about 30 seconds. Season with a pinch of salt and the crushed red pepper and cook, stirring, for 2 minutes. Add the Rabbit Ragù and ¾ cup of the reserved braising liquid. Stir in the Scarpetta Tomato Sauce, then simmer until the liquid in the pan is reduced by half.

Cook the Ricotta Cavatelli until not quite tender. Reserve 1 cup of the pasta cooking water, then drain the pasta, and add the pasta to the sauté pan, tossing it with the ingredients in the pan. Add some of the reserved pasta cooking water if the sauce looks very dry, and cook until the pasta is just tender and has absorbed the flavors of the sauce. Take the pan off the heat and add the butter, 2 tablespoons olive oil, and the Parmigiano-Reggiano. Toss vigorously to emulsify. Season to taste with salt, then add the arugula and toss gently to combine. Divide among serving bowls and sprinkle with a little additional Parmigiano-Reggiano.

RABBIT RAGÙ

MAKES ABOUT 3 CUPS

Extra-virgin olive oil

1 whole rabbit (about 3 pounds), cut into pieces

Kosher salt and freshly ground black pepper

¼ cup thinly sliced guanciale

1 cup chopped onion

½ cup chopped celery

½ cup chopped carrot

4 cloves garlic, peeled

¼ teaspoon crushed red pepper

4 fresh sage leaves

1 cup dry white wine

2 plum tomatoes, quartered

¼ cup dried porcini mushrooms, soaked in 1 cup warm water

4 cups Chicken Stock (page 310)

Heat a convection oven to 325°F or a conventional oven to 350°F.

In a large saucepan or Dutch oven, heat 2 tablespoons olive oil over medium-high heat. Season the rabbit well all over with salt and black pepper. In batches so as not to crowd the pan, brown the rabbit pieces well all over, adding more oil as needed. Transfer the seared rabbit to a rimmed baking sheet. Add the guanciale, lower the heat to medium, and cook, stirring, until the fat begins to render, about 30 seconds. Add the onions, celery, and carrots, and cook, stirring occasionally, until the vegetables are tender and lightly browned, about 5 minutes. Add the garlic, crushed red pepper, and sage, and cook, stirring occasionally, for 2 minutes. Add the wine and tomatoes. Lift the dried porcini out of the soaking water and add them. Pour in the soaking liquid, leaving any sediment behind. Cook, stirring, until the liquid has reduced by three-quarters, about 10 minutes. Return the rabbit to the pot and add the stock. Bring, to a simmer, cover, transfer to the oven, and cook until the meat is falling off the bone, about 1 hour.

Let the rabbit cool in the liquid. When cool enough to handle, remove the rabbit from the braising liquid (reserve the braising liquid) and take the meat off the bones. Strain the liquid; add 1 cup to the rabbit and reserve 1 cup.

RICOTTA CAVATELLI

SERVES 4 TO 5

At the restaurant, we use a cavatelli machine to shape these guys, which means we can crank out of lot of these tender dumplings quite fast. It's not an expensive piece of equipment, and it just clamps onto the end of a table or counter, but it is quite specialized, so most people don't have one. Shaping them by hand takes a lot more time but can be fun if you have someone helping you and maybe a glass of wine, too.

12 ounces ricotta cheese

½ cup "00 flour" (see page 123)

½ cup semolina flour

½ teaspoon kosher salt

In a medium bowl, mix all of the ingredients. The dough may feel very dry and seem difficult to combine at first, but keep working the dough and it will combine nicely. Refrigerate the dough for at least 1 hour to let the moisture of the ricotta evenly disperse throughout the dough.

Divide the dough in half and roll each piece through a pasta machine. Start on the widest setting and roll until about ¼ inch thick (on our machine, that's the 6 setting).

Lightly flour a rimmed baking sheet with semolina flour.

Shape the dough sheets into cavatelli using a cavatelli machine or by hand. To shape by hand, cut the sheet of pasta into 1-inch strips, then cut those into ½ x 1-inch strips. Using a gnocchi board, place the rectangle of pasta at the top of the board. Using the side of your thumb, gently smear the pasta down the board; the piece should take on a hollow center with sides that are just barely touching, sort of like an open tube. As you work, transfer the cavatelli to the baking sheet in a single layer. Freeze on the baking sheet until hard; this makes the pasta easier to handle. Once rock-hard, transfer the pasta to freezer bags or other airtight containers. (The cavatelli will keep, frozen, for up to 2 weeks.)

ORECCHIETTE WITH BOAR SAUSAGE, FAVA, AND MINT

This is a twist on the orecchiette with sausage and broccoli rabe that I grew up on. Though we didn't have boar sausage in our family version, it's quite common in Tuscany and is becoming more available here. You can substitute high-quality sweet Italian sausage, however, if you like.

SERVES 6

1 pound wild boar sausage, removed from casings

3 ounces pancetta, chopped very finely

1 tablespoon fennel seeds, toasted (see page 89) and ground

1½ teaspoons crushed red pepper

Kosher salt

2 tablespoons extra-virgin olive oil

1 cup sliced shallots

1 clove garlic, sliced

1 pound orecchiette

1 cup fava beans, blanched (see page 194)

1 cup peas, blanched (see page 194)

2 tablespoons (1 ounce) unsalted butter, cut into pieces

1 cup pea shoots

½ cup freshly grated Parmigiano-Reggiano cheese

2 tablespoons coarsely chopped fresh mint

In a stand mixer fitted with the dough hook, mix the sausage, pancetta, fennel, and crushed red pepper until combined. Cover and refrigerate for at least 4 hours and up to 24 hours to let the flavors meld.

Bring a large pot of well-salted water to a boil. Heat the olive oil in a large sauté pan over medium heat. Spread half of the sausage mixture over half of the pan in a thin patty. (Reserve the other half of the sausage for future good eating; it freezes well.) Cook the sausage undisturbed to brown one side.

At the same time, on the other side of the pan, add the shallots and cook, stirring occasionally until tender, about 3 minutes. Add the garlic and continue to cook until the shallots are a deep brown, another 5 minutes. Use a spoon or spatula to mix the sausage well with the shallots and garlic, and continue to cook until the sausage no longer looks raw.

which wine? A crisp and mineral-style Chardonnay with nuances of spice and delicate toasty aromas should bring harmony to the full flavors of this pasta. Try the Cuvée Bois Les Crêtes from Val d'Aosta.

Cook the ravioli until not quite tender. Using a wire skimmer or large slotted spoon, transfer the ravioli to the sauté pan. Toss gently but well to coat, and let the ravioli finish cooking. Add the grated Parmigiano-Reggiano and the chives and toss gently.

Divide the ravioli among warm, large, shallow serving bowls and drizzle the brown butter over them. Using an immersion blender, froth the *brodo*. Spoon about ¼ cup of broth and froth over the ravioli. Shower generously with shaved white truffles, if you like.

NOTES: *It's always a good idea to save the rinds from Parmigiano-Reggiano, because they add extra flavor and richness to stews, soups, and other slow-cooked dishes. The rinds freeze well, so just pop them into a freezer bag and forget about them until you want to add one to whatever you're cooking.*

Lecithin, widely used in commercially prepared foods, has made its way to the professional kitchen, becoming a staple of many chefs and, increasingly, home cooks. A natural product derived from egg yolks, soybeans, and corn, it acts as a stabilizer and emulsifier. It helps give whole-grain products a light and tender texture, keeps chocolate and candies from crystallizing, keeps aïoli and mayonnaise emulsified, and, in the case of foams, keeps the foam foamy for longer. Available at most health-food stores (it's also a nutritional supplement believed to offer a number of health benefits) and through mail order, it's a cool addition to your pantry. Once you get some, you will find all kinds of uses for it.

FRESH PASTA, BUT FROZEN, TOO

I always freeze my fresh pasta before cooking it. I know that sounds sacrilegious, but freezing actually makes fresh pasta cook up better. When submerged in simmering water, the frozen-fresh pasta does not absorb as much liquid as would just-made pasta. It holds its shape without expanding so much that it becomes flabby, and its flavor does not become diluted with excess water. Freezing pasta is also practical; you can make your pasta well ahead of serving it and then cook it in mere minutes. If the pasta is frozen well (that is, if the freezer temperature remains consistent), it will still be tender and supple when cooked. All of the pasta we serve at Scarpetta is made fresh and then frozen—even if we plan to serve the pasta the day it's made. This goes for filled pasta as well, and maybe even more so. Fresh-frozen pasta is stronger and so less likely to split apart as it cooks.

RICOTTA AND TRUFFLE RAVIOLI

MAKES ABOUT 70 RAVIOLI

1 cup ricotta cheese, drained if very wet	Pinch of nutmeg, preferably freshly grated
¼ cup freshly grated Parmigiano-Reggiano cheese	Kosher salt and freshly ground black pepper
1 large egg yolk	All-purpose flour, for dusting
½ teaspoon preserved truffles	Fresh Pasta dough (page 129)

In a small bowl, combine the ricotta, Parmigiano-Reggiano, egg yolk, preserved truffles, and nutmeg. Season to taste with salt and black pepper. (The filling may be made up to 1 day ahead and kept covered and refrigerated. Let it warm up a bit at room temperature before using.) Transfer the filling to a pastry bag fitted with a plain 3/8- or 1/2-inch tip.

Lightly flour a rimmed baking sheet. Roll the pasta out into sheets as directed on page 129; strive for the thinnest setting on your machine, but if the dough starts to tear, the second-to-last setting is fine.

Work with one sheet at a time, and keep the others covered with plastic wrap to prevent them from drying out. Very lightly brush a little water over the entire sheet. Pipe about 1-teaspoon dollops of filling at 2-inch intervals along a strip about 1 inch from the bottom of the sheet. (Alternatively, use a small spoon to drop the filling onto the sheet.)

Lift the bottom edge of the sheet up and lay it over the filling. Using your thumbs and index fingers, gently pinch between each mound of filling to eliminate any trapped air.

With a pastry wheel or pizza cutter, cut away the filled strip of pasta, then cut between each mound of filling to make individual pieces. Repeat to make more ravioli. As you work, transfer the filled pasta to the baking sheet in a single layer. Freeze on the baking sheet until hard; the freezing makes the pasta easier to handle. Once rock-hard, transfer them to freezer bags or other airtight containers. (The ravioli will keep, frozen, for up to 2 weeks.)

TALEGGIO MEZZALUNA WITH MORELS AND NEW POTATOES

Taleggio is one of my favorite cheeses. Its strong (some would say stinky) aroma gets mellowed in this lovely pasta. When they are in season, we use spring garlic or ramps in place of the scallions. Be sure to clean the morels carefully, as they can hold a lot of grit.

which wine? This Taleggio-filled pasta has an incredibly flavorful interior with a creamy texture and pungent aroma. The cheese imparts the essence of the Italian countryside in Lombardy, so pair it with a Valtellina Superiore red wine made with the Nebbiolo grape. With its sweet bouquet and expansive palate, it should create a remarkable match.

SERVES 4

Kosher salt

1 cup diced new potatoes, preferably a mix of red, white, and purple

1 sprig fresh thyme, plus ½ teaspoon chopped fresh thyme

1 clove garlic, smashed

2 tablespoons extra-virgin olive oil

⅓ cup sliced scallions

20 fresh morel mushrooms

60 pieces Taleggio Mezzaluna (page 158)

1½ tablespoons unsalted butter

Finely freshly grated Parmigiano-Reggiano cheese, for serving

---

Bring a large pot of well-salted water to just under a boil.

Bring a small saucepan of well-salted water to a boil. Add the potato, thyme sprig, and garlic, and cook until just tender, about 5 minutes. Drain and reserve.

Heat the olive oil in a large sauté pan over medium-high heat. Add the scallions and cook, stirring, for 30 seconds. Add the mushrooms, potatoes, and the chopped thyme, and cook, stirring occasionally, for 3 to 4 minutes to bring out the flavors.

Meanwhile, cook the pasta, adjusting the heat so that the water does not boil vigorously.

Add the butter and about ½ cup of the pasta water to the sauté pan. When the *mezzaluna* are just shy of tender, gently transfer them to the sauté pan; a spider or a large wire skimmer is a good tool for this. Let the *mezzaluna* finish cooking for another 1 minute or so.

Divide the pasta among wide, shallow serving bowls. Top with the vegetables and finish with Parmigiano-Reggiano.

TALEGGIO MEZZALUNA

MAKES ABOUT 80 PIECES

This makes a little more than you need for the recipe, but leftover pasta can be kept frozen for future good eating. Try it tossed with the Concentrated Tomato Sauce on page 181.

5 to 6 ounces Taleggio cheese, rind removed and cheese cut into small cubes, at room temperature

3 tablespoons (1½ ounces) mascarpone cheese

1 large egg yolk

½ tablespoon preserved truffles

Fresh Pasta dough (page 129)

In a stand mixer fitted with the paddle attachment, combine the Taleggio and mascarpone on medium speed until smooth, about 3 minutes. You want to be sure the cheeses are well homogenized before adding the egg (don't worry; you can't overmix).

Add the yolk and mix until well combined, then add the truffles and mix briefly to combine. (The filling may be made up to 2 days ahead and kept covered and refrigerated. Let it come to room temperature before using.) Transfer the filling to a pastry bag fitted with a plain ⅜- or ½-inch tip.

Roll the pasta out into sheets as directed on page 129; strive for the thinnest setting on your machine, but if the dough starts to tear, the second-to-last setting is fine.

Lightly flour a rimmed baking sheet. Cut the sheets of dough lengthwise into 2½-inch strips. Work with one strip at a time, and keep the others covered with plastic wrap to prevent them from drying out. Very lightly brush a little water over the entire strip. Pipe about ½-teaspoon dollops of filling at 2-inch intervals just a little bit above the middle of the strip. (Alternatively, use a small spoon to drop the filling onto the strip.)

Lift the bottom edge of the strip and bring it to meet the top, letting it fall loosely over the filling. Using the pinky side of each hand, gently pat the area close to each mound of filling to coax out any trapped air. Position a 2-inch round cookie cutter over the filling and folded edge of the dough so that one-third of the cookie cutter hangs below the folded edge and the filling is approximately centered. Press to cut shapes that are mostly round but with a straight bottom, like half-moons. Repeat to make more half-moons. As you work, transfer the filled pasta to the baking sheet in a single layer. Freeze the pasta on the baking sheet until hard; the freezing makes them easier to handle. Once they are rock-hard, you can transfer them to freezer bags or other airtight containers. (The *mezzaluna* will keep, frozen, for up to 2 weeks.)

SALT YOUR PASTA WATER WELL

A very basic element for making pasta taste its best is often given short shrift. The pasta cooking water must be amply salted. My mother advised salting the water "until it tastes like soup," and she was right. A couple tablespoons of salt, preferably kosher salt, which dissolves quickly, usually does the trick.

SHORT RIB AND BONE MARROW AGNOLOTTI WITH HORSERADISH BROWN BUTTER AND HERBED BREAD CRUMBS

A pasta filled with braised short ribs is both a dream for our customers, who get to enjoy the deeply flavored, sensuous filling, and for Scarpetta's bottom line, because we can use those pieces of irregularly shaped short rib we wind up with after cutting the meat neatly for the short rib and farro appetizer on page 81. Shredded and tossed with a rich sauce and bone marrow, what would have been otherwise wasted becomes this amazing filling for one of our most popular dishes.

SERVES 4

FOR THE BROWN BUTTER

8 tablespoons (4 ounces) unsalted butter

1 tablespoon prepared horseradish, plus more as needed

Juice of ½ lemon

FOR SERVING

Kosher salt

72 pieces Short Rib and Bone Marrow Agnolotti (page 162)

2 tablespoons unsalted butter

½ teaspoon chopped fresh flat-leaf parsley

Pinch of crushed red pepper

Herbed Bread Crumbs (page 355)

Freshly grated horseradish

28 thin slices garlic crisped in hot olive oil (optional)

Shaved Parmigiano-Reggiano cheese

FOR THE BROWN BUTTER: In a small saucepan, melt the butter over medium heat. Continue to cook until well browned. Add the horseradish and lemon juice, taste, and add more horseradish if desired (horseradish can vary in potency, and you want this to have some kick to counter the sweetness of the pasta filling). Keep the butter warm.

TO SERVE: Bring a large pot of well-salted water to a boil. Lower the heat to a rapid simmer and cook the Short Rib and Bone Marrow Agnolotti until just tender. Reserve some of the pasta cooking water, then gently drain the pasta. Return the pasta to the pot and toss gently with the butter, parsley, and crushed red pepper, adding up to ¾ cup of the pasta cooking water to moisten the pasta.

Divide the pasta among serving plates. Drizzle the brown butter over the pasta. Sprinkle with Herbed Bread Crumbs, grated horseradish, and the crisped garlic, if using, and finish with a few shaving of Parmigiano-Reggiano.

SHORT RIB AND BONE MARROW AGNOLOTTI

MAKES ABOUT 144 AGNOLOTTI

We use short ribs in this meaty filling, and they are essentially the "leftovers" from a short rib appetizer we make. Feel free to use whatever braised meat you happen to have left over at your house for the filling. This makes a lot of agnolotti, but you can portion them and freeze them if you don't use them all at once.

FOR THE FILLING

1 tablespoon extra-virgin olive oil

½ white onion, chopped

1 tablespoon granulated sugar

2 tablespoons red wine vinegar, plus more as needed

3 cups chopped Braised Short Ribs (page 320)

1 cup Chicken Reduction (page 315)

2 ounces bone marrow (see Note)

2 tablespoons chopped fresh flat-leaf parsley

Kosher salt

¼ cup freshly grated Parmigiano-Reggiano cheese

10 cloves Pickled Garlic (page 334)

FOR THE PASTA

"00" flour (see page 123), as needed

Agnolotti Dough (page 165)

FOR THE FILLING: In a medium saucepan, heat the olive oil over medium heat. Add the onions and cook, stirring occasionally, until deep brown, about 12 minutes. Stir in the sugar, then add the vinegar. Cook, stirring, for 2 minutes. Add the short ribs and ½ cup of the Chicken Reduction. Increase the heat so that the liquid is at a simmer and cook, stirring occasionally, until the liquid has reduced and the mixture has become sticky, about 5 minutes. Add the remaining ½ cup Chicken Reduction and cook until the filling comes together and is deeply rich and beefy. Take the pan off the heat and add the bone marrow, parsley, and 1 teaspoon salt. Cook, stirring, until the bone marrow has melted into the sauce. Transfer to a food processor while still hot and purée until smooth, about 1 minute. Add the Parmigiano-Reggiano and Pickled Garlic, and purée again. Season to taste with salt, if needed, and adjust with more vinegar, if necessary. Let cool to room temperature before using. (The filling may be made up to 2 days ahead and kept covered and refrigerated.)

which wine? Red wine is the (perhaps obvious) choice for this dish. In Piedmont, intense and rich food is the norm, so a Nebbiolo-based wine, maybe one from Sandrone or even a blend from Angelo Gaja, like Sito Moresco, makes good sense.

FOR THE PASTA: Line a rimmed baking sheet with parchment paper and flour it lightly. Set the pasta machine on its widest setting. Cut the Agnolotti Dough into 4 pieces. Work with one piece at a time, and wrap the others in plastic wrap to prevent them from drying out. Very lightly flour the piece of dough and run it through the pasta machine twice. Fold it in half and run it through again. Do that a couple more times; this serves as a final kneading.

Set the machine to the next level of thickness and run the piece of dough through again. Keep running it through the machine, adjusting the rollers to a thinner setting until the sheet is as thin as you can roll it without tearing. Transfer the sheets to a lightly floured work surface. (You can stack them if well floured.)

Fill a pastry bag fitted with a plain ⅜- to ½-inch tip with the filling. Working with one sheet at a time (keep the others covered with plastic wrap), very lightly brush a little water over the entire sheet. Pipe about 1-teaspoon dollops of filling at 1-inch intervals along a strip about 1 inch from the bottom of the sheet. (Alternatively, use a small spoon to drop the filling onto the sheet.)

Lift the bottom edge of the sheet up and lay it over the filling. Using your thumbs and index fingers, gently pinch between each mound of filling to eliminate any trapped air.

With a pastry wheel or pizza cutter, cut away the filled strip of pasta, then cut between each mound of filling to make individual pieces. As you work, transfer the filled pasta to the baking sheet in a single layer. Freeze on the baking sheet until hard; the freezing makes the pasta easier to handle. Once rock-hard, transfer them to freezer bags or some airtight containers. (The agnolotti will keep, frozen, for up to 2 weeks.)

NOTE: *Ask your butcher for bone marrow, or buy beef bones with the marrow inside and heat them in the oven just long enough to loosen the marrow so you can scoop it out.*

AGNOLOTTI DOUGH

MAKES ABOUT 2 POUNDS

This Piemontese style of dough, made with egg yolks only, is a very rich recipe, and the dough usually has a gorgeous golden hue (depending on how deeply colored the yolks are). It can be a little more difficult to handle than my conventional fresh pasta dough, but the results are ethereal.

1½ cups "00" flour (see page 123), plus more as needed

1½ teaspoons kosher salt

12 large egg yolks

1 tablespoon extra-virgin olive oil

In a stand mixer fitted with the dough hook, combine the flour and salt on low speed. Add the egg yolks and olive oil and continue to mix with the machine on low speed. Once the flour is incorporated, increase the speed to medium-low and mix/knead the dough for 5 minutes. Lightly flour your work surface. Dump the dough onto the surface and continue to knead for a couple more minutes.

Wrap the dough well in plastic wrap and let it rest in the refrigerator for at least 1 hour before rolling it. This rest allows the flour to be fully absorbed by the wet ingredients for a smooth, tender dough. (You can make the dough up to 1 day ahead of rolling it; keep it covered and refrigerated.)

DUCK AND FOIE GRAS RAVIOLI WITH MARSALA SAUCE

I have served this exact same dish for many years now, and still people do not get tired of it. Like the restaurant itself, it manages to be both elegant and comforting.

1 cup Marsala

1 cup Ruby Port

⅓ cup red wine

1 cup Chicken Reduction (page 315)

Kosher salt

60 pieces Duck and Foie Gras Ravioli (page 168)

8 tablespoons (4 ounces) unsalted butter, cut into pieces

Pinch of crushed red pepper

1 tablespoon freshly grated Parmigiano-Reggiano cheese

Pinch of finely sliced fresh chives

which wine? Why not try a wonderful Lagrein? It can be deliciously plummy, earthy, and chewy, dark and full-bodied but not heavy, with a pronounced minerally edge that should work extremely well with the slight gaminess of the duck.

In a small saucepan, combine the Marsala, Port, and red wine and cook over medium-high heat until reduced by half. Add the Chicken Reduction and cook over medium-high heat until reduced to a sauce-like consistency that coats the back of a spoon. (The reduction can be made 2 days ahead; cover and refrigerate, and reheat gently before using.)

Bring a large pot of well-salted water to just under a boil. Reheat the Marsala sauce if necessary. Cook the Duck Ravioli until not quite tender, reserving some of the pasta cooking water.

Meanwhile, in a large sauté pan combine the butter and crushed red pepper with 1 cup of the pasta cooking water and bring to a simmer over medium heat to melt the butter. Add the ravioli and toss gently to coat, adding more pasta water if necessary. Add the Parmigiano-Reggiano and chives and toss gently. Divide the ravioli among large serving plates and drizzle each with about 1 tablespoon of the sauce.

which wine? A
medium-body rosé wine
with an aromatic fresh-
ness should blend well
with this dish. Campania
makes some good ones,
like Marisa Cuomo Rosato
Costa d'Amalfi, or even try
Villabella Chiaretto from
Veneto.

TO SERVE: Bring a pot of well-salted water to a boil. Put the shrimp and the mussels in a large sauté pan. Add the green beans, the mussel cooking liquid, and the 1 tablespoon olive oil to the sauté pan and gently warm over medium-low heat, stirring occasionally.

Meanwhile cook the Pisarei until not quite tender, about 5 minutes. Using a slotted spoon, transfer the pasta to the sauté pan. Add a little of the cooking water to the pan and increase the heat to medium-high. Cook until the Pisarei are cooked through, about 2 minutes. Add the chives and toss gently. Divide among serving bowls and finish with a drizzle of olive oil.

NOTE: *Tiny rock shrimp are sweeter than most shrimp, with a lobster-like texture and taste, but if you can't get them, you can substitute conventional shrimp (cut them into thirds).*

MY CULINARY HOLY TRINITY

Even a casual reading of the recipes in this cookbook will demonstrate my love for the aromatic ingredients that I use as a flavor base in most of my savory cooking: fresh thyme, crushed red pepper, and olive oil. From marinating chicken to steaming mussels to roasting vegetables, these three ingredients almost always have a role to play. But you don't taste the end result and think, "This tastes like thyme," or "This dish is spicy." Instead the red pepper and thyme work together to create a base layer of flavor, expressed through the fat of the olive oil, that makes these recipes taste like they can only have come from Scarpetta.

PISAREI

MAKES 2 POUNDS

Pisarei are kind of a cross between a dumpling, gnocchi, and pasta. Made with a combination of flour and bread crumbs seasoned with fresh herbs, the humble pasta has a sturdy texture and a great flavor. They are dense, however, so a small portion is all you need. While you might be able to get away with using those bread crumbs that come in the round carton for this recipe, the homemade ones below put those to shame. You will make more than you need, but the bread crumbs will keep for weeks at room temperature and longer if sealed airtight and frozen.

4 cups panko bread crumbs or homemade dried bread crumbs

2 tablespoons finely chopped fresh flat-leaf parsley

1 tablespoon finely chopped fresh basil

1½ teaspoons finely chopped fresh oregano

½ teaspoon garlic powder

½ teaspoon onion powder

Kosher salt

3 cups "00" flour (see page 123), plus more as needed

⅔ cup hot water

3 large eggs

¼ cup extra-virgin olive oil

Heat a convection oven to 325°F or a conventional oven to 350°F. On a rimmed baking sheet, combine the panko with the parsley, basil, oregano, garlic powder, onion powder, and ¼ teaspoon salt. Bake until the panko is golden brown, about 20 minutes. Let cool, and then grind in a food processor to a fine consistency.

In a stand mixer fitted with the paddle attachment, combine 2 cups of the flavored bread crumbs, the flour, the hot water, eggs, olive oil, and 2 teaspoons salt. Mix until the dough comes together, adding additional water 1 teaspoon at a time, if needed.

Lightly dust a rimmed baking sheet with flour. Roll the dough into a log about 1½ inches around. Cut the log into quarters. Work with one piece at a time, and keep the other pieces covered with plastic wrap to prevent them from drying out. Roll the log segment out until about ½ inch around. Using a sharp knife, cut the rope on a diagonal into pieces about ½ inch long. Transfer the Pisarei to the baking sheet in a single layer. Repeat with the remaining dough. Freeze the Pisarei on the baking sheet until hard. Once they are rock-hard, you can transfer them to a freezer bag or other airtight container. (They'll keep, frozen, for 1 month.)

RABBIT WITH PAN-ROASTED PARSNIPS AND HERBED SPAETZLE

When I was younger, I cooked for a while in Germany, where I fell in love with spaetzle. It's enjoyed there as a side dish, but I think it makes an excellent pasta course. This is a very rustic, very soothing dish. At the restaurant, we finish it with a Parmesan froth, but it doesn't really need it, because between the rabbit, the parsnips, and the hit of mint, there is plenty of exciting flavor.

Extra-virgin olive oil

1 whole rabbit (about 3 pounds), cut into pieces

Kosher salt

6 cloves garlic, very thinly sliced, plus 1 whole clove, peeled

3 sprigs fresh thyme

2 sprigs fresh rosemary

Pinch of crushed red pepper

5 plum tomatoes, 3 seeded and coarsely chopped, 2 peeled (see page 22), seeded, and cut into small dice

½ cup dry white wine

1½ cups Chicken Reduction (page 315)

2 cups diced (½-inch) parsnips (from about 4 parsnips)

Herbed Spaetzle (page 177)

½ cup freshly grated Parmigiano-Reggiano cheese

3 tablespoons chopped fresh mint

1 teaspoon chopped fresh flat-leaf parsley

1 teaspoon chopped fresh chives

Heat a convection oven to 325°F or a conventional oven to 350°F.

In a large ovenproof sauté pan, heat 2 tablespoons olive oil over medium-high heat. Season the rabbit well all over with salt and sear, skin side down, until well browned, 5 minutes. Turn the pieces over and brown the other side. Remove the rabbit from the pan; discard the excess oil in the pan but do not wipe the pan clean.

Add the sliced garlic, 2 sprigs of the thyme, the rosemary, and crushed red pepper and cook over medium-high heat until fragrant, about 1 minute. Add the coarsely chopped tomatoes and season with a couple pinches of salt. Cook, stirring occasionally, until the tomatoes release their liquid, about 3 minutes. Add the rabbit back to the pan and let it mingle with the other flavors for 1 to 2 minutes. Add the wine, pouring it over the rabbit in the pan. Cook until most of the alcohol is cooked away; you'll know when that happens because the flavor of the dish will be sweeter and less acidic, about 4 minutes. Add the Chicken Reduction, cover, transfer the pan to the oven, and cook, basting the rabbit occasionally, until the rabbit is nice and tender but not falling off the bone, about 50 minutes.

Remove the rabbit from the pan and reserve the sauce. When the rabbit is cool enough to handle, take the meat off the bones in chunks. Chop the meat into pieces of about 1 inch and reserve.

Pass the sauce through a fine-mesh strainer; you should have about 1½ cups. (The rabbit may be cooked up to 2 days ahead; refrigerate the meat and the sauce separately, covered.)

To serve, put the sauce in a large sauté pan and heat over low heat. Add the rabbit and reheat it gently. Meanwhile, in a medium sauté pan over medium-high heat, heat 1 tablespoon olive oil. Add the whole garlic clove and the remaining thyme sprig. Cook until the garlic sizzles and colors slightly. Add the parsnips and cook, turning occasionally, until just tender and a light golden color, 3 to 4 minutes.

Transfer the parsnips to the pan with the rabbit and cook together for a couple of minutes to let flavors meld. Add the Herbed Spaetzle and toss. Add the finely diced tomatoes, Parmigiano-Reggiano, mint, parsley, and chives, and cook, tossing occasionally, until the spaetzle is heated through. Taste and season with additional salt, if needed.

HERBED SPAETZLE

SERVES 6

Spaetzle are little noodles native to Germany (as well as Alto Adige), where I lived for a while as a young cook. I love their irregular shape and soothing flavor. These herbed spaetzle taste amazing with the rabbit, but if you want a more classic version for another dish, simply omit the herbs.

¾ cup whole milk

3 large eggs

2 cups all-purpose flour, sifted

Kosher salt

1 teaspoon finely chopped fresh chives

1 teaspoon finely chopped fresh flat-leaf parsley

1 teaspoon finely chopped fresh rosemary

1 teaspoon finely chopped fresh thyme

Extra-virgin olive oil

2 tablespoons unsalted butter (if reheating as a side dish)

In a stand mixer fitted with the paddle attachment, combine the milk and the eggs on low speed until the egg yolks break up. Add the flour and 1 teaspoon salt and mix on low speed until a thick, pancake-like batter forms. Add the chives, parsley, rosemary, and thyme, and mix until well incorporated, 1 to 2 minutes. Transfer the batter to a smaller bowl (to fit more easily in the fridge), cover with plastic wrap, and refrigerate for 30 minutes to let the batter rest.

Bring a pot of well-salted water to a boil and have nearby a bowl of ice water and a rimmed baking sheet. Working over the boiling water and using a rubber spatula, press the batter in batches through the holes of a perforated broiling pan insert, a colander, or the large holes of a box grater. The dough will form small dumplings as it drops into the water. Allow the spaetzle to rise to the surface and float for about 30 seconds before transferring it to the ice water with a slotted spoon or spider. (To keep the ice and spaetzle separated, set a sieve in the ice water and put the spaetzle in that.) Transfer the cooled spaetzle to the baking sheet and continue cooking the rest of the batter. (If you are not using the cooked spaetzle right away, toss it with a little olive oil and refrigerate, covered in plastic wrap, for up to 2 days.)

Reheat the spaetzle by following the directions in the recipe calling for it. Or, for a delicious side dish, heat a large sauté pan over medium-high heat and add 2 tablespoons olive oil and the butter. When the butter is melted, add the spaetzle and cook, tossing occasionally, until golden brown, about 2 minutes. Season to taste.

SPINACH AND RICOTTA GNUDI WITH CONCENTRATED TOMATO SAUCE

Made with what could otherwise be a filling for a ravioli—namely ricotta cheese and spinach—these little dumplings are incredibly tender and light. Despite the ethereal quality of these *gnudi*, they pair well with a tomato sauce made more intense by the addition of *strattu*, a tomato concentrate from Sicily that I absolutely adore. When you see these soft, pale *gnudi* (pronounced with a silent "g," making it sound just like you think) contrasted with the red and intense sauce, you will probably agree that there's something sexy about it.

SERVES 4

1 teaspoon extra-virgin olive oil

5 ounces baby spinach, tough stems removed

1 pound ricotta cheese, preferably sheep's milk, drained if very wet

2 large egg yolks

1 ounce Parmigiano-Reggiano cheese, finely grated

¼ cup "00" flour (see page 123), plus more as needed

3 tablespoons panko bread crumbs

Pinch of nutmeg, preferably freshly grated

1 teaspoon kosher salt

Freshly ground black pepper

Concentrated Tomato Sauce (page 181)

1 tablespoon chopped fresh basil

Shaved Parmigiano-Reggiano cheese, for serving

In a sauté pan large enough to hold the spinach, heat the olive oil over medium heat. Add the spinach and cook, turning occasionally with tongs, until completely wilted. Let cool, and then use your hands to squeeze the spinach very dry. Chop the spinach very, very finely.

In a stand mixer fitted with the paddle attachment, combine the ricotta, egg yolks, and spinach. Add the Parmigiano-Reggiano, flour, panko, nutmeg, salt, and about 15 grinds of pepper, and combine until just incorporated. The dough should feel moist but should not stick to your hands; if it does, add a little more flour. Let the dough rest for 10 minutes.

While the dough rests, bring a small saucepan of salted water to a boil. Roll a piece of the dough into a ball about the size of a golf ball, and cook for 3 to 4 minutes to test for texture. If the *gnudi* is too soft to hold its shape, add more flour to the dough. Refrigerate

which wine? This traditional Tuscan dish calls for an expressive Vernaccia, perhaps one with more texture and weight as opposed to a simpler style. Look for the single vineyard selections from Falchini or Fattorie Melini.

the dough for about 1 hour; this allows it to hydrate and will make shaping the dough easier.

Shape the spinach-ricotta mixture into golf ball–size balls (about 28 total). Refrigerate if not using right away. Otherwise, bring a large saucepan of well-salted water to a gentle boil.

In a large sauté pan, reheat the Concentrated Tomato Sauce.

Boil the *gnudi* for 3 minutes. Using a slotted spoon, transfer the *gnudi* to the pan with the sauce and roll around in the sauce to coat; you may need to add up to 1/3 cup additional pasta cooking water to the pan to loosen the sauce. Divide among serving plates and finish with a sprinkling of the chopped basil and the shaved Parmigiano-Reggiano.

NOTE: *You can shape the* gnudi *and keep them refrigerated for a few hours before boiling and serving.*

CONCENTRATED TOMATO SAUCE

MAKES ABOUT 1 CUP

1 cup Scarpetta Tomato Sauce (page 322)

2 tablespoons stratto (see Note) or high-quality tomato paste

Pinch of crushed red pepper

2 tablespoons extra-virgin olive oil

In a large sauté pan, warm the Scarpetta Tomato Sauce over medium-low heat. Whisk in the *stratto*, chopping up the dense paste with your whisk as you go, and the crushed red pepper. The sauce will thicken considerably. Continue cooking, whisking occasionally, until the sauce is a uniform color and texture, about 5 minutes. If necessary, thin out with a little water, preferably pasta cooking water, 1 tablespoon or so at a time; you want a thick sauce that is silky, with a nice flow. Whisk in the olive oil. Reserve the sauce off the heat until ready to serve.

NOTE: *The addition of* stratto, *a concentrated tomato sauce from Sicily, gives the sauce a more intense flavor and deeper color in mere minutes.*

BLACK TRUFFLE RISOTTO

Risotto can be fickle and requires a lot of attendance, so we don't feature it on the menu at Scarpetta, but we do make it for special tasting menus during truffle season, when we can give a dish like this the attention it deserves. Made with egg yolks and preserved truffles, this risotto is very luxurious, and I love how the yolks add their golden hue to the rice. If you can get your hands on a fresh truffle, a bit shaved over the risotto just as it's being served is amazing. You inhale and you're in heaven.

SERVES 4 TO 6

3 tablespoons extra-virgin olive oil (just enough to coat the pan)

3 tablespoons finely chopped shallot

1½ teaspoons finely chopped garlic

Pinch of crushed red pepper

Kosher salt

2½ tablespoons (1¼ ounces) unsalted butter

1½ cups Vialone Nano rice (see Note)

½ cup dry white wine

4 to 5 cups Chicken Stock (page 310)

1½ teaspoons chopped fresh thyme

½ cup freshly grated Parmigiano-Reggiano cheese

1 tablespoon preserved truffles

2 large egg yolks

In a 4-quart saucepan, heat the olive oil over medium heat. Add the shallot, garlic, crushed red pepper, and a pinch of salt and cook, stirring, until fragrant, about 1 minute. (Take the pan off the heat if the garlic starts to brown.) Add 1 tablespoon of the butter, lower the heat to medium-low, and cook, stirring occasionally, until the shallot is very tender, 5 minutes.

Add the rice and cook, stirring, for 1 minute to toast it lightly. Increase the heat to medium, add the wine, and cook until most of the wine is gone.

Add 1 cup of the stock and cook, stirring, until almost all of the liquid has been absorbed and evaporated. Add another 1 cup stock and increase the heat so that there is a fair amount of bubbling on the surface (this agitation helps release the starch as the rice cooks). Cook, stirring, until almost all of the liquid has been absorbed. To see if it's time to add more liquid, drag the spoon through the rice; if the liquid doesn't immediately fill in the space, it's time to add more. Add another 1 cup or so of stock and the thyme. Continue to

cook, stirring and adding more stock as needed, until the risotto looks creamy but the rice is still al dente, about 18 minutes.

Take the risotto off the heat. Add the remaining 1½ tablespoons butter, the Parmigiano-Reggiano, and the truffles, and stir well. Stir the egg yolks well, then stir them in until well combined; it's okay if the risotto looks very loose at this point, because it will thicken as it cools a bit. Divide the risotto among wide, shallow serving bowls.

NOTE: *I find that sometimes in risotto, you just get too much starch; the dish turns out mushy, the rice grains barely distinguishable. Now, some people really like that style, but I prefer a looser risotto, one in which each rice grain is distinct even while the overall impression of the dish is smooth and supple. Vialone Nano rice, which you can find in well-stocked supermarkets as well as Italian groceries, helps ensure that result.*

which wine? For this risotto, you could go in two different directions: a Chardonnay-based wine that's not too oaky, with a lovely acidity to balance the richness of the dish; or a Barolo or Barbaresco, which have tannic structures that will definitely elevate the flavors of the risotto.

SECONDI

FISH AND MEAT

I DON'T KNOW ABOUT YOU, but I often have the experience when I am eating out that all of the fun and exciting flavors disappear when the appetizers are cleared. That is not true with these dishes. Crafted so that there are many varied layers of flavors and textures, the main courses at Scarpetta stay exciting until the last bite. As with everything we present, the goal is to include different flavor profiles that interplay to create a balanced whole. Indeed, I think some of our customers may be surprised when they see all of the different elements that go into making up just one plate. That's because those disparate elements come together in such a way that the dish just makes sense. Though the making of it may have included many steps, what's set down on the table seems like a simple dish. The elements work in such harmony that the food is easy to "get."

What I set out to do in all of the recipes in this book is to demonstrate exactly how we make a dish at Scarpetta. That means shortcuts and substitutions are few and far between. After all, what is the sense of working to make the dish if it does not deliver on the promise of tasting like the dish that we serve at the restaurant? With the exception of the big family-style roasts, such as the pork roast on page 242 and the rib eye on page 252, most of these main course recipes have multiple elements to prepare for the plate. Aside from the protein, which is usually very simply cooked, most of the dishes include a delicate vegetable purée smeared across the plate. It's partly a visual reminder of the meaning of the name *Scarpetta*—that swipe people make with their bread across the plate when they want to sop up every last bit of something delicious. But it's not just there for whimsy. The purée also adds a base note of flavor and some additional texture to the plate, and it often winds up being that bit of deliciousness people mop up with their last morsel of bread. As you look to make these recipes, you may be tempted to leave it out. Please don't.

Most of these dishes also include a few roasted, sautéed, or pickled vegetables, a deeply flavored sauce, and some fresh herbs or tender greens. When you see all that as one dish, it can seem overwhelming to execute. But if you think about it, it's really something home cooks do all the time when entertaining; they make a protein (often with gravy), a starchy side (think mashed potatoes), and a green vegetable. At Scarpetta, we simply take that notion and elevate it so that all of the components come together in a more refined way.

When you read through this chapter and pick out the recipes you want to make for a special dinner, know that because these recipes come from a working kitchen, most of the elements can—and indeed often must—be made in advance, which makes the final preparation go quickly. Enjoy.

BLACK COD WITH CONCENTRATED TOMATOES AND CARAMELIZED FENNEL

This is one of these dishes that sells well at every Scarpetta location. It's never been off the menu, but over the years it has evolved as we add layers of flavor. The tomato "paint," for instance, infuses the cod with the flavors of tomato as well as garlic, capers, and oregano. The fennel comes at you in four different ways: toasted and ground seeds, tender roasted fennel bulb, fennel fronds, and fennel pollen, which though small in amount adds the perfect finish.

SERVES 4

FOR THE TOMATO PAINT

Extra-virgin olive oil

⅓ cup diced onion

3 cloves garlic, chopped

2 tablespoons capers, rinsed and coarsely chopped

3 cups canned tomatoes, drained and crushed

1 sprig fresh oregano

1 teaspoon fennel seeds, toasted (see page 89) and ground

Kosher salt

FOR SERVING

4 cod fillets, 5 to 6 ounces each

Kosher salt

Extra-virgin olive oil

Braised Fennel (page 189)

8 pieces Concentrated Tomatoes (page 324)

1 tablespoon chopped fresh chives

Flaked sea salt

¼ teaspoon fennel pollen (see Note, page 194)

2 tablespoons micro fennel or fennel fronds

Trucioleto Sauce (page 317)

FOR THE TOMATO PAINT: Heat a convection oven to 325°F or a conventional oven to 350°F.

Heat 1 tablespoon olive in a medium saucepan over medium heat. Add the onion, and cook, stirring occasionally, until soft and starting to brown around the edges. Add the garlic and capers and cook, stirring, for 2 minutes. Increase the heat to medium-high and add the tomatoes and oregano. Stir well to combine, and bring to a simmer. Transfer to the oven and cook, stirring every 10 minutes, until reduced and quite thick, about 40 minutes. Remove from the oven and stir in the fennel seeds. Transfer to a food processor, purée until smooth, and season to taste with kosher salt. (The paint can be made 2 days ahead; cover and refrigerate.)

which wine? For this rich, flaky, white-fleshed fish, choose a rich white wine like those made from grapes found on the slopes of Mount Etna in Sicily. Try an Etna Bianco; the blend, with citrus, mint, and minerals and excellent density, should be texturally perfect for the cod.

TO SERVE: Heat a convection oven to 450°F or a regular oven to 475°F.

Heat a large, ovenproof sauté pan over high heat. Season the flesh side of the cod well with kosher salt. Add 2 tablespoons olive oil to the pan and, when hot, add the cod, skin side down. Using a pastry brush, brush the top and sides of the cod with the tomato paint. Transfer the cod to the oven and cook for 8 minutes. Turn the cod over and brush a light coating of the paint onto the skin and the sides. Return the cod to the oven and cook until just cooked through, 2 to 4 minutes depending on thickness.

Meanwhile, heat 2 tablespoons olive oil in another large, ovenproof sauté pan over medium heat. Add the Braised Fennel in a single layer and cook undisturbed until beautifully browned, 2 to 3 minutes. Turn the fennel slices over and place 2 Concentrated Tomatoes on each slice. Transfer the pan to the oven to heat through for 4 minutes.

HOW TO COOK FISH PERFECTLY EVERY TIME

Like most endeavors, cooking a fillet of fish so that it's perfectly golden or crisp on the outside and tender inside takes practice. But there are also a few techniques and tips that help guarantee good results. At Scarpetta, the pan gets heated first until very hot, and only then is a good amount of oil added to the pan. The fish goes into the pan skin side down and does not get touched until that first side has beautiful color or, if it's skin on, is crispy. To turn the fish, a flexible spatula works best (tongs can be too rough on the fish). You also don't want to actually lift the fish out of the pan, as too much handling can make flaky fish fall apart. Instead, use the spatula to lift one edge of the fish up and turn it over to the other side. If the fish is sticking, chances are it has not cooked on that first side long enough; give it another minute and try turning again. Sometimes we finish cooking the fish in the oven, mainly to make room on the stove for more fish to be seared, but also because the oven can cook the fish more evenly.

Divide the fennel and tomato among serving plates. Sprinkle with the chives and a tiny pinch of flaked sea salt. Place the roasted cod, skin side up, on the tomatoes and fennel. Sprinkle each with a tiny pinch of flaked sea salt and fennel pollen. Top with a tiny handful of micro fennel. Spoon a few tablespoons of the Trucioleto Sauce on the plate around the fish, and drizzle with a little olive oil.

BRAISED FENNEL

SERVES 4 AS A SIDE DISH

This braised fennel is so simple but so good. For a vegetarian main course, brown the fennel as directed and serve with some Concentrated Tomatoes (page 324) and a generous sprinkling of black olives.

1 large or 2 small bulbs fennel, trimmed

1 tablespoon extra-virgin olive oil

Pinch of crushed red pepper

Kosher salt

Heat a convection oven to 375°F or a conventional oven to 400°F.

Slice the fennel vertically through the core to get 4 slices, each ½ inch thick. (Reserve any remaining fennel for another use.)

In a roasting pan or baking dish just large enough to hold the fennel in a single layer, drizzle the olive oil and sprinkle the crushed red pepper over the bottom. Lay the fennel planks in the pan and season lightly with salt. Add ¼ cup water, cover the pan tightly with aluminum foil, and bake until tender, about 30 minutes. (The fennel can be braised 1 day ahead. Cover and refrigerate.) Caramelize as directed in the black cod recipe on page 187, or simply reheat in a low oven.

STRIPED BASS WITH CELERY ROOT PURÉE, CHARRED ONION, SPRING GARLIC, AND PICKLED LEEK VINAIGRETTE

The vinaigrette that we serve this bass with acts almost like a chimichurri, brightening the charred flavors from the onion and the fish. It's really bright and beautiful. The earthy celery root keeps the dish grounded.

SERVES 4

2 endives, split in half lengthwise

2 spring onions, halved

8 scallions, trimmed to 4 inches

Extra-virgin olive oil

1 tablespoon chopped fresh thyme

Pinch of crushed red pepper

Kosher salt

4 skin-on, wild striped bass fillets, about 5 ounces each

Freshly ground black pepper

1 cup Celery Root Purée (page 328), heated

¼ cup Spring Garlic and Pickled Leek Vinaigrette (page 191)

Microgreens (optional)

Heat a grill or grill pan to medium-high. (If using a grill pan, heat the oven to 350°F.)

Toss the endives, spring onions, and scallions with 3 tablespoons olive oil, the thyme, and crushed red pepper. Season well with salt and grill until charred and tender, moving the vegetables to a cooler side of the grill (or lowering the heat on the grill pan) as needed.

With a sharp knife, score just the skin of the bass. Season the bass on both sides with salt and black pepper and lightly coat it with olive oil.

With a paper towel dampened with olive oil, oil the grill (or grill pan). Place the fish skin side down on the hottest part of the grill. Cook for 1½ minutes undisturbed, then rotate the fish 45 degrees to get nice-looking grill marks on the skin side. Cook for another 1½ minutes. (If the grill is hot enough, the fish should not stick. If it seems to be sticking, leave it for another minute before trying

which wine? The grilled fish, with its delicate meat and smoky components, will be surely complemented by a Pecorino wine from Le Marche, whose crisp, dry style and nutty overtones should enhance the flavors of the dish.

to move it.) Turn the fish over and cook on the other side for 2 minutes. Transfer to a cooler spot on the grill to finish cooking, another 5 to 6 minutes. (If using a grill pan, transfer the fish to the oven to finish cooking, another 5 to 6 minutes.)

To serve, divide the Celery Root Purée among serving plates, smearing it across the center of the plate. Place the charred vegetables in a line down the center of the plate. Top with the fish, skin side up. Spoon 1 tablespoon of the Spring Garlic and Pickled Leek Vinaigrette over each plate, top with a few microgreens, if using, and serve.

SPRING GARLIC AND PICKLED LEEK VINAIGRETTE

MAKES ABOUT 1½ CUPS

This makes more than you need for the striped bass recipe, but the vinaigrette, which will last up to 5 days covered and refrigerated, would also be fantastic drizzled over grilled steak.

6 ounces spring garlic (see Note), trimmed and very thinly sliced (about 2 cups)

Extra-virgin olive oil

Kosher salt

⅓ cup Pickled Leeks (page 336), plus 2½ tablespoons of the pickling liquid

½ cup chopped fresh flat-leaf parsley

½ cup chopped fresh chives

½ teaspoon crushed red pepper

In a small saucepan, combine the spring garlic with 1 cup olive oil and heat over medium heat. Simmer until the garlic is soft, about 30 minutes. Season to taste with salt, remove from the heat, and let cool to room temperature. (The garlic will keep, submerged in the olive oil and covered and refrigerated, for 1 week. Warm it at room temperature before using.)

Mince the Pickled Leeks and transfer them to a small bowl along with the pickling liquid. Take the spring garlic out of the oil it cooked in (reserve the oil for other uses) and add it to the leeks. Add the parsley, chives, crushed red pepper, and ½ teaspoon salt. Slowly whisk in ⅓ cup olive oil. (The vinaigrette will keep, covered and refrigerated, for 3 days. Let warm at room temperature before using.)

NOTE: *If spring garlic (see page 203) is not available, use 1½ cups sliced leeks and 5 cloves garlic in its place.*

FENNEL- AND CITRUS-SPICED ROASTED BLACK COD WITH BACCALÀ MANTECATO

With its fragrant spice rub featuring lemon and anise, the cod is quite delicious on its own. But it becomes spectacular when paired with *baccalà mantecato*, a Venetian specialty that's similar to brandade but more like a thick, creamy sauce. Roasted cherry tomatoes cut through all that richness and add a pop of color to the plate.

SERVES 4

FOR THE SPICES

1 tablespoon Dried Lemon Zest (page 351) or high-quality purchased dried lemon zest

1½ teaspoons fennel seeds

1 teaspoon anise seeds (not star anise)

¼ teaspoon crushed red pepper

½ teaspoon fennel pollen (see Note)

2 tablespoons flaked sea salt

FOR SERVING

¾ cup Baccalà Mantecato (page 195)

4 black cod fillets, about 5 ounces each

Kosher salt

Extra-virgin olive oil

4 small sprigs fresh thyme

12 very thin garlic slices

4 ounces chanterelle mushrooms, trimmed

16 asparagus spears, preferably thin ones, trimmed to 3 inches and blanched (see page 194)

12 to 16 pieces Roasted Cherry Tomatoes (page 323)

1 tablespoon chopped fresh flat-leaf parsley

Freshly ground black pepper

2 tablespoons Black Olive Oil (page 344)

FOR THE SPICES: In a small sauté pan, toast the Dried Lemon Zest, fennel seeds, anise seeds, and crushed red pepper over medium heat, stirring occasionally, until fragrant, 2 to 3 minutes. Transfer the spices to a spice grinder, add the fennel pollen, and grind finely. If not using right away, let cool to room temperature, and store airtight. Mix 1 tablespoon of the spices with the flaked sea salt to be used as finishing salt and reserve it separately from the rest of the spices. (Both spice mixes will keep for months, tightly covered, but their aroma and intensity will lessen over time.)

TO SERVE: Heat a convection oven to 375°F or a conventional oven to 400°F.

BLANCHING

The point of blanching is to set color in a vegetable or to help loosen its skin for peeling. In most cases, the vegetables will be cooked further to get to their optimum tenderness. To blanch, bring a pot of salted water to a boil and fill a bowl with ice water. Boil the vegetables for 1 minute, then transfer to the ice water to stop the cooking. If a recipe calls for a vegetable to be cooked to a certain doneness ahead of time, the technique is the same, but the vegetable should cook for a little longer, as directed.

Warm the *Baccalà Mantecato* over low heat, if necessary.

Pat the cod dry, lightly dust both sides with just a little of the unsalted spice mix, and season lightly with kosher salt. Heat 1 tablespoon olive oil in a large sauté pan over high heat, add the cod skin side down, and top each fillet with 1 sprig thyme and 3 slices garlic. Immediately transfer to the oven to cook until just cooked through, 8 to 12 minutes depending on thickness.

Meanwhile, heat 1 tablespoon olive oil in a medium sauté pan over high heat. Add the mushrooms, season lightly with kosher salt, and cook, stirring occasionally, until nicely browned on all sides, about 4 minutes. Add the asparagus, Roasted Cherry Tomatoes, and parsley and cook, stirring occasionally, to heat through. Season with kosher salt and black pepper to taste.

Divide the vegetables among serving plates. Using about 3 tablespoons of the *mantecato* per plate, dollop it over and around the vegetables. Place the fish, skin side up, on the vegetables. Drizzle a little Black Olive Oil over everything and finish with a pinch of the spices mixed with sea salt.

NOTE: *Fennel pollen, long a part of culinary tradition in northern Italy, is exactly what it sounds like: granules of pollen harvested from the buds of flowering fennel plants. Just a little bit not only adds its own sweet, licorice-like notes, but it also boosts the overall flavor of the dish. Look for it in specialty markets—it's becoming more widely available—or by mail order.*

BACCALÀ MANTECATO

MAKES ABOUT 3 CUPS

The name of the dish comes from the Italian verb *mantecare*, which means "to stir vigorously" or whip so as to create a creamy consistency, which is exactly what you do to the cod to create this thick sauce. The recipe makes more than you need for the dish, but it will keep for 3 days covered with plastic wrap and refrigerated and is delicious slathered on grilled bread.

2 cups whole milk

2 cloves garlic, lightly smashed

4 ounces fingerling potatoes, peeled and thinly sliced

1 sprig fresh thyme

8 ounces salt cod, preferably homemade (page 196), cut into large chunks

¼ cup extra-virgin olive oil

Kosher salt

In a medium saucepan over medium heat, combine the milk, garlic, potatoes, and thyme. Bring to a simmer and cook until the potatoes are soft, about 10 minutes. Add the salt cod and poach until falling apart, 5 to 7 minutes.

Meanwhile, fill a large bowl with several inches of ice water.

Working over a bowl to collect the liquid, drain the salt cod, then transfer the fish to a blender and remove the thyme. Add enough of the reserved poaching liquid to just cover the solids, and purée until smooth, adding more poaching liquid as needed until the purée is the consistency of yogurt, about 3 minutes. With the machine running, slowly add the olive oil until emulsified. Taste and season with salt if needed.

Transfer to a bowl and put the bowl in the ice water to cool quickly. If not using right away, cover and refrigerate. (It will keep, covered and refrigerated, for 3 days.)

HOMEMADE SALT COD

MAKES ABOUT 8 OUNCES

You can buy salt cod, but this homemade version is more supple and not as strongly flavored.

¾ cup kosher salt

¼ cup granulated sugar

10 ounces Atlantic cod fillet, skin and blood line removed

Mix together the salt and sugar.

Put a cooling rack over a rimmed baking sheet and cover it with cheesecloth. Sprinkle a layer of the salt and sugar mixture over the cheesecloth, about ¼ inch thick. Place the cod on top and put the rest of the salt and sugar mixture over the fish, brushing away any piles from the edges of the fish. Cover loosely with the cheesecloth and refrigerate for 12 hours; the fish should be firm but not stiff. Rinse the cure off under running water and pat the fish dry with paper towels. Wrap in plastic wrap and refrigerate for at least 24 hours to allow the cure to penetrate the fish evenly. (It will keep, covered and refrigerated, for 1 week, or frozen for up to 2 months.)

SLOW-COOKED LOBSTER WITH RICOTTA DUMPLINGS, PEA SHOOTS, CHERRY TOMATOES, AND TARRAGON OIL

The key to this recipe is to slowly cook the lobster so that it gets that great melt-in-your-mouth texture. Paired with soft ricotta cheese dumplings and cherry tomatoes, this is summer eating at its best.

SERVES 4

FOR THE DUMPLINGS

1 pound fresh ricotta cheese, preferably sheep's milk, drained if very wet

2 large egg yolks

¼ cup panko bread crumbs

3 tablespoons plus 1 teaspoon all-purpose flour

Kosher salt and freshly ground black pepper

Extra-virgin olive oil, as needed

FOR THE LOBSTER

2 lobsters, 1½ pounds each

FOR SERVING

Extra-virgin olive oil

20 cherry tomatoes

1 cup Lobster Broth (page 311)

6 tablespoons (3 ounces) unsalted butter, cut into pieces

1 teaspoon fresh lemon juice

Crushed red pepper

Kosher salt

2 cloves garlic, thinly sliced

1 cup pea shoots

1 tablespoon chopped fresh chives

Juice of ½ lemon

Tarragon Oil (page 345)

FOR THE DUMPLINGS: Line a rimmed baking sheet with parchment paper. In a medium bowl, combine the ricotta, egg yolks, panko, and flour. Season to taste with salt and black pepper. Refrigerate the dough for at least 10 minutes to make it easier to handle.

Meanwhile, bring a large saucepan of well-salted water to a gentle boil. Fill a large bowl with ice water.

Using two teaspoons, shape the ricotta mixture into quenelles (see page 79), transferring them to the baking sheet as you go. (You will

need 20 quenelles.) In batches, boil the dumplings for 7 minutes, then gently transfer to the ice water and let cool for 20 minutes. (This makes the dumplings easier to handle and less prone to falling apart when mixed with everything else. At this point, the dumplings may be drained, tossed with olive oil, and refrigerated for up to 2 days.)

FOR THE LOBSTER: Bring a large pot of water to a boil. Fill a large bowl with ice water.

which wine? To complement the sweet lobster flavor, pour a wine with a complete bouquet, like a Chardonnay from northern Italy with enough richness and intensity to be in harmony with the ricotta.

Separate the large claws from the bodies. Boil the bodies for 1½ minutes, then transfer them to the ice water. (The lobster will not be fully cooked at this point.) Boil the claws for 6 minutes, then shock in the ice water. Remove the lobster meat from the shells (reserve the shells for making stock). Split the tails in half lengthwise, then cut each half into thirds. Cut the claws in half and reserve. If not using the lobster meat right away, cover and refrigerate for up to 1 day.

TO SERVE: Heat a convection oven to 325°F or a conventional oven to 350°F.

In a large sauté pan over medium-high heat, heat 1 tablespoon olive oil. Add the cherry tomatoes and cook, stirring occasionally, until their skins blister, about 5 minutes. Remove from the pan, let cool slightly, and peel them.

Put the lobster meat in a medium ovenproof sauté pan. Add ¼ cup of the Lobster Broth, 2 tablespoons of the butter, 2 tablespoons olive oil, the lemon juice, and a pinch of crushed red pepper. Season lightly with salt, transfer the pan to the oven, and cook, basting the lobster with the butter and oil from the pan every few minutes, until the lobster is no longer translucent and is firm to the touch, 8 to 12 minutes (begin checking early so you don't overcook the lobster).

Meanwhile, heat 2 tablespoons olive oil in a large sauté pan over medium-high heat. Add the garlic and a pinch of crushed red pepper and cook, swirling the garlic in the pan, until the garlic just begins to turn golden. Add ½ cup of the Lobster Broth and cook for 1 minute, then add the tomatoes and the dumplings. Lower the heat to medium and gently cook for 2 minutes, adding more Lobster Broth if the pan is dry. Add the remaining 4 tablespoons butter, swirling it in the pan to emulsify the sauce. Add the lobster meat, turning it over in the sauce to coat it well. Add the pea shoots, chives, and lemon juice and stir gently to combine. Divide among serving plates and drizzle each plate with a little of the Tarragon Oil.

CRISPY BLACK BASS WITH PORCINI BRODETTO

This dish marries the deep woodsy flavor of dried porcini mushrooms with a seafood stew. A sip of the earthy yet briny broth makes you feel like you're at the edge of the forest overlooking the ocean. Contrasting the brothy stew is perfectly cooked fillet of crisp-skinned black bass. At Scarpetta, we always have fish bones ready for a pot of broth, but you can buy these from your fishmonger (if he or she doesn't give them to you for free). Same with the additional shrimp shells you will need. You will make more *brodetto* than you will need, but you can freeze any left over.

SERVES 4

FOR THE SHRIMP

4 very large shrimp (12 to 15 per pound), peeled (save the shells for the brodetto), deveined, and cut in half lengthwise

Extra-virgin olive oil

1 tablespoon chopped fresh flat-leaf parsley

Pinch of crushed red pepper

FOR THE BRODETTO

Extra-virgin olive oil

1 cup fennel pieces (this can be scraps, such as fennel tops)

½ cup chopped spring garlic bulbs (reserve the tops for serving)

6 ounces shrimp shells (from about 2 pounds shrimp)

8 ounces fish bones, preferably from black bass

1 cup sliced cremini mushrooms

½ ounce dried porcini mushrooms

2 quarts Chicken Stock (page 310)

Kosher salt

FOR SERVING

Extra-virgin olive oil

½ cup finely diced spring garlic tops

½ cup julienned baby fennel

½ cup julienned spring onion (or substitute scallions)

Kosher salt

Pinch of crushed red pepper

1 cup cooked fregola (see Note, page 215)

2 tablespoons diced (¼ inch) potatoes, preferably purple ones

1 ounce garlic scapes, sliced finely on a bias and blanched (see page 194)

1 tablespoon chopped fresh flat-leaf parsley

4 skin-on black bass fillets, about 5 ounces each

FOR THE SHRIMP: In a small bowl, toss the shrimp with 1 table-spoon olive oil, the parsley, and the crushed red pepper. Cover, refrigerate, and marinate for at least 3 hours and up to 24 hours.

FOR THE *BRODETTO*: Heat 1 tablespoon olive oil in a large saucepan or stockpot over medium-high heat. Add the fennel and spring garlic, and cook, stirring, until tender, about 3 minutes. Add the shrimp shells and cook, stirring occasionally, until bright red and aromatic, about 3 minutes. Add the fish bones, cremini and porcini mushrooms, and the stock, and bring to a boil. Lower the heat and simmer, skimming off foam occasionally, for 30 minutes.

Strain through a fine-mesh strainer into a clean saucepan and cook over medium-high heat until reduced to about 4 cups, about 5 minutes. Using an immersion blender to combine, slowly add 2 tablespoons olive oil to the *brodetto* and mix until emulsified. Season to taste with salt. (The *brodetto* may be made up to 2 days ahead; keep it covered and refrigerated, and reheat gently before using.)

TRULY SEASONAL INGREDIENTS

Few things excite a chef more than working with truly seasonal ingredients in the short window when they're available. When spring garlic is at the farmers' market, we scoop it up. Spring garlic looks a little like a scallion, with small bulbs attached to floppy greens; it has a gentle garlic flavor.

TO SERVE: Heat a convection oven to 400°F or a conventional oven to 425°F. Reheat the *brodetto* if necessary.

In a large sauté pan, heat 2 tablespoons olive oil over medium heat. Add the spring garlic tops, fennel, spring onion, 1 teaspoon salt, and the crushed red pepper. Cook, stirring occasionally, until the vegetables are tender and sweet, about 5 minutes. Add the fregola, the potatoes, and 2 cups of the *brodetto*, and increase the heat to medium-high. Cook, stirring occasionally, until almost all of the liquid is absorbed or reduced, about 4 minutes. Add the garlic scapes, potatoes, shrimp, and parsley, and cook, stirring occasionally, until the shrimp are cooked through, about 2 minutes. Taste for seasoning, and add additional salt if needed. Stir in 2 tablespoons olive oil.

Heat a large sauté pan over medium-high heat. Add 1 tablespoon olive oil to the pan. Season both sides of the bass with salt. Add the bass, skin side down, to the pan, then transfer to the oven. Cook for 5 minutes, then turn the fish over and cook until just medium-rare—a cake tester inserted into the fish should meet no resistance—about another 30 seconds.

Divide the fregola mixture among serving plates. Place the bass, skin side up, on top. Pour some warm *brodetto* over the bass and serve.

TURBOT WITH MUSSELS, CAVOLO NERO, SALSIFY, AND PROSECCO EMULSION

Turbot has a beautiful flavor and a slightly gelatinous quality that I just love. A study in contrasts, this dish is mostly monochromatic—the fish, the purée, the mushrooms, and the froth are all shades of white—except for the dramatic dashes of darkness from the *cavolo nero* (black cabbage, often called lacinato kale or dinosaur kale). To brighten up these deep flavors, finish the plate with a Prosecco froth that's easily made using an immersion blender.

SERVES 4

FOR THE MUSSELS

Extra-virgin olive oil

1 clove garlic, sliced

3 sprigs fresh thyme

Kosher salt

Pinch of crushed red pepper

20 mussels, preferably P.E.I.

FOR THE CABBAGE AND MUSHROOMS

Extra-virgin olive oil

2 medium shallots, chopped

2 cloves garlic, chopped

1 tablespoon chopped fresh thyme

Pinch of crushed red pepper

1 pound hon-shimeji mushrooms (see page 48)

Kosher salt

4 ounces cavolo nero, stemmed, blanched (see page 194), and cut into 1½-inch strips

Freshly ground black pepper

FOR THE PROSECCO EMULSION

1 lemon

2 cups Prosecco

1½ teaspoons granulated sugar

¼ teaspoon kosher salt

1½ teaspoons lecithin (see Note, page 155)

FOR SERVING

Pan-Roasted Salsify (page 206)

2 tablespoons chopped fresh flat-leaf parsley

½ teaspoon fresh thyme leaves

Crushed red pepper

4 turbot fillets, 4 to 5 ounces each

Kosher salt

Extra-virgin olive oil

1 cup Salsify Purée (page 330)

FOR THE MUSSELS: Heat 1 tablespoon olive oil in a large sauté pan over medium heat. Add the garlic and cook, stirring, until it sizzles. Add the thyme, 1 teaspoon salt, the crushed red pepper, and the mussels. Add ¼ cup water and increase the heat to medium-high. Cover and cook, shaking the pan occasionally, until the mussels open, about 5 minutes.

which wine? A more delicate white is the way to go here. Try not to overwhelm the fish, so choose a crisp white with a balanced texture, like a Verdicchio from Le Marche.

Put a colander in a bowl and drain the mussels, reserving the cooking liquid. When cool enough to handle, remove the mussels from their shells, collecting any juices with the cooking liquid. Reserve the mussels and their liquid. (The mussels may be steamed earlier in the day. Cover and refrigerate the mussels and the cooking liquid until ready to use.)

FOR THE CABBAGE AND MUSHROOMS: In a large sauté pan over medium-low heat, heat 1 tablespoon olive oil. Add the shallots and garlic, and cook, stirring occasionally, until tender but not colored, adjusting the heat as needed, about 5 minutes. Add the thyme and crushed red pepper and cook for 1 minute. Add 2 tablespoons olive oil and increase the heat to medium. Add the mushrooms, season lightly with salt, and cook, stirring, until tender, about 3 minutes. Add the *cavolo nero*, and cook, stirring occasionally, until very tender. If the vegetables look dry, add water as needed, a little at a time. Season to taste with additional salt and black pepper, remove from the heat, and reserve.

FOR THE PROSECCO EMULSION: Use a vegetable peeler to peel wide strips of zest from the lemon. In a medium saucepan, combine the zest with the Prosecco, sugar, and salt. Heat over medium-high heat until the liquid just begins to boil. Remove the pan from the heat and let the zest steep for 10 minutes. Remove the zest and transfer the liquid to a blender. Add the lecithin and blend briefly. Strain through a fine-mesh strainer into a clean saucepan and keep warm. (You can make the emulsion up to 8 hours ahead. Cover and refrigerate it; reheat it to just warm before using.)

TO SERVE: Add the Pan-Roasted Salsify to the cabbage and mushrooms and heat over medium heat, stirring occasionally, until warmed through. Add the mussels and just enough of the reserved cooking liquid to moisten everything. Toss to combine, and cook just until the mussels are heated through. Stir in the parsley and keep warm.

Heat a large sauté pan over medium-high heat. Sprinkle the thyme and a few flakes of crushed red pepper over each fillet and season with salt. Add 1 tablespoon oil to the pan and, when hot, add the fish to the pan, skin side down, and cook undisturbed for 3 minutes. Turn over and cook for another 1 minute. Remove the fish from the pan and keep warm.

Spread about 3 tablespoons of the Salsify Purée on each serving plate. Divide the vegetables and mussels among the plates. Top with the fish, skin side up, and a drizzle of olive oil. Using an immersion blender, froth the Prosecco emulsion, and spoon the bubbles and a little bit of the liquid over the fish.

PAN-ROASTED SALSIFY

SERVES 4 AS A SIDE DISH

Salsify unpeeled looks rough. Similar to a parsnip in size, though a little skinnier, salsify has a tough tan skin and is usually sold with some of its shaggy roots intact. But beneath that coarse exterior is a bright white root with a flavor that's much milder than you might expect—more akin to an artichoke than a root vegetable.

1 tablespoon extra-virgin olive oil

1 pound salsify, peeled, sliced on the bias ¼ inch thick, and blanched (see page 194; about 2 cups)

1 clove garlic, peeled

1 sprig fresh thyme

In a medium sauté pan, heat the olive oil over medium-high heat. Add the salsify and cook, turning occasionally, until just tender, about 4 minutes. Add the garlic clove and the thyme sprig, and cook, stirring to infuse the flavors, until the garlic sizzles and colors slightly. Remove the garlic and thyme before serving the salsify.

DIVER SCALLOPS WITH PINE NUT GREMOLATA AND ASPARAGUS

When Nina, chef de cuisine at Scarpetta Miami, first made this dish for me to try, I told her to put it on the menu that day. It's that good.

SERVES 4

FOR THE GREMOLATA

½ cup extra-virgin olive oil

1 clove garlic, peeled

1 cup finely chopped fresh flat-leaf parsley

3 tablespoons pine nuts, toasted (see page 89)

1½ teaspoons finely grated lemon zest

¾ cup Pickled Ramps (page 335) or Pickled Leeks (page 336)

Flaked sea salt

FOR THE SCALLOPS

12 large diver scallops (10 per pound)

2 tablespoons extra-virgin olive oil

1 teaspoon chopped fresh thyme

Pinch of crushed red pepper

FOR SERVING

Extra-virgin olive oil

12 green asparagus spears, peeled, trimmed to 2-inch lengths, blanched, and shocked (see page 194)

8 blue foot mushrooms or other wild mushrooms, halved

Radish Confit (page 209)

1 teaspoon chopped fresh flat-leaf parsley

Kosher salt and freshly ground black pepper

1 cup Celery Root Purée (page 328)

FOR THE GREMOLATA: Heat the olive oil in a small saucepan over low heat. Using a rasp-style grater, grate the garlic into the oil and warm gently for 5 minutes, adjusting the heat as needed to keep the garlic from coloring. Remove from the heat and transfer the garlic and oil to a bowl. Add the parsley, pine nuts, lemon zest, and Pickled Ramps, and season with flaked sea salt to taste. (The gremolata may be made earlier in the day; cover and refrigerate, and let warm up a bit at room temperature before serving.)

FOR THE SCALLOPS: Remove the muscle from the side of each scallop and discard. In a small bowl, combine the olive oil, thyme, and crushed red pepper. Add the scallops and gently toss to coat. Cover and refrigerate for at least 1 hour and up to 4 hours.

TO SERVE: In a medium sauté pan, heat 1 tablespoon olive oil over medium-high heat. Add the asparagus, mushrooms, and the radishes from the Radish Confit, and cook, stirring occasionally, until slightly browned, 3 to 5 minutes. Stir in the parsley and remove from the heat.

Heat a large sauté pan over high heat, and add 2 tablespoons olive oil. Remove the scallops from their marinade, season with kosher salt and black pepper, and add them to the pan. Let them cook undisturbed until a deep brown crust develops on one side, about 1½ minutes. Turn each scallop over and cook, basting occasionally with the oil in the pan, until the scallops are medium-rare, about another 1½ minutes.

Divide the Celery Root Purée among large serving plates, smearing it across the middle of the plate. Place the vegetables randomly on the plates, then place the scallops on the purée. Top each scallop with about 1 tablespoon of the gremolata.

RADISH CONFIT

MAKES ¼ CUP

If you have only ever had radishes raw, these cooked ones will be a revelation.

12 to 16 baby radishes, or 1 or 2 regular radishes, cut into 8 to 12 thin wedges depending on size

1 cup extra-virgin olive oil, plus more as needed

1 sprig fresh thyme

Crushed red pepper

Kosher salt

In a small saucepan, cover the radishes with the olive oil. Add the thyme and crushed red pepper, and season lightly with salt. Cook over low heat, stirring occasionally, until tender, about 10 minutes; the time will vary depending on the size of the radishes. The radishes will keep, covered and refrigerated, for 3 days.

BRANZINO WITH SAFFRON-SCENTED SHELLFISH STUFATO AND BROCCOLI DI CICCO

With its saffron flavor, this stew-like dish is a play on bouillabaisse. And like a good pot of bouillabaisse, the flavors in this dish build: The clams and mussels when cooked provide the base for a broth that infuses the *stufato* with its of-the-sea flavors. In Los Angeles, broccoli di Cicco, an heirloom broccoli that hails originally from Italy, is often at the farmers' market. Broccoli rabe makes a great substitute if you can't find it.

SERVES 4

FOR THE SHRIMP

2 tablespoons extra-virgin olive oil

½ teaspoon chopped fresh rosemary

½ teaspoon chopped fresh flat-leaf parsley

Pinch of crushed red pepper

8 rock shrimp, peeled (see Note)

FOR THE MUSSELS AND CLAMS

1 tablespoon extra-virgin olive oil

1 clove garlic, sliced

3 sprigs fresh thyme

1 teaspoon kosher salt

Pinch of crushed red pepper

12 mussels, preferably P.E.I.

12 littleneck clams

FOR THE BROTH

Extra-virgin olive oil

1 cup diced leeks (white and light green parts)

½ cup sliced shallots

2 cloves garlic, thinly sliced

½ teaspoon saffron threads

2 plum tomatoes, cut into medium dice

Kosher salt

FOR THE STUFATO

Extra-virgin olive oil

¼ cup diced leeks, blanched (see page 194)

¾ cup diced (¼-inch) Yukon gold potatoes, blanched (see page 194)

½ pound broccoli di Cicco or broccoli rabe, blanched (see page 194)

1 cup cherry tomatoes, preferably Sun Gold, halved

2 tablespoons chopped fresh flat-leaf parsley

Kosher salt

FOR SERVING

4 branzino fillets, 5 to 6 ounces each

Kosher salt and freshly ground black pepper

Extra-virgin olive oil

Smoked Paprika Oil (page 341)

FOR THE SHRIMP: In a small bowl, combine the olive oil with the rosemary, parsley, and crushed red pepper. Add the shrimp and toss to combine. Cover and refrigerate for at least 3 hours and up to 24 hours.

FOR THE MUSSELS AND CLAMS: Heat the oil in a large sauté pan over medium heat. Add the garlic and cook until it sizzles. Add the thyme, salt, crushed red pepper, mussels, and clams. Add ¼ cup water and increase the heat to medium-high. Cover and cook until the clams and mussels open, about 5 minutes. Meanwhile, put a colander in a bowl. When almost all of the clams and mussels have opened, drain them in the colander, reserving the cooking liquid. When cool enough to handle, remove the clams and mussels from their shells, collecting any juices, and reserve. Decant the cooking liquid into a measuring cup, leaving any sediment behind in the bowl. Add the juices collected from shucking the clams and mussels and enough water, if needed, to make 2 cups.

FOR THE BROTH: In a large saucepan, heat 1 tablespoon olive oil over medium heat. Add the leeks, shallots, and garlic, and cook, stirring occasionally, until tender but not colored, about 5 minutes. Crumble in the saffron and cook, stirring occasionally, until very fragrant, 1 to 2 minutes. Add the tomatoes and a pinch of salt and cook until the tomatoes are soft and broken down, about 3 minutes. Add the broth from the mussels and clams and 1 cup water and bring to a boil. Lower the heat to a simmer and cook for 30 minutes. Strain the broth through a fine-mesh strainer and reserve. You will have about 2 cups.

FOR THE *STUFATO*: Heat 1 tablespoon olive oil in a large sauté pan over medium heat. Add the leeks and cook, stirring occasionally, until tender but not browned, about 3 minutes. Add the potatoes and the broth and bring to a simmer, stirring occasionally, to work some of the starch into the broth. Continue cooking until the liquid has reduced by about two-thirds, 5 to 7 minutes. Add the shrimp, mussels, broccoli di Cicco, and tomatoes, and cook over

which wine? The aromatic flavors of the saffron and the delicacy of the fish require a wine with a spicy texture, like a generous Verdicchio from Umani Ronchi or Saltarelli.

medium heat for 2 minutes. Add the parsley and 1 tablespoon olive oil, and season to taste with salt. The liquid should be brothy but not too loose. Keep the *stufato* warm while you cook the fish.

TO SERVE: Heat a large sauté pan over high heat. Season the branzino with salt and black pepper. Add 1 tablespoon olive oil to the pan, then add the branzino, skin side down. Cook, undisturbed, until the skin is crispy, about 6 minutes. Turn the fish over and cook for another 1 minute.

Divide the *stufato* among wide, shallow serving bowls. Place a branzino fillet, skin side up, on top. Finish with a light drizzle of Smoked Paprika Oil.

NOTE: *Tiny rock shrimp are sweeter than most shrimp, with a lobster-like texture and taste, but if you can't find them, you can substitute conventional shrimp (cut them into thirds).*

SOFT-SHELL CRABS WITH SPRING VEGETABLE FRICASSEE

In Venice, soft-shell crabs, known there as *molecche*, are also a favorite seasonal treat. In this dish, the crab is surrounded by beautiful spring vegetables and an aromatic broth. Because *molecche* are tinier than our crabs, we like to cut our crabs into smaller pieces, which also adds more of the soft-shell flavor to the overall dish.

SERVES 4

Kosher salt

6 white asparagus spears, tough ends trimmed and peeled

6 green asparagus spears, tough ends trimmed and peeled

2 cups cipollini onions

½ cup fregola (see Note)

Extra-virgin olive oil

3 soft-shell crabs, cleaned (see opposite) and quartered

12 cockles or other small clams

4 cups Crab Stock (page 313)

2 leeks (white and light green parts), cut into thin rounds, rinsed, and patted dry

1 large shallot, thinly sliced lengthwise

1 ounce guanciale, cut into julienne

Pinch of crushed red pepper

4 ounces (about 2 cups) white hon-shimeji mushrooms (see page 48), cleaned and trimmed, or slivered shiitake mushrooms

1½ cups thawed frozen sweet peas or fresh peas, blanched (see page 194)

¼ cup heavy cream

1 tablespoon chopped fresh tarragon

which wine? A lovely, crisp Sauvignon Blanc would work extremely well here. Look for one with a style that emphasizes the varietal's greener quality; its mineral, almost saline notes should bring out the sweetness of the crabmeat.

Bring a skillet of salted water to a boil. Fill a bowl with ice water. Blanch the white asparagus for 1 minute, then transfer to the ice water to stop the cooking. Drain and pat dry. Cut off about 1½ inches from the tops of the white and the green asparagus and reserve. Cut the rest of the spears on a sharp bias ¼ inch thick. Reserve.

Blanch the cipollini as you did the white asparagus, then peel and quarter.

Bring a medium saucepan of well-salted water to a boil. Add the fregola and cook until just barely tender, about 6 minutes. Drain and spread on a rimmed baking sheet to cool.

HOW TO CLEAN SOFT-SHELL CRABS

For the freshest "softies," they must be alive when you buy them. If you are going to make them the second you get home, you can have the fishmonger clean them for you; if not, you should clean them yourself. To clean a crab, cut off the head approximately ¼ inch below the eyes. Press on the crab a little to squeeze out an unpleasantly flavored green bubble. Remove the gill filaments on each side of the crab by peeling back the pointed soft shell and scraping these inedible gills out with a paring knife. On the belly side, bend back the apron (or tail flap) and pull it off using a slight twisting motion.

Heat 2 tablespoons olive oil in a large sauté pan over medium-high heat. When the pan starts smoking, remove from the heat and add the crabs. Immediately put the pan back on the heat and cook until the crabs form a hard crust on one side, about 1 minute. Add the cockles and 2 cups stock. Cover the pan and cook, shaking the pan occasionally, until the cockles open. Take off the heat and reserve.

In a large sauté pan, heat 1 tablespoon olive oil over medium-high heat. Add the leeks, shallot, guanciale, and crushed red pepper. Season lightly with salt and cook, stirring, until the guanciale becomes fragrant and the leeks and shallots are tender, about 5 minutes. Add the mushrooms, peas, white and green asparagus, and cipollini, and cook for 5 minutes to blend the flavors, adjusting the heat as necessary and adding additional Crab Stock as necessary to keep the vegetables from browning. Add the fregola, crabs, cockles, and any liquid in the pan. Lower the heat and cook, stirring occasionally and adding additional stock as necessary, until the fregola has released its starch and the sauce has thickened, 7 to 9 minutes. Stir in the heavy cream and tarragon and cook just until the cream is hot. Divide everything among serving plates, saving the crab for last so it's on top.

NOTE: *Fregola is a tiny toasted pasta similar to couscous. A Sardinian specialty, fregola is made by rubbing coarse semolina flour and water together to create little pellets. You can usually find it at specialty food stores and Italian markets. Israeli couscous can sub for it in most recipes, if you can't find it.*

GUANCIALE-WRAPPED HALIBUT WITH MORELS, ASPARAGUS, AND SMOKED POTATO SAUCE

Halibut is a lean fish that's easy to overcook, which is why wrapping it with guanciale (or *lardo* or pancetta, either of which can take the place of the guanciale) is such genius. As the fish cooks, the fat in the guanciale bastes it and its own flavors season the fish. The idea of serving the fish with smoked potatoes came from Freddy, my chef in Los Angeles, and I love it. At the restaurant, we pour the sauce over the fish tableside.

SERVES 4

FOR THE SAUCE

2 cups applewood chips, soaked in water for 4 hours (for cold-smoking the potatoes)

4 fingerling potatoes, cooked in salted water until just tender

1 cup peeled, diced (½-inch) russet potato

Extra-virgin olive oil

½ cup sliced shallots

1 sprig fresh thyme

Kosher salt

1½ to 2 cups Chicken Stock (page 310)

FOR THE HALIBUT

Extra-virgin olive oil

1 teaspoon chopped fresh thyme

Pinch of crushed red pepper

4 halibut fillets, about 5 ounces each

6 ounces thinly sliced guanciale

FOR SERVING

Extra-virgin olive oil

1 tablespoon diced shallots

2 ounces fresh morel mushrooms

8 ounces asparagus, trimmed, peeled, cut into 2-inch lengths, and blanched until tender (see page 194)

Pinch of crushed red pepper

1 tablespoon chopped fresh chives

1 teaspoon fresh thyme leaves, plus 1 sprig fresh thyme

Kosher salt

1 clove garlic, lightly smashed

FOR THE SAUCE: Cold-smoke the cooked fingerlings and the raw diced potatoes together as directed on page 70. Reserve the fingerlings. Smoke the raw potatoes a second time. (The potatoes can be smoked 1 day ahead and kept covered and refrigerated.)

Heat 1 tablespoon olive oil in a medium saucepan over medium-low heat. Add the shallots and thyme, season with salt, and cook, stirring, until the shallots are tender but not colored, about 10 minutes. Add the diced potato to the pan and cook, stirring occasionally, until it starts to become translucent, adjusting the heat so the potato

which wine? A light- to medium-bodied red would work here because of the dish's smoky flavors and the richness from the guanciale. A Pinot Nero, with its spicy notes, wild ribs, and gamey undertones, would be an excellent choice. Look for one from Trentino, like Poyer & Sandri Pinot Nero Selezione.

doesn't brown. Add 1½ cups of the stock, bring to a simmer, and cook until the potatoes are tender. Transfer to a blender and purée, adding a little more stock if necessary to make a loose sauce. With the machine running, slowly add 2 teaspoons olive oil and blend to emulsify. Season to taste with salt. (The sauce can be made 1 day ahead. Once cool, cover and refrigerate; reheat gently to serve.)

FOR THE HALIBUT: On a rimmed dish large enough to hold the halibut, combine 2 tablespoons olive oil, the thyme, and crushed red pepper. Add the halibut and turn to coat it. Cover and refrigerate for at least 1 hour and up to 4 hours.

On a clean surface or on parchment paper, lay out about 10 slices guanciale in two overlapping rows. Place a fillet on the guanciale and wrap the fish tightly with it. Repeat with the rest of the guanciale and fillets. Refrigerate the wrapped fish for at least 30 minutes and up 4 hours.

TO SERVE: Heat a convection oven to 350°F or a conventional oven to 375°F. Slice the smoked fingerlings in half lengthwise, and reheat the smoked potato sauce if necessary.

In a medium sauté pan, heat 2 tablespoons olive oil over medium heat. Add the shallots and cook, stirring, until tender and browned, about 5 minutes. Add the morels and cook, stirring, for 3 minutes. Add the fingerling potatoes, asparagus, and crushed red pepper and cook for another 2 minutes. Stir in the chives and thyme leaves. Season to taste with salt and keep warm.

Meanwhile, heat a large, ovenproof sauté pan over high heat. Add 2 tablespoons olive oil and the halibut. Cook both sides until golden brown. Add the thyme sprig and garlic to the pan, transfer the pan to the oven, and cook until medium, about 7 minutes.

Divide the vegetables among serving plates and place the halibut on top of the vegetables. Pour a few tablespoons of the smoked potato sauce around the fish. Finish with a drizzle of olive oil.

SPICED HALIBUT WITH ALMONDS, ARTICHOKES, AND MINT

This recipe is all about spring: from the bright green of the mint pesto to the emblematic vegetables in the accompaniment (baby artichokes, baby carrots, and fava beans glazed with lemony goodness) to the slight floral flavor of the easy-to-make nut and spice coating for the fish. On their own, each of the dish's components is really good. Yet the true magic happens when they come together on the plate, and the colors, textures, and flavors get to play together. We also do this recipe as a vegetarian option without the fish.

SERVES 4

FOR THE SPICES

½ cup raw almonds

1 teaspoon ground cardamom

½ teaspoon crushed red pepper flakes

1 teaspoon kosher salt

1 teaspoon chopped fresh thyme

FOR THE ARTICHOKES

¾ cup fresh lemon juice, plus more as needed

½ cup dry white wine

8 baby artichokes

3½ cups Vegetable Broth (page 314)

Extra-virgin olive oil

Kosher salt

FOR SERVING

Extra-virgin olive oil

Roasted Baby Carrots (page 337)

¼ cup fava beans or soybeans, blanched (see page 194)

2 teaspoons finely chopped fresh flat-leaf parsley

Crushed red pepper

4 halibut fillets, about 5 ounces each, preferably square

Kosher salt

2 cloves garlic, crushed

2 sprigs fresh thyme

¼ cup Mint Pesto (page 223)

FOR THE SPICES: Grind the almonds, cardamom, crushed red pepper, and salt in a spice grinder until finely ground. Add the thyme. (This makes more than you will need for the recipe, but you can freeze the extra; it's delicious on chicken as well as fish.)

FOR THE ARTICHOKES: In a medium saucepan, combine the lemon juice and wine. Trim the artichokes, slice them in half though the stem, remove the choke if necessary (if they are true babies, there should be no choke), and put them in the lemon and wine as you work to keep them from browning. Add the broth, ¼ cup olive oil, and ½ teaspoon salt. Cover with a cut piece of parchment paper or a plate to keep the artichokes submerged, and bring to just under a simmer over medium heat. Cook until tender (a cake tester or skewer should go in and out of an artichoke easily), about 20 minutes. Remove from the heat and allow the artichokes to cool in the liquid. (The artichokes may be cooked a few hours before serving and left at room temperature, submerged in the liquid.)

TO SERVE: Heat a convection oven to 300°F or a conventional oven to 325°F.

Drain off all but about 1 cup of the artichoke cooking liquid. Add ¼ cup olive oil to the artichokes and stir over medium heat to emulsify the oil and liquid. Add the Roasted Baby Carrots, fava beans, parsley, and crushed red pepper, and cook, stirring occasionally, until most of the liquid has reduced and been absorbed by the vegetables. The sauce that's left should be like a glaze.

Meanwhile, season the halibut on both sides with a little salt and a few flakes of crushed red pepper. Dip one side in the spice mix, tamping down on the fish lightly to help the spices stick. Heat a large sauté pan over medium-high heat. Add enough olive oil to coat the pan well. Add the fish, spice side down, and cook, undisturbed, until golden brown on the spice side, 2 to 3 minutes. Turn the fish over, add the garlic and thyme to the pan, transfer the pan to the oven, and cook until medium, about 7 minutes.

Smear 1 tablespoon of the Mint Pesto across the center of each serving plate. Divide the vegetables, as well as any remaining liquid in the pan, among the plates, placing them in the center as well. Place a fillet, spice side up, on top of the vegetables. If there is any liquid remaining in the pan, drizzle it over each serving; otherwise drizzle just a little olive oil over each to finish.

MINT PESTO

MAKES ABOUT 1 CUP

This pesto, while delicious with the halibut, would also work well as a condiment for grilled lamb. At the restaurant, we blanch the mint before making the pesto because the blanching helps the mint hold its color, and then the pesto can be made up to 2 days ahead and refrigerated. But if you plan to use the pesto on the same day you make it, it's perfectly fine to skip that step.

3 cups fresh mint leaves

1 clove garlic, chopped

½ teaspoon kosher salt

½ cup extra-virgin olive oil, plus more as needed

2 tablespoons pine nuts, toasted (see page 89)

Combine the mint, garlic, and salt in a blender. Add the olive oil and purée until smooth. Add the pine nuts and purée until the texture is somewhat thick and paste-like, with some small pieces of nuts. If the mixture is very stiff, add oil a little bit at a time, and purée. (If not using right away, cover and refrigerate for up to 2 days. Let the pesto come to room temperature before serving.)

ROAST CHICKEN WITH FEGATO SAUCE

This is the only chicken dish I make at Scarpetta, and so I make the bird its very best with super-crispy skin, juicy and tender meat, and a sauce made rich with the giblets, of which the strongest flavor comes from the liver (*fegato* in Italian). Boning the chicken makes it cook evenly, which gets every inch of skin beautifully browned. Eating boneless chicken is a pleasure, too.

SERVES 4

FOR THE SPICES AND CHICKEN

5 whole star anise

1 teaspoon whole cloves

1 teaspoon whole cumin seeds

1½ teaspoons ground nutmeg

1 whole chicken (3 to 3½ pounds), giblets removed and reserved, chicken cut in half and boned (see page 227)

FOR THE SAUCE

Reserved giblets

2 cups Chicken Reduction (page 315)

1 tablespoon extra-virgin olive oil

1½ tablespoons finely chopped shallots

Kosher salt

Crushed red pepper

¼ teaspoon finely chopped fresh rosemary

¼ teaspoon finely chopped fresh thyme

2 tablespoons dried currants

FOR SERVING

1 tablespoon plus 1 teaspoon finely chopped fresh chives

2 tablespoons olive oil

Kosher salt and freshly ground black pepper

Creamy Polenta (page 77)

Roasted Baby Carrots (page 337)

FOR THE SPICES: In a small sauté pan over medium heat, toast the star anise, cloves, and cumin seeds, stirring occasionally, until fragrant, 2 to 3 minutes. Add the nutmeg and toast briefly. Transfer to a spice grinder and grind finely. Rub the spices all over the flesh (not the skin) of the chicken. Cover and refrigerate for at least 4 hours (preferably longer) and up to 24 hours.

FOR THE SAUCE: Finely mince the chicken liver, heart, and gizzard.

SICILIAN SPICED DUCK BREAST WITH PRESERVED ORANGE

Duck is really more like steak than chicken, and so it takes well to bold seasonings like this spice rub. I don't know if you will ever find this exact mix of spices in Sicily, but it tastes like you should. Fragrant orange helps cut the richness of the meat and that crispy skin. We use the zest and juice in the sauce and serve the duck with some preserved oranges, which also add a tangy saltiness to the plate.

which wine? This dish, with spices and orange flavor, is akin to tagines from North Africa, where there are numerous plantings of Carignan, so a full-bodied red would do nicely. Perhaps a blend like Shardana from Santadi, a Sardinian wine with flavors of tar, smoke, spices, and black olives.

SERVES 4

FOR THE SPICES AND DUCK

4 pieces Dried Orange Zest (page 351)

2 tablespoons fennel seeds

2 tablespoons sweet paprika

1 teaspoon crushed red pepper

¼ teaspoon broken pieces from a whole cinnamon stick

¼ teaspoon sweet smoked paprika (*pimentón*)

4 boneless, skin-on duck breasts, about 6 ounces each

FOR THE SAUCE

1 orange

Extra-virgin olive oil

½ cup thinly sliced shallots

Kosher salt

Pinch of crushed red pepper

2 cups Chicken Reduction (page 315)

1 sprig fresh rosemary

1 sprig fresh thyme

1 clove garlic, smashed

FOR SERVING

Kosher salt

Extra-virgin olive oil

Roasted Baby Beets (page 338), quartered

Roasted Baby Carrots (page 337)

1 tablespoon chopped fresh chives

8 slices Quick Preserved Orange (page 352)

Flaked sea salt

FOR THE SPICES: In a small sauté pan, toast the Dried Orange Zest, fennel seeds, sweet paprika, crushed red pepper, cinnamon, and smoked paprika over low heat, shaking the pan occasionally, until fragrant, 2 to 3 minutes. Let cool briefly, then grind finely in a spice grinder.

With a sharp knife, trim the duck breasts of excess fat and score the skin side of the duck in a diamond pattern, being careful not to cut all the way through to the meat. Turn the breasts over and season the flesh side only of the duck with 1 tablespoon of the spices. Cover and refrigerate for at least 4 hours and up to 24 hours.

FOR THE SAUCE: Using a vegetable peeler, zest the orange in wide strips, then juice the orange; reserve the zest and the juice. Heat 2 tablespoons olive oil in a small saucepan over medium heat. Add the shallots, season lightly with kosher salt, and cook, stirring occasionally, until tender, sweet, and browned, about 10 minutes. Add the crushed red pepper and the orange juice and cook until the juice is reduced by half. Add the Chicken Reduction and simmer for 10 minutes. Stir in the rosemary, thyme, garlic, and orange zest. Remove from the heat and allow to steep for 10 minutes. Strain the sauce into a small saucepan, bring to a simmer over medium-high heat, and cook until reduced to a nice saucy consistency. Whisk in 1 tablespoon olive oil and season to taste with kosher salt. (The sauce can be made 2 days ahead; store covered and refrigerated.)

TO SERVE: Heat a convection oven to 300°F or a conventional oven to 325°F. Reheat the sauce if necessary.

Season the duck breasts all over with kosher salt. Heat 1 tablespoon olive oil in a large sauté pan over medium heat. Add the duck breasts, skin side down, and cook to slowly render the fat for 5 minutes. As the fat accumulates, remove it from the pan by tilting the pan and scooping some out with a spoon. When the skin is lightly browned, transfer the pan to the oven and cook until medium-rare (125°F on an instant-read thermometer), 8 to 12 minutes. Remove the pan from the oven, flip the breasts over, and let rest in the pan for 10 minutes.

Meanwhile, in a medium sauté pan, heat 1 tablespoon olive oil over medium heat and reheat the Roasted Baby Beets and Roasted Baby Carrots until hot. Toss with the chives and keep warm.

Divide the Quick Preserved Orange slices among serving plates. Place the beets and carrots on the oranges. Slice the duck breasts lengthwise and lay the slices on top of the vegetables. Drizzle about 2 tablespoons of the sauce over each plate. Finish with a sprinkling of sea salt.

ROASTED BONE-IN VEAL CHOP WITH SEMOLINA GNOCCHI

Everyone associates a big veal chop with Italian restaurants. Here is our take on the classic.

FOR THE VEAL CHOPS

4 bone-in rib veal chops, 10 to 12 ounces each, frenched

¼ cup extra-virgin olive oil

2 cloves garlic, sliced

Leaves from 1 sprig fresh rosemary

¼ teaspoon crushed red pepper

FOR THE SAUCE

Extra-virgin olive oil

1 cup sliced shallots

Kosher salt

¼ cup coarsely chopped fresh rosemary

¼ cup sliced Quick Preserved Lemon (page 352), plus 1 tablespoon julienned Quick Preserved Lemon

5 cloves garlic, lightly smashed

½ teaspoon crushed red pepper

4 cups Chicken Reduction (page 315), simmered over medium-high heat until reduced to 2 cups

FOR SERVING

4 cloves garlic, smashed

4 sprigs fresh thyme

2 sprigs fresh rosemary

Extra-virgin olive oil

Kosher salt and freshly ground black pepper

1 teaspoon fresh lemon juice

Roasted Baby Beets (page 338), quartered

Roasted Baby Carrots (page 337)

1 tablespoon chopped fresh flat-leaf parsley

4 pieces Semolina Gnocchi (page 234)

½ cup mixed tender fresh herb leaves, such as chervil, chives, mint, parsley, and tarragon; small leaves left whole, large leaves torn into pieces

Flaked sea salt

FOR THE VEAL: Put the veal chops on a rimmed baking sheet or in a baking dish. In a small bowl, combine the olive oil, garlic, rosemary, and crushed red pepper, and pour it over the veal. Turn the meat in the marinade to coat, cover, and refrigerate for at least 4 hours and up to 24 hours.

which wine? A Castellare I Sodi di San Niccolò made with Sangiovese and Malvasia Nera, with its dark cherries and incense and a mineral-infused finish, would be a great choice.

FOR THE SAUCE: In a medium saucepan, heat 1 tablespoon olive oil over medium heat. Add the shallots and a pinch of kosher salt, and cook, stirring occasionally, until tender and golden, 3 to 5 minutes. Add the rosemary, the ¼ cup Quick Preserved Lemon, garlic, and crushed red pepper. Cook, stirring occasionally, for 2 minutes. Add the Chicken Reduction and bring to just below a boil. Remove from the heat and let the flavors steep, stirring occasionally. Taste the sauce. If not full and rich flavored, return the sauce to the heat to reduce a little more to intensify the flavors. Strain through a fine-mesh strainer. Whisk in ¼ cup olive oil and the julienned Quick Preserved Lemon, taste, and season with additional kosher salt if necessary. Keep the sauce warm for serving.

TO SERVE: Heat a convection oven to 250°F or a conventional oven to 275°F.

Put the garlic, thyme, and rosemary on a rimmed baking sheet just large enough to hold the chops. Heat 1 tablespoon olive oil in a large sauté pan over high heat. Season the veal chops well with kosher salt and black pepper. In batches, add the veal chops to the pan and brown well on both sides. Transfer the chops to the baking sheet, placing them on top of the herbs and garlic. Pour ¼ cup olive oil over the veal chops, transfer the baking sheet to the oven, and cook, turning the chops about every 5 minutes and basting them with the olive oil in the pan, until an instant-read thermometer inserted into the thickest part of a chop reads 135°F for medium-rare and 140°F for medium, 18 to 25 minutes. Remove the chops from the oven and let rest for 8 minutes.

In a small bowl, whisk the lemon juice with 1 tablespoon olive oil. Divide the Roasted Baby Beets and the Roasted Baby Carrots among serving plates and sprinkle the parsley over them. Put a piece of Semolina Gnocchi next to the vegetables. Place 1 chop on each plate over the gnocchi. Toss the mixed herbs with the lemon juice and olive oil, and put a tiny handful of the salad on top of each veal chop. Pour 2 to 3 tablespoons of the sauce over each plate and drizzle with some of the pan juices. Finish each plate with a tiny sprinkling of sea salt.

SEMOLINA GNOCCHI

MAKES 12 PIECES

When I was a kid, we ate semolina and milk for breakfast the way other kids ate oatmeal. So whenever I make this, it brings me back, at least until I add the cheese and the chives that make it delicious for dinner. I like to serve it with roasted or braised meats. If you have any left over, you can serve slices topped with Mushroom Fricassee (page 74) or Roasted Cherry Tomatoes (page 323).

Cooking spray, for the pan (optional)

7 cups whole milk

2 teaspoons kosher salt

1 cup semolina flour

¼ cup freshly grated Parmigiano-Reggiano cheese, plus more for serving

2 tablespoons finely chopped fresh chives

1½ tablespoons unsalted butter, plus more for serving

Spray a 9 x 13-inch rimmed baking sheet with cooking spray or line it with parchment paper.

In a medium saucepan, bring 6 cups of the milk to a boil. Whisk in the salt and the semolina. Continue whisking for a minute or so over the high heat. Lower the heat to a simmer and cook, whisking often. As the mixture begins to thicken, slowly add the remaining 1 cup milk. Continue cooking, whisking occasionally, until the floury taste is cooked off and the mixture has thickened, about 20 minutes. Stir in the Parmigiano-Reggiano, chives, and butter, and pour into the baking dish. Refrigerate until firm, about 1 hour.

Just before serving, cut the gnocchi into pieces and place the pieces on a baking sheet. Top each with a dab of butter and a sprinkling of Parmigiano-Reggiano and broil briefly just to melt the butter and the cheese.

PANCETTA-WRAPPED PORK TENDERLOIN WITH APPLES AND TURNIPS

I love this dish because it takes some of the most humble ingredients—pig jowl and turnips—and transforms them into a fine-dining experience. The jowl, while not labor-intensive, needs time in the brine and the oven, so plan to start it a couple days ahead. This is a great fall dish.

SERVES 4

4 ounces pancetta, thinly sliced

1 small pork tenderloin (about 1½ pounds)

Extra-virgin olive oil

2 sprigs fresh thyme

1½ sprigs fresh rosemary

2 cloves garlic, lightly smashed

1 cup peeled and diced (¼-inch) turnip

Kosher salt and freshly ground black pepper

1 cup peeled and diced (¼-inch) apple

1 cup Butternut Squash Purée (page 329), reheated if necessary

4 (1 x 3-inch) pieces Fresh Guanciale Confit (page 238), at room temperature

Lentils with Pickled Mustard Seeds (page 236)

Heat a convection oven to 225°F or a conventional oven to 250°F.

On a clean work surface, unroll the slices of pancetta and lay the strips out, slightly overlapping them. Place the tenderloin at one end of the strips and roll the pancetta around the tenderloin. Using kitchen string, tie the tenderloin at intervals to keep the pancetta secure.

Heat 1 tablespoon olive oil in a large, ovenproof sauté pan over medium-high heat. Add the pork tenderloin and cook on all sides until the pancetta is lightly browned. Take the pork out of the pan, wipe it clean, then add 1 tablespoon olive oil, the thyme, 1 sprig of the rosemary, and 1 clove of the garlic. Put the pork back in the pan and transfer to the oven. Cook, turning the tenderloin every 4 minutes, until medium (135°F to 140°F on an instant-read thermometer), about 12 minutes.

Meanwhile, heat 1 teaspoon olive oil in a medium sauté pan over medium-high heat. Add the turnips, season with salt and black pepper, and cook, stirring occasionally, until lightly browned and about

The lentils here are as much a sauce as they are an accompaniment. They give the plate loads of texture and, thanks to the tangy mustard seeds, help cut the richness of the guanciale confit. You can definitely make these ahead of serving, as they taste even better the day after they're made.

halfway cooked, 5 to 8 minutes. Add the apple, the remaining ½ sprig rosemary, and the remaining garlic clove, and cook, stirring occasionally, until the turnip is tender, about 5 minutes.

In a small sauté pan, heat 1 teaspoon olive oil over high heat. Add the Fresh Guanciale Confit, fat side down, and cook until nicely browned and heated through, 1 to 2 minutes.

Cut the string away from the pork tenderloin and slice it into 12 pieces. Smear ¼ cup Butternut Squash Purée across each serving plate. Put about 2 tablespoons of the turnips and apples on different spots on the plate. Place 1 piece of the confit, browned side up, on each plate. Divide the pork tenderloin among the plates and drizzle the Lentils with Pickled Mustard Seeds over everything.

LENTILS WITH PICKLED MUSTARD SEEDS
MAKES ABOUT 1 CUP

½ cup lentils du Puy	½ cup finely diced shallots
1 sprig fresh thyme, plus 1 tablespoon leaves	Kosher salt
1½ sprigs fresh rosemary	3 cups Chicken Reduction (page 315)
1 clove garlic, lightly smashed	1 tablespoon Dijon mustard
Extra-virgin olive oil	5 tablespoons Pickled Mustard Seeds (page 331)
½ cup finely diced carrot	Pinch of crushed red pepper
½ cup finely diced celery	

In a small saucepan, cover the lentils with 2 inches cold water. Add the thyme sprig, 1 sprig of the rosemary, and the garlic. Bring to a simmer over medium-high heat and cook, adjusting the heat and adding more water as necessary, until just al dente. Drain.

Meanwhile, in a medium saucepan, heat 1 tablespoon olive oil over medium heat. Add the carrot, celery, and shallots; season lightly with salt, and cook, stirring, until tender but not browned, 5 to 8 minutes. Add the lentils, Chicken Reduction, and the remaining ½ sprig rosemary. Bring to a simmer and cook until the lentils are tender, about 10 minutes. Stir in the mustard, Pickled Mustard Seeds, thyme leaves, and the crushed red pepper. Season to taste with salt. Remove the whole sprigs and garlic cloves before serving. (The lentils can be made up to 3 days ahead. Let cool, then cover and refrigerate. Reheat gently to serve.)

FRESH GUANCIALE CONFIT

SERVES 6 TO 8

If you don't see pork jowl at the market, ask your butcher to order it. It's an inexpensive cut, but cooked long and low it becomes this tender and luscious piece of meat. This makes a lot, but confit can be frozen for future good eating. I like to chop some up and cook it with onions and potatoes, like a little stew.

1 cup kosher salt

½ cup granulated sugar

10 cloves garlic, peeled

½ bunch fresh thyme

4 dried bay leaves

1 tablespoon plus ½ teaspoon whole black peppercorns

4 pounds pork jowls

2 teaspoons cumin seeds

½ teaspoon whole cloves

½ teaspoon yellow mustard seeds

2 teaspoons sweet paprika

½ teaspoon ground cinnamon

2 quarts duck fat

Extra-virgin olive oil, as needed

In a large pot, combine the salt, sugar, garlic, thyme, bay leaves, and the 1 tablespoon black peppercorns with 1 gallon water. Bring to a boil, let cool to room temperature, and refrigerate until cool. Submerge the pork jowls in the brine and refrigerate for 1 hour.

Meanwhile, in a small sauté pan, toast the cumin seeds, cloves, mustard seeds, and the remaining ½ teaspoon black peppercorns over medium heat until fragrant, 2 to 3 minutes, then transfer to a spice grinder and grind finely. Transfer to a small bowl and add the paprika and cinnamon.

Heat a convection oven to 325°F or a conventional oven to 350°F.

Remove the jowls from the brine, pat dry, and season all over with the spices.

Put the duck fat in a heavy-based pot large enough to hold the pork jowls. Nestle the pork jowls in the fat; if the fat doesn't fully cover the jowl, add enough olive oil to cover.

Cook in the oven until simmering, about 30 minutes, then lower the temperature to 300°F (325°F for a conventional oven), and cook until a long carving fork can be easily inserted into the pork, 4 to 5 hours.

Let cool for 20 minutes, then transfer the pork to a rimmed baking sheet in a single layer with about 1 inch of space around each piece. Place a second baking sheet on top, weight it with about 10 pounds (cans of tomatoes make good weights), and refrigerate overnight.

Trim the jowls and cut them into 1 x 3-inch rectangles. If there is an excessive amount of fat, trim some away but leave at least ¼ inch on top. (The jowls will keep, covered and refrigerated, for 3 days; they can also be frozen for up to 2 months. Thaw in the refrigerator.) Use the jowls as directed in the recipe, or cook, skin side down, in a sauté pan over medium heat until the skin is nicely browned and the jowls are heated through.

SPICE-CRUSTED VEAL RIB EYE

In this recipe, veal roast, preferably with its fat cap still on, gets coated with a bold spice rub that includes star anise, smoked paprika, and Szechuan peppercorns. It then gets deeply and darkly seared before finishing in a low oven, which keeps the delicate meat from drying out. I've made this exact same recipe with pork loin, but it just doesn't compare to the regal texture of tender veal. Serve the roast with some Creamy Polenta (page 77) or Semolina Gnocchi (page 234).

which wine? Choose a wine with soft tannins and a core of spices, like a Pinot Nero from northern Italy. These wines, though less fruity than New World Pinot Noirs, always possess fragrant layers of red cherries, cinnamon, and cloves, which will provide superb aromatics for the veal.

SERVES 4 TO 6

1 tablespoon crushed red pepper

1 tablespoon whole Szechuan peppercorns

1 tablespoon coriander seeds

1½ teaspoons cumin seeds

1½ teaspoons sweet smoked paprika (pimentón)

2 whole star anise or 1½ teaspoons ground

1 (3- to 4-pound) veal rib eye roast, trimmed but with the fat cap left on, and tied

Extra-virgin olive oil

Kosher salt

5 or 6 sprigs fresh thyme

5 or 6 cloves garlic, peeled

In a small skillet, toast the crushed red pepper, Szechuan peppercorns, coriander seeds, cumin seeds, smoked paprika, and star anise over medium heat until fragrant, 2 to 3 minutes. Let cool, then transfer to a spice grinder and grind finely.

Coat the veal well all over with a thick layer of the spices. An easy way to do this is to spread the spices out on a rimmed baking sheet and roll the roast in the rub, tamping the spices on so they stick. Let the veal sit at room temperature for 1 hour or refrigerate for up to 24 hours. (Remove the veal from the refrigerator about a half hour before roasting.)

Heat a convection oven to 250°F or a conventional oven to 275°F. If you have a flattop griddle large enough to accommodate the whole veal roast, heat that over medium-high heat. If not, cut the roast in half so it can fit into a large skillet and heat the skillet. Add enough olive oil for a light coating. Season the veal all over with salt and sear it until well browned on all sides. Transfer to a roasting pan or a large rimmed baking sheet. Drizzle about ¼ cup olive oil over the meat and add the thyme and garlic to the pan. Finish cooking the roast in the oven, basting the veal occasionally, until it registers 135°F on an instant-read thermometer inserted into the thickest part of the roast, about 50 minutes. Transfer the roast to a cutting board and let it rest in a warm place for 15 minutes before slicing it into thick slices.

MOLASSES- AND BALSAMIC-GLAZED SLOW-ROASTED PORK

I think of this dish as a marriage between my family's New England roots (my dad grew up in Maine and remembers using molasses as a condiment, pouring it over a biscuit-topped chicken stew) and my Italian heritage on my mother's side (we had balsamic vinegar in the pantry long before it became fashionable here in the United States). These two ingredients come together in a glaze that makes this pork irresistible. I mean it: You put a piece of this pork in front of me and I can't help myself. Serve this big roast with your favorite sides.

SERVES 6 TO 8

Extra-virgin olive oil

½ small onion, quartered

5 sprigs fresh thyme

½ cup balsamic vinegar

1 cup Chicken Reduction (page 315)

1 cup unsulfured molasses

2 tablespoons dry mustard

Pinch of crushed red pepper

1 (5-bone) pork loin roast, about 4 pounds, preferably Berkshire pork, chine bones removed

Kosher salt

2 small sprigs fresh rosemary

2 cloves garlic, sliced thinly

Heat just enough olive oil to coat the bottom of a small saucepan over medium heat. Add the onion and 1 sprig of the thyme and cook, stirring occasionally, for 5 minutes to develop the flavors. Add the vinegar, increase the heat to medium-high, and cook until reduced to about 1/3 cup, 1 to 2 minutes. Add the Chicken Reduction and continue to cook until the mixture has thickened enough to coat the back of a spoon. Strain through a fine-mesh strainer into a bowl. Stir in the molasses, mustard, and crushed red pepper.

Heat a convection oven to 500°F or a conventional oven to 525°F. (If you have a second oven, heat it to 250°F for convection and 275°F for conventional.)

Set the pork on a rack over a rimmed baking sheet. If the pork has its fat cap on, lightly score the fat using just the weight (no additional pressure) of a very sharp knife. Season the pork lightly all over with salt. Reserve about ½ cup of the molasses mixture for serving and coat the roast with the rest. Let stand for 30 minutes, occasionally brushing the molasses that runs off the meat back over it.

Roast the pork in the 500°F oven (525°F conventional oven) for 10 minutes.

If you do not have a second oven heating, reduce the oven temperature to 250°F (275°F for a conventional oven). Take the pork out of the oven and carefully add water to the bottom of the pan to keep the meat moist as it continues to cook. Top the roast with the remaining 4 sprigs of thyme, the rosemary, and the garlic slices, and season again lightly with salt. If you have a second oven already heated, put the pork in there. If not, allow the oven temperature to reduce for 10 minutes before returning the roasts to the oven.

Continue cooking, basting the meat occasionally and adding a little more water as needed, until an instant-read thermometer inserted into the thickest part of the roast registers 145°F, about 2 hours. Remove the pork from the oven and allow it to rest for 20 minutes before serving.

Serve the pork as either bone-in chops or boneless slices. For the latter, cut the entire loin away from the bones in one piece, and then slice across the grain. Brush the chops or slices with the additional reserved molasses mixture and serve.

which wine? With sweet-and-sour components, the rule is almost always to serve an aromatic white like a Gewürztraminer. Its sweet-fruit perfume and honey, candied orange, and ginger flavors meld together with the fatty components of the pork. Tramin and Cantina Terlano are some of the more complex ones.

SCARPETTA'S ROASTED PORCHETTA

This is not a traditional porchetta in any way, shape, or form, but it's really spectacular. We often make this for events—a slice of this tender meat with its crispy skin makes everybody happy. To cut the richness, consider serving it with some spicy sautéed broccoli rabe on the side. Though the porchetta does not need a lot of hands-on time, you do need to start it at least 2 days ahead of serving it to account for the brining and drying times.

SERVES 8

FOR THE BRINE AND PORK

40 cloves garlic, lightly smashed

1 bunch fresh thyme

6 tablespoons dried juniper berries

3 tablespoons whole black peppercorns

2 tablespoons fennel seeds

1½ cups kosher salt

½ cup lightly packed light or dark brown sugar

½ whole pork belly, 7 to 8 pounds

FOR THE SPICE RUB

1 tablespoon dried juniper berries

1 tablespoon whole black peppercorns

2 tablespoons fennel seeds

1 teaspoon ground nutmeg

2 tablespoons chopped fresh thyme

4 cloves garlic, coarsely chopped

FOR THE BRINE: In a large pot, combine the garlic, thyme, juniper berries, peppercorns, and fennel seeds with 1 gallon water. Bring to a boil, and simmer for 10 minutes to bring out the flavor of the aromatics and spices. Remove from the heat, whisk in the salt and sugar, and let cool to room temperature.

Put the pork in a large roasting pan and pour the brine over it. Cover and refrigerate for 24 hours.

FOR THE SPICE RUB: In a medium sauté pan over medium heat, toast the juniper berries, peppercorns, and fennel seeds until fragrant, 2 to 3 minutes. Transfer to a small bowl and add the nutmeg. Add the thyme and garlic and toss to combine.

which wine? A medium-weight, unoaky dry red should be your first choice. Though popular throughout Italy, porchetta hails from the Lazio region (around Rome), so that might be a place to start. Cesanese del Piglio comes to mind; its sweet wild herbs, tobacco, and juicy dark berries should be well suited for the richness of the pork. Look for Corte dei Papi Colle Ticchio.

Remove the pork from the brine and pat it dry. Pat the spice rub on the flesh side only of the pork belly, using just what adheres; you may have some spice rub left over. Put the pork skin side up on a large rimmed baking sheet and refrigerate it, uncovered, for 24 hours to dry out.

To serve, heat a convection oven to 450°F or a conventional oven to 475°F.

Roll the pork belly lengthwise into a cylinder and secure the roll with kitchen string, tying it at intervals along the length of the roll. With a cake tester or skewer, prick the skin all over; this helps the skin get nice and crispy. Fit a roasting rack on a rimmed baking sheet, put the pork belly on the roasting rack, and roast for 10 minutes. Baste the pork, rotate the pan 90 degrees, and continue to roast, basting the pork and rotating the pan 90 degrees every 5 minutes, for another 25 minutes. (Turning the pan ensures that the skin will crisp evenly.)

Turn the oven down to 300°F (325°F for a conventional oven) and cook, rotating the pan every 15 minutes, until the pork reads 155°F on an instant-read thermometer, about 2 hours.

Let the pork rest for 30 to 40 minutes before cutting off the string and slicing it about ¾ inch thick.

AUSTRALIAN WAGYU STEAK WITH POTATOES, ROASTED MUSHROOMS, AND PARMESAN

Steak and potatoes. What's not to like? This is simple, honest fare. The key to making it outstanding lies in the execution.

SERVES 4

FOR THE STEAKS

¼ cup extra-virgin olive oil

6 sprigs fresh thyme

4 sprigs fresh rosemary, torn into pieces

4 cloves garlic, sliced

Pinch of crushed red pepper

4 New York strip steaks, preferably Australian Wagyu, 8 to 10 ounces each, 1½ to 2 inches thick

FOR SERVING

2 cloves garlic, lightly smashed

2 sprigs fresh rosemary, torn into pieces

2 sprigs fresh thyme

Kosher salt and freshly ground black pepper

Extra-virgin olive oil

2 tablespoons thinly sliced shallots

12 Roasted Baby Potatoes (page 339), cut in half

4 cups mixed wild mushrooms, cut into 1- to 2-inch pieces

Crushed red pepper

1½ teaspoons thinly sliced fresh chives

Parmigiano-Reggiano cheese, for shaving

1 cup Trucioleto Sauce (page 317), reheated if necessary

Flaked sea salt

FOR THE STEAKS: In a container large enough to hold the steaks, combine the olive oil, thyme, rosemary, garlic cloves, and crushed red pepper. Add the steaks and turn to coat. Refrigerate for at least 4 hours and up to 8 hours. Let warm at room temperature for 30 minutes before cooking.

TO SERVE: Heat a convection oven to 250°F or a conventional oven to 275°F. Put the garlic, rosemary, and thyme on a large rimmed baking sheet.

Heat a large sauté pan over high heat. Season the steaks well on both sides with kosher salt and black pepper. Add 2 tablespoons olive oil

which wine? Because of the high fat content of this meat, a well-structured red, like the ones produced from vines grown on the coast of Tuscany, will complement it nicely. Look for a blend like Bolgheri Orma or Giusto di Notri from Tua Rita.

to the pan. In batches if necessary, add the steaks to the pan, making sure there is room around each. Cook the steaks until deep brown on one side, about 1½ minutes. Flip and brown the other side. Transfer the steaks to the baking sheet. Drizzle 2 tablespoons olive oil over the steaks and finish cooking in the oven, turning the steaks over every 5 minutes, until medium-rare (120°F on an instant-read thermometer), about 15 minutes. Let rest for 5 minutes before slicing.

Meanwhile, heat 1 tablespoon olive oil in a small saucepan over medium heat. Add the shallots and cook, stirring occasionally, until tender and browned, about 10 minutes. Heat 2 tablespoons olive oil in a large sauté pan over high heat. Add the Roasted Baby Potatoes, cut side down, and cook undisturbed until they start to brown and crisp, 1 to 2 minutes. Add the mushrooms, season with kosher salt and a pinch of crushed red pepper, and cook, stirring once or twice, until the mushrooms begin to brown and crisp on their edges, 2 to 4 minutes. Stir in the shallots and chives and keep warm.

Slice the steaks ¼ inch thick and divide among serving plates, fanning the slices out. Top with the mushrooms and potatoes and about 6 pieces shaved Parmigiano-Reggiano. Pour about ¼ cup Trucioleto Sauce onto each plate. Finish with a sprinkle of sea salt and a drizzle of olive oil and serve immediately.

SEARING AND SLOW-ROASTING MEAT

The steak we serve at Scarpetta is different from the steak you get at most restaurants. Instead of gradations of doneness, the inside of our steak is the same beautiful rosy red from the middle of the steak to the very edge. That's because I use a method that is not only astoundingly consistent but is also easily replicated at home: a quick sear for color and flavor and then a finish in a very, very low oven. It's almost impossible to overcook steak when you make it this way. The slow cooking relaxes the muscle so that it cooks up tenderly and evenly. An added benefit is that you can get the rest of the meal together in the time it takes for the meat to gently finish cooking in the oven.

DRY-AGED STEAK WITH SMOKED EGGPLANT PURÉE

A dry-aged piece of beef has a remarkable depth of flavor, and it's worth treating yourself to one now and again. What I love about this dish is that you get the beefiness of the steak, the smokiness of the eggplant, and then—pop—a sweet roasted tomato, which has just the right amount of acid to cut through all that caveman flavor.

SERVES 4

3 cloves garlic, 2 sliced, 1 thinly sliced

2 sprigs fresh rosemary

2 sprigs fresh thyme, plus ½ teaspoon leaves

4 dry-aged New York strip steaks, 8 to 10 ounces each

Kosher salt and coarsely ground black pepper

2 tablespoons grapeseed or canola oil

Extra-virgin olive oil

1 cup thinly sliced shallots

Pinch of crushed red pepper

Roasted Cherry Tomatoes (page 323), warm or at room temperature

½ teaspoon thinly sliced fresh chives

2 cups Smoked Eggplant Purée (page 252), reheated if necessary

¾ cup Red Wine Sauce (page 318), reheated if necessary

Flaked sea salt

Heat a convection oven to 250°F or a conventional oven to 275°F.

Put the 2 cloves sliced garlic, the rosemary, and thyme sprigs on a large rimmed baking sheet.

Heat a large sauté pan over high heat. Season the steaks well with kosher salt and black pepper. Add the grapeseed oil to the pan. In batches if necessary, add the steaks, making sure there is room between each. Cook until deep brown on one side, about 1½ minutes. Flip and brown the other side. Transfer the steaks to the baking sheet. Drizzle 2 tablespoons olive oil over the steaks and finish cooking in the oven, turning the steaks over every 5 minutes, until medium-rare (120°F on an instant-read thermometer), about 15 minutes. Let rest for 5 minutes before slicing.

In a medium saucepan, heat ½ cup olive oil over low heat. Add the shallots, season with kosher salt, and cook, stirring occasionally,

A full-bodied Cabernet Sauvignon would be the obvious choice here for most people. But instead, opt for an Aglianico wine grown on volcanic soil. Full of dark berries and sweet balsamic notes, it gradually brings complexity to the meat. Definitely try one from Campania, like Galardi Terra di Lavoro or Terredora di Paolo Taurasi.

until soft and sweet but not colored, about 10 minutes. Stir in the thinly sliced garlic, the thyme leaves, and the crushed red pepper. Add the Roasted Cherry Tomatoes and cook, gently tossing, until heated through, about 2 minutes. Take the pan off the heat, stir in the chives, and keep warm.

Divide the Smoked Eggplant Purée among serving plates. Slice the steak in half, if you like, and place on top of the eggplant. Top with the tomatoes and shallots and drizzle the Red Wine Sauce over and around the steak. Finish with a tiny sprinkle of sea salt.

SMOKED EGGPLANT PURÉE

MAKES ABOUT 3 CUPS

Great with steak, this purée also makes a great dip.

2 globe eggplants, about 1½ pounds each

Extra virgin olive oil

2 cups thinly sliced shallots

2 cloves garlic, thinly sliced

1 sprig fresh thyme

Pinch of crushed red pepper

2 cups applewood chips, soaked in water for 4 hours for smoking

Heat a convection oven to 350°F or a conventional oven to 375°F, Line a rimmed baking sheet with aluminum foil.

Light two gas burners to high and place the eggplants directly on the burners. Using tongs to turn the eggplants, char them on all sides until well blackened. (Alternatively, broil the eggplants, turning them with the tongs, until blackened and charred on all sides.) Place the eggplants on the baking sheet and bake until very tender, about 1 hour. When cool enough to handle, cut the eggplants in half lengthwise and scoop out the flesh. (Discard the skin.) It's okay if a little charred skin gets into the flesh while scooping.

Heat 2 tablespoons olive oil in a large saucepan over medium-low heat. Add the shallots and cook, stirring occasionally, until very soft, about 10 minutes. Add the garlic, thyme, and crushed red pepper. Stir in the eggplant, and cook for another 5 to 7 minutes.

Take the eggplant off the heat and cold-smoke twice, as directed on page 70. Before the second smoke, stir the eggplant to expose new surface area to the smoke.

Transfer the eggplant to a blender and purée. With the machine running, slowly add 2 tablespoons olive oil and blend until emulsified. (The purée will keep, covered and refrigerated, for 3 to 4 days. Reheat gently before serving.)

SPICE-RUBBED BONE-IN RIB EYE

This is a big hunk of meat, and it looks just awesome. I love that it delivers on its promise, too. The spice rub and the heat of the sear creates flavors that are truly compelling.

SERVES 4 TO 6

1½ teaspoons whole allspice berries

1½ teaspoons cumin seeds

1½ teaspoons yellow mustard seeds

¾ teaspoon whole Szechuan peppercorns

½ teaspoon crushed red pepper

1 tablespoon plus 1 teaspoon sweet smoked paprika (*pimentón*)

5 sprigs fresh rosemary

1 (2-bone) rib eye steak, 3 pounds

3 cloves garlic, smashed

2 sprigs fresh thyme

Kosher salt

Extra-virgin olive oil

Flaked sea salt

In a small sauté pan over medium heat, toast the allspice berries, cumin seeds, mustard seeds, Szechuan peppercorns, and crushed red pepper until fragrant, 2 to 3 minutes. Take the pan off the heat and add the paprika and the leaves from 2 sprigs of the rosemary. Let cool slightly before grinding finely in a spice grinder. (Once cooled, the spices will keep for weeks if stored airtight.)

Rub the rib eye all over with 1 tablespoon of the spices. Cover and refrigerate for at least 4 hours and up to 8 hours.

Heat a convection oven to 225°F or a conventional oven to 250°F. Remove the steak from the refrigerator and let sit at room temperature for 30 minutes before cooking. Put the garlic, thyme, and the remaining 3 sprigs rosemary on a large rimmed baking sheet.

Heat a medium ovenproof sauté pan over high heat. Season the meat all over with kosher salt. Add 3 tablespoons olive oil to the pan and immediately place the steak in the pan. Cook the steak

which wine? Rather than pairing this with a classic Cabernet Sauvignon–based wine, go for a classic indigenous Italian varietal like the one from Graci Quota 600, a red wine produced from ungrafted vines of Nerello Mascalese grown on the slopes of Mount Etna in Sicily; it has a supple palate, spicy dark fruits, and a slightly tannic finish. Or go with an Aglianico from I Feudi di San Gregorio.

undisturbed until a nice dark crust forms, about 2 minutes. Flip the steak over and sear the other side. Transfer to the baking sheet and finish cooking in the oven, flipping the rib eye over every 10 minutes, until an instant-read thermometer inserted into the thickest part of the steak reads 120°F for medium-rare, about 1 hour.

Let rest for 15 minutes on a cutting board. To carve, run your knife along the bone to cut away the meat. (Reserve the bone for serving.) Cut the steak at a 45-degree angle into ½-inch slices. Place the meat next to the bone on a large platter, sprinkle with sea salt, drizzle with olive oil, and serve.

COLORADO LAMB CHOPS WITH ROSEMARY-LEMON JUS, PARSNIP PURÉE, AND HAZELNUT CRUMBLE

This is one of those dishes where I can't imagine any of the parts of the whole not being on the plate. The rosemary and lemon in the jus cuts through the gaminess of the lamb just beautifully, while the parsnip purée adds such an interesting layer, with its earthy flavor playing off the sweetness of the hazelnuts.

SERVES 4 TO 6

FOR THE MARINADE

2 (8-bone) lamb racks, 1 to 1½ pounds each, frenched

½ cup extra-virgin olive oil

6 cloves garlic, crushed

3 sprigs fresh rosemary

Pinch of crushed red pepper

FOR THE JUS

1 tablespoon extra-virgin olive oil

4 ounces lamb scraps or lamb stew meat

2 shallots, sliced

3 sprigs fresh rosemary

Pinch of crushed red pepper

1 cup Chicken Reduction (page 315)

FOR THE CRUMBLE

5 tablespoons granulated sugar

3 tablespoons (1½ ounces) unsalted butter

2 tablespoons light corn syrup

¾ cups whole hazelnuts

2 teaspoons kosher salt

¾ teaspoon baking soda

FOR SERVING

12 baby carrots

6 cloves garlic, lightly smashed

5 sprigs fresh thyme

Extra-virgin olive oil

Kosher salt and freshly ground black pepper

2 sprigs fresh rosemary

Parsnip Purée (page 326)

4 ounces yellow foot mushrooms or other wild mushrooms, cut into 1-inch pieces following their natural shapes

2 tablespoons chopped fresh flat-leaf parsley

2 teaspoons fresh micro mint leaves or chopped fresh mint

A Nero di Troia from Puglia, with its smoky and gamey flavors, will provide plenty of textural mouthfeel for the lamb. Try one from Rivera or Botromagno, which would provide a generous long finish.

FOR THE MARINADE: Place the lamb racks on a small rimmed baking sheet or in a baking dish. In a small bowl, combine the olive oil, garlic, rosemary, and crushed red pepper. Pour the marinade over the racks, cover, and refrigerate, turning the racks occasionally, for at least 6 hours and up to 24 hours.

FOR THE JUS: In a medium saucepan, heat the olive oil over medium-high heat. Add the lamb scraps and cook on all sides until deeply browned, 5 to 8 minutes. Lower the heat to medium, add the shallots, and cook, stirring occasionally, until the shallots are deeply browned, about 10 minutes. Add the rosemary and crushed red pepper and cook until fragrant, about 1 minute. Add the Chicken Reduction and bring to a boil. Lower the heat to a simmer and cook for 30 minutes, skimming off and discarding any fat that collects on the surface. Strain through a fine-mesh strainer. (The jus may be made up to 2 days ahead; cover and refrigerate, and reheat gently before serving.)

FOR THE CRUMBLE: Line a rimmed baking sheet with a silicone liner or parchment paper.

In a medium saucepan over medium-high heat, bring the sugar, butter, corn syrup, and 2 tablespoons water to a boil. Stir in the hazelnuts and cook, stirring occasionally, until the sugar is golden, about 15 minutes. Stir in the salt and baking soda and cook until light brown, 1 to 2 minutes. Carefully pour onto the baking sheet and let cool completely. Break the brittle into pieces, put the pieces in a food processor, and pulse to make coarse crumbs. Alternatively, put the pieces in a heavy-duty plastic bag and smash them with a rolling pin or meat pounder. (The crumble can be made 1 day ahead; store in an airtight container at room temperature.)

TO SERVE: Heat a convection oven to 250°F or a conventional oven to 275°F. On a small rimmed baking sheet or ovenproof sauté pan, toss the carrots, 2 of the garlic cloves, and 1 sprig of the thyme with enough olive oil to coat well. Season with salt and pepper and roast until tender and lightly browned, about 50 minutes.

Meanwhile, wipe the marinade off the lamb and season well with salt and pepper. In a large sauté pan, heat ¼ cup olive oil over medium-high heat. Add the lamb and sear on all sides until dark brown, about 5 minutes. Remove the lamb from the pan and discard the oil. Add the lamb back to the pan, fat side up, and add the remaining 4 garlic cloves, the remaining 4 thyme sprigs, the rosemary, and ¼ cup olive oil. Put the pan in the oven and cook, basting and rotating the meat occasionally, until an instant-read thermometer inserted into the rack reads 130°F, 20 to 30 minutes. Let rest for 15 minutes before slicing.

Meanwhile, reheat the Parsnip Purée and the jus if necessary.

In a medium sauté pan, heat 1 tablespoon olive oil over medium-high heat and cook the mushrooms, stirring occasionally, for 2 minutes. Add the carrots and parsley and cook for another 1 minute.

Smear about 2 tablespoons of the Parsnip Purée over each warm serving plate. Divide the mushrooms and carrots among the plates, placing them on the purée. Cut the lamb racks into single chops and divide the chops among the plates. Drizzle each plate with about 1 tablespoon of the jus. Sprinkle with the hazelnut crumble and garnish with a pinch of mint.

MOIST ROASTED CAPRETTO (BABY GOAT)

I almost always have goat on the menu at Scarpetta New York; if not this exact dish, then maybe as a *ragù* for a pasta. People just love it. This version is truly all about the goat.

SERVES 4 TO 6

FOR THE GOAT

Extra-virgin olive oil

6 cloves garlic, 4 sliced thinly, 2 cloves smashed

3 sprigs fresh rosemary

Crushed red pepper

3 pounds baby goat leg and shoulder

Kosher salt and freshly ground black pepper

1 cup dry white wine

½ cup Chicken Reduction (page 315)

Goat Stock (page 263), reheated if necessary

FOR SERVING

Extra-virgin olive oil

2 shallots, sliced thinly

Kosher salt

4 ounces pancetta, diced

8 ounces fingerling potatoes, blanched until tender (see page 194), cut into ¼-inch dice

8 ounces broccoli rabe, trimmed, blanched (see page 194), and cut into 2-inch pieces

1 tablespoon finely sliced fresh chives

Pinch of crushed red pepper

FOR THE GOAT: In a small bowl, combine ¼ cup olive oil with the sliced garlic, 2 sprigs of the rosemary, and ¼ teaspoon crushed red pepper. Put the goat on a rimmed baking sheet or in a baking dish and rub the marinade all over it. Cover with plastic wrap and refrigerate for at least 8 hours and up to 24 hours.

Heat a convection oven to 450°F or a conventional oven to 475°F. Remove the goat from the refrigerator and let sit at room temperature for 30 minutes before cooking.

Heat a large flameproof roasting pan over high heat. Wipe off the goat pieces; reserve the marinade. Season the meat all over with salt and black pepper. Add ¼ cup olive oil to the roasting pan, then add the goat and brown on all sides, about 6 minutes. Remove the meat from the pan and pour off the oil. Put the pan over medium

which wine? Sardinia is known for many wonderful things, one of them being delicious goat dishes, so it makes sense to pair this goat dish with a Carignano/Syrah blend from the region. Shardana's 2007 Valli di Porto Pino has ripe red fruit and grilled herb flavors and a nice tannic quality that goes perfectly with the goat.

heat, add ¼ cup olive oil, the reserved marinade, ½ teaspoon crushed red pepper, the smashed garlic cloves, and the remaining rosemary sprig. Cook, stirring, until fragrant, about 1 minute. Add the wine, and cook, stirring and scraping up the bits on the bottom of the pan, until the liquid in the pan is almost gone and what's left starts to emulsify with the oil. Add the Chicken Reduction and ¾ cup of the Goat Stock and bring to a boil. Return the goat pieces to the roasting pan and baste with the liquid.

Transfer the pan to the oven. Every 8 minutes, baste the meat and check the level of the liquid in the pan; you want it about ¼ inch up the sides of the meat. Add up to 1 cup of Goat Stock every time you check on the goat to maintain that level. After 1 hour, reduce the oven temperature to 350°F (375°F for a conventional oven) and continue to baste and monitor the liquid level at 10-minute intervals. Continue this process until the meat starts to release from the bone on the ends. (If you use up all of the Goat Stock before the goat is done, use water.) Test for doneness by pushing the back of a spoon against the meat; when it gives and does not bounce back, the goat is done. Cooking time can vary, but begin checking after a total cooking time of 1 hour.

Remove the goat from the oven and let cool slightly. Transfer the sauce to a narrow, tall saucepan and skim the excess fat from the top. Season to taste with salt only if needed; there should be enough from the initial seasoning and from the continual reduction of the sauce, which intensifies all flavors, including salt.

When cool enough to handle, cut the meat from the bone in large pieces, then cut those pieces into 2-inch cubes and reheat it in the sauce. (The goat may be cooked 2 days ahead, and it tastes better for it. Let it cool to room temperature, then refrigerate the meat and sauce together.)

TO SERVE: Heat a convection oven to 350°F or a conventional oven to 375°F.

MOIST ROASTING

I like to cook large pieces of meat and fish using a method that's really a hybrid of roasting and braising, in which I brown a large piece of meat in a little oil and then cook it uncovered in a little liquid in a pretty hot oven. I call this "moist roasting" because the moisture in the oven cooks the meat very tenderly, but the high temperature also continues to brown the meat's exposed surfaces. By keeping a small amount of liquid in the pan and adding more throughout the process, there is a constant reduction and a deepening of flavors. One of the signs of this happening is that the color of the liquid and the meat becomes darker. As the meat gets basted, a thin layer of sauce that remains on the meat after basting reduces and caramelizes before the next basting occurs. The end result is a moist, tender, and flavorful piece of meat as well as a deep, complex sauce that has an amazing silkiness.

In a small sauté pan, heat 1 tablespoon olive oil over medium-low heat. Add the shallots, season lightly with salt, and cook, stirring occasionally, until tender and browned, about 10 minutes. Remove from the heat and reserve.

In a medium ovenproof sauté pan, combine the roasted goat meat, 2 cups of the sauce, and 2 tablespoons olive oil. Transfer to the oven and heat, basting occasionally, for 6 minutes.

Meanwhile, heat 2 teaspoons olive oil in a large sauté pan over medium heat. Add the pancetta and cook, stirring occasionally, until the pancetta starts to color, about 2 minutes. Add the potatoes and cook, tossing occasionally, until the potatoes become crispy, about 2 minutes. Add the broccoli rabe and reserved shallots and cook, stirring, for 2 minutes. Add the chives and the crushed red pepper and season to taste with salt.

Divide the vegetables among serving plates. Divide the goat meat among the plates and pour a few tablespoons of the sauce on each plate. Finish with a drizzle of olive oil.

GOAT STOCK

MAKES 2 QUARTS

1 pound goat bones

The flavor from the young goat is so clean and pure that you do not need any other ingredients to make this stock, which allows the flavor of the goat to come through without being gamy. Ask your butcher for goat bones.

In a large stockpot, combine the bones with 2½ quarts water. Bring to a simmer over medium-high heat. Reduce the heat so the liquid is lightly bubbling, and gently simmer, skimming off any foam or impurities that rise to the surface, for 3 hours.

Strain through a fine-mesh strainer. (The stock may be made 2 days ahead. Once it has cooled, cover and refrigerate it. It can also be frozen for up to 2 months.)

ASH-SPICED VENISON WITH POLENTA DUMPLINGS, CRANBERRIES, AND CONCORD GRAPE REDUCTION

In Italy, some cured meats are aged under ash. That was my inspiration for this dish, which turns spices to ash and then uses that mixture to coat the venison.

SERVES 4

FOR THE SPICE ASH

2 sticks cinnamon, broken into pieces (about 3 tablespoons)

2 tablespoons whole Szechuan peppercorns

2 tablespoons dried juniper berries

9 whole star anise

2 teaspoons whole cloves

4 pieces venison loin, about 5 ounces each

FOR SERVING

Extra-virgin olive oil

Kosher salt

2 cloves garlic, smashed

2 sprigs fresh rosemary

4 pieces Polenta Dumplings (page 266)

½ cup thinly sliced shallots

8 ounces Brussels sprouts, trimmed and sliced very thinly

20 dried cranberries, soaked in water to rehydrate

Pinch of crushed red pepper

½ cup warm Parsnip Purée (page 326)

Flaked sea salt

½ cup Concord Grape Reduction (page 267)

FOR THE SPICE ASH: Heat the broiler to high. Put the cinnamon, Szechuan peppercorns, juniper berries, star anise, and cloves on a small rimmed baking sheet or in a small ovenproof sauté pan and broil until dark black and gray (like hot charcoal), about 5 minutes. (If they catch on fire, blow out the fire and return the spices to the oven.) If, after 5 minutes, some of the spices are blackened and others are not, remove the blackened ones and return the others to the broiler. Let cool, then finely grind in batches in a spice grinder. The mixture will keep, stored airtight, indefinitely.

Rub the venison all over with ¼ cup of the spice ash, and shake off any excess. Refrigerate for at least 4 hours and up to 24 hours.

TO SERVE: Heat a convection oven to 225°F or a conventional oven to 250°F.

Heat 2 tablespoons olive oil in a medium ovenproof sauté pan over medium-high heat. Season the venison all over with kosher salt and add it to the hot pan. Cook undisturbed until a slight crust forms on one side, about 30 seconds. Turn and cook each side to give it a nice crust all over. Remove the venison from the pan and wipe the pan clean. Return the venison to the pan along with the garlic cloves, rosemary, and another 2 tablespoons olive oil. Transfer the pan to the oven and cook until medium-rare (120°F on an instant-read thermometer), 10 to 15 minutes. Remove the venison from the pan and allow to rest for 5 minutes.

Meanwhile, in a medium sauté pan, heat 1 tablespoon olive oil over high heat. Add the Polenta Dumplings and cook until golden brown on one side. Turn the dumplings over and cook the other side. Transfer to the oven to keep warm.

In a large sauté pan, heat 1 tablespoon olive oil over medium-high heat. Add the shallots and cook, stirring, until tender and browned, about 5 minutes. Lower the heat to medium, add the Brussels sprouts, and cook until tender, 2 to 3 minutes. Drain the cranberries and add them and the crushed red pepper to the pan. Stir and cook for another 1 to 2 minutes to warm the cranberries. Season to taste with kosher salt.

Divide the Parsnip Purée among serving plates, smearing it across the middle of each plate. Top with the Polenta Dumplings and the Brussels sprouts. Slice the venison ½ inch thick and place the slices on top of the vegetables. Top with a tiny pinch of sea salt and a drizzle of olive oil. Pour 2 to 3 tablespoons of the Concord Grape Reduction on each plate.

POLENTA DUMPLINGS

MAKES 12 SQUARES

This is a great way to use up leftover polenta.

¾ cup finely sliced bacon

1 cup thinly sliced shallots

1 sprig fresh thyme

Kosher salt

1½ cups Creamy Polenta (page 77), at room temperature or cold

1 cup panko bread crumbs

⅓ cup plus 2 tablespoons all-purpose flour

2 large egg yolks

2 tablespoons chopped fresh chives

Line a shallow baking dish or rimmed baking sheet with parchment paper or plastic wrap. In a medium sauté pan over medium-low heat, cook the bacon until it starts to brown. Add the shallots and thyme and cook until the shallots are well browned, about 10 minutes. Remove the thyme sprig, season with salt, and transfer to a stand mixer fitted with the paddle attachment. Mix in the polenta, panko, flour, egg yolks, chives, and ½ teaspoon salt. Transfer to the baking dish and spread 1 inch thick. Refrigerate for 2 hours. (The polenta can be made up to 2 days ahead; keep it covered and refrigerated.) When ready to use, cut the polenta into 2-inch squares.

CONCORD GRAPE REDUCTION

MAKES ABOUT 2 CUPS

This makes more than you need for the Ash-Spiced Venison, but it freezes well. It's also delicious with duck and lamb.

2 tablespoons extra-virgin olive oil

1 cup thinly sliced shallots

Pinch of crushed red pepper

2 sprigs fresh thyme

1 cup Concord grapes, or ¼ cup Concord grape juice

2 tablespoons red wine vinegar

2 cups Chicken Reduction (page 315)

In a medium saucepan, heat the olive oil over medium heat. Add the shallots and cook, stirring occasionally, until the shallots are well browned, about 10 minutes. Add the crushed red pepper and thyme and cook, stirring, until fragrant, about another 1 minute. Add the grapes and cook, stirring occasionally, until the grapes start to burst and most of their liquid has reduced, about 5 minutes. (If using grape juice, cook it until it is reduced by half, about 3 minutes.) Add the vinegar and cook until the pan is almost dry, about 6 minutes. Add the Chicken Reduction and bring to a boil. Lower the heat, simmer for 15 minutes, then strain immediately. If the mixture seems too thin, return it to medium-high heat and continue to cook until you get a nice sauce-like consistency. (The reduction can be made 2 days ahead and kept covered and refrigerated; reheat gently before serving.)

I'VE NEVER BEEN A BIG FAN OF ITALIAN DESSERTS. Most feel like they're trying too hard. Such sweetness and heft. The recipes that follow may not be your typical tiramisu or cannoli (and some are based on French and Spanish desserts, too), yet they all exemplify what I do love about savory Italian cooking: the importance of seasonality, a balance of textures and flavors on the plate, the attention to detail. Though some of these recipes include many components—something cold, something smooth, something crunchy—they all come together on the plate as naturally as can be. You get the most bang by making and serving all the different elements, but you can pare the desserts down as you like. We make our own sorbets and gelatos, but you can substitute the same flavor (or similar) of high-quality purchased products. But if you have an ice-cream machine, do try making ours, because the flavors are dynamite.

You can certainly serve wine with any and all of these desserts. From Passito di Pantelleria to a Vin Santo from Tuscany to a Recioto from Veneto, there's an Italian dessert wine for everyone's palate. The rule of thumb here is to choose a wine with similar flavor components as the dessert and with an equally or higher level of sweetness than the dessert.

DOLCI

LINGERING

VANILLA CARAMEL BUDINO WITH SALTED CARAMEL SAUCE

Budino is Italian for "pudding," and though the custard is delicious—smooth, creamy, and rich—what makes this dessert outstanding is the topping of warm, salty, caramel that gets poured over it. At the restaurant, we serve the *budino* in small glass cups so the contrasting layers are visible. To reinforce the salty-sweet nature of the *budino*, we top it with whipped cream and a teeny sprinkle of flaked sea salt. Over the top? Maybe. Delicious? Definitely.

SERVES 6 TO 8

FOR THE BUDINO

4 large egg yolks

1⅓ cups plus 2 tablespoons heavy cream

1½ cups plus 2 tablespoons whole milk

¼ cup cornstarch

1 teaspoon kosher salt

1 vanilla bean, split

1 cup granulated sugar

8 tablespoons (4 ounces) unsalted butter, at room temperature

FOR SERVING

½ cup heavy cream

1 teaspoon confectioners' sugar

¼ teaspoon vanilla extract

Salted Caramel Sauce (page 273), reheated if necessary

Gianduja Crumble (optional; page 274)

Flaked sea salt

FOR THE BUDINO: Fill a large bowl with ice water.

In a medium bowl, whisk together the egg yolks, the 2 tablespoons cream, the 2 tablespoons milk, and the cornstarch.

In a medium saucepan, combine the remaining 1½ cups cream, the remaining 1½ cups milk, and the kosher salt. Open the vanilla bean and, with the tip of a paring knife, scrape the seeds into the saucepan. Add the pod as well and bring the mixture to a simmer over medium heat.

In another medium saucepan, heat the granulated sugar over medium-high heat, stirring occasionally with a wooden spoon or heatproof spatula, until the sugar melts and becomes dark brown. Remove the sugar from the heat and slowly stir in the warm cream mixture (be careful, as it will bubble and sputter) until well incorporated.

Whisk a small ladleful of the warm cream mixture into the egg yolk mixture a little at a time. Then slowly mix the egg yolk mixture into the saucepan. Cook, stirring, until a thick custard forms.

Strain through a fine-mesh strainer into a large heatproof measuring cup (you will have about 3¾ cups) or a bowl. Whisk in the butter until melted.

While the custard is still warm, divide it among serving bowls or cups (we use plain juice glasses), filling them no more than three-quarters full. Cover with plastic wrap, pressing it onto the surface to prevent a skin from forming, and refrigerate for at least 2 hours and up to 2 days.

TO SERVE: In a medium bowl, combine the heavy cream, confectioners' sugar, and vanilla extract and whisk to medium peaks. Pour 2 to 3 tablespoons of the Salted Caramel Sauce over each custard and top with a spoonful of the Gianduja Crumble, if you like. Top with a dollop or quenelle (see page 79) of whipped cream and a pinch of sea salt.

SALTED CARAMEL SAUCE

MAKES ABOUT 1 CUP

This is addictingly good stuff. Try a little over your favorite vanilla ice cream. The caramel sauce may be made ahead and refrigerated. Reheat it gently (to about 130°F).

¾ cup heavy cream

1½ teaspoons kosher salt

½ vanilla bean, split

8 tablespoons (4 ounces) unsalted butter, cut into pieces

1 cup granulated sugar

In a small saucepan, combine the cream and salt. Open the vanilla bean and scrape the seeds into the cream with the tip of a paring knife. Add the pod to the saucepan as well, and bring the cream to a simmer over medium heat.

Meanwhile, combine the butter and sugar in a medium saucepan, and cook, stirring occasionally with a wooden spoon or heatproof spatula, until the butter and sugar have melted and are a deep amber color. (The caramel will bubble and look strange as it cooks. Once the sugar melts and the moisture from the butter evaporates, the mixture should become thin and glossy.) Remove the sugar from the heat and carefully add the hot cream; it will bubble and spurt but will settle down. Stir well to combine, then strain though a fine-mesh strainer. The sauce will keep, covered and refrigerated, for at least 1 week. Reheat it gently before using.

GIANDUJA CRUMBLE

MAKES ABOUT 1½ CUPS

This chocolate and hazelnut crumble adds some fun texture to the *budino*, but it's also great with ice cream. *Feuilletine* is part of every pastry chef's arsenal and is essentially paper-thin wafer baked until crispy. It's most often broken up and used to add crisp texture to all kinds of desserts. You can find it where baking supplies are sold. Or you can use a substitution that, while not as fancy, adds that same great crunch: cornflakes.

3 ounces milk chocolate, chopped

3 ounces hazelnut praline paste

3 ounces feuilletine or cornflakes

Line a rimmed baking sheet with a silicone liner or parchment paper.

In a double boiler or a bowl set over (but not touching) a saucepan of simmering water, melt the chocolate and praline paste together, stirring occasionally. With a heatproof rubber spatula, fold in the *feuilletine*, then spread the mixture out on the baking sheet and freeze until hard.

Break into pieces and transfer to a stand mixer fitted with the paddle attachment. With the bowl guard on (or holding up some plastic around the bowl as a shield), mix on high speed to crumble the chocolate into pea-size pieces. Keep the crumble refrigerated until just before serving.

PUMPKIN POTS DE CRÈME WITH CONCORD PRESERVES AND CINNAMON FROTH

This dessert calls to mind the cooling days of the grape harvest. Indeed, grapes are featured three ways: in the preserves, a tablespoon of which gets hidden between layers of the custard and its light and creamy cinnamon topping; in a sorbet; and in a slice of *schiacciata all'uva* (a sweet, grape-stuffed bread) served along with the custard. Do plan to make this in the fall, when Concord grapes, those deep, dark eating grapes often made into jelly and jam, are available.

SERVES 6 TO 8

FOR THE CUSTARD

2 cups heavy cream

2 cups whole milk

1 tablespoon crumbled whole cinnamon stick

2 whole cardamom pods, smashed to expose their seeds

2 whole cloves

1 whole star anise

½ teaspoon ground cinnamon

⅛ teaspoon ground ginger

⅛ teaspoon ground nutmeg

1¼ cups granulated sugar

12 large egg yolks

2 cups canned pumpkin purée

FOR THE PRESERVES

12 ounces Concord grapes

1 tablespoon verjus or white wine

¼ teaspoon finely grated lemon zest

½ lemon

¼ cup plus 1 tablespoon granulated sugar

1 teaspoon powdered pectin

FOR THE CINNAMON FROTH

2 gelatin sheets

1½ cups whole milk

¾ cup heavy cream

1 tablespoon ground cinnamon

1 orange

¼ cup plus 2 tablespoons granulated sugar

4 large egg yolks

FOR SERVING

Salted Pumpkin Seeds (page 278)

Concord Grape Sorbet (page 278)

Schiacciata all'Uva (page 279)

Heat a convection oven to 250°F or a conventional oven to 275°F.

FOR THE CUSTARD: Combine the cream and milk in a medium saucepan and bring to a simmer over medium heat.

Meanwhile, in a small sauté pan, toast the cinnamon stick pieces, the cardamom, cloves, and star anise, stirring occasionally, until fragrant, 2 to 3 minutes. Add them and the ground cinnamon, ginger, and nutmeg to the milk and cream. Bring to a boil, then lower the heat to a simmer and cook for 2 minutes. Take the pan off the heat and let the spices steep for about 5 minutes. Add the sugar and stir to dissolve. Strain though a fine-mesh strainer into a large bowl. Whisk in the egg yolks and the pumpkin purée, then pass the mixture thorough a clean fine-mesh strainer.

Pour the custard into individual ramekins or other heatproof serving dishes. (At the restaurant, we use heatproof water glasses and fill each with about 1/2 cup custard.) Put the custards in a roasting pan, add enough water to come halfway up the sides of the ramekins, and cover loosely with aluminum foil. Bake until the custard is mostly set, with a little jiggle left in the center, 35 to 40 minutes depending on the size of your serving dish. Let cool at room temperature, then cover and refrigerate for at least 4 hours and up to 24 hours. The custard will continue to set as it cools.

FOR THE PRESERVES: Put the grapes in a blender and pulse on the lowest speed until the grapes are broken up and the liquid appears slightly purple. Transfer to a small saucepan and add the verjus and lemon zest, and squeeze the juice from the 1/2 lemon into the pan. Stir to combine and cook over medium heat. Mix the sugar and the pectin together well and add it to the grapes, stirring vigorously as you do so. Add 3 tablespoons water and bring to a boil. Lower the heat to a simmer and cook until the mixture forms thick bubbles around the edge, 2 to 3 minutes, then strain through a fine-mesh strainer. Cool to room temperature, then cover with plastic wrap and refrigerate for up to 3 days.

FOR THE CINNAMON FROTH: Fill a small bowl with ice water. Soak the gelatin sheets in the water for 5 to 10 minutes.

Meanwhile, combine the milk, cream, and cinnamon in a medium saucepan. Using a vegetable peeler, peel 4 wide strips of zest from the orange and add them to the pan. (Reserve the rest of the orange for another use.) Bring to a simmer, then take off the heat, cover, and let steep for 15 minutes. Strain through a fine-mesh strainer into a clean saucepan and reserve.

Fill a medium bowl with ice water.

In a small bowl, whisk together the sugar and the egg yolks. Whisk ¼ cup of the warm cinnamon cream into the yolks, then whisk all of the yolks back into the cream. Heat the cream over medium heat and bring the mixture to just under a boil. Remove the gelatin sheets from the ice water and squeeze to wring out any excess water. Add the gelatin to the saucepan and stir to dissolve. Transfer to a bowl and place the bowl in the ice water to cool the cream quickly. Transfer to a whipped cream canister with 2 chargers. Shake very vigorously and refrigerate until needed.

TO SERVE: Put a tablespoon of the Concord preserves on each custard. Cover with the whipped cinnamon froth. Put each custard on a serving plate and place 2 teaspoons of the Salted Pumpkin Seeds down on the plate. Put a scoop or quenelle (see page 79) of the Concord Grape Sorbet on the pumpkin seeds, and next to that, a small slice of the *Schiacciata all'Uva*.

SALTED PUMPKIN SEEDS

MAKES 2 CUPS

This makes a lot, but they are great for snacking.

½ cup extra-virgin olive oil

2 cups pumpkin seeds

2 tablespoons flaked sea salt

Line a small rimmed baking sheet with paper towels. Heat the olive oil in a medium saucepan over medium-high heat until smoking. Add the pumpkin seeds all at once and stir continuously until the seeds start popping. Continue to cook until they start turning brown in spots. Stir in the salt and pour onto the baking sheet to cool.

CONCORD GRAPE SORBET

MAKES 1 QUART

This is a truly seasonal sorbet, as you can only find Concord grapes in the fall. Make it while you can.

2 pounds Concord grapes

2 lemons

1 cup simple syrup (see page 282)

1 cup light corn syrup

Combine all of the ingredients in a blender and purée. Freeze according to your ice-cream maker's directions.

SCHIACCIATA ALL'UVA

SERVES 8 TO 10

This sweet flatbread is often made in Tuscany during the wine grape harvest. Try to find seedless Concord grapes for this.

¾ cup granulated sugar

½ cup plus 2 tablespoons (2½ ounces) all-purpose flour

½ cup plus 2 tablespoons cornmeal, preferably bramata (see page 77)

1½ teaspoons baking powder

Grated zest of 1 orange

½ cup heavy cream

½ cup whole milk

5 large egg yolks, lightly beaten

¼ cup Marsala

1 teaspoon vanilla extract

10 tablespoons (5 ounces) unsalted butter, melted

1 pound seedless Concord grapes, cut in half

Heat a convection oven to 350°F or a conventional oven to 375°F.

In a stand mixer fitted with the paddle attachment, combine the sugar, flour, cornmeal, baking powder, and orange zest on low speed. Add the cream, milk, egg yolks, Marsala, and vanilla extract, and mix until combined. Add the butter and mix until emulsified. Add the grapes and mix briefly to disperse.

Press the dough into a 9 x 13-inch baking pan and bake until well browned on the bottom, about 20 minutes. Serve warm or at room temperature.

BLACK PLUM TART

When plums are in season, this is the tart to make. We make this in a 4 x 14-inch rectangular tart pan because we like how the slices look on the plate. If you want to make a round tart, choose a 9½-inch pan, which has about the same volume and area. Serve the tart with White Peach Sorbet (page 283), if you like.

SERVES 6

FOR THE DOUGH

4¾ cups (19 ounces) all-purpose flour

2 cups confectioners' sugar

2 sticks plus 5 tablespoons (10½ ounces) cold unsalted butter, cut into pieces

2 large eggs

⅛ cup ice water

FOR THE FILLING

5 tablespoons (2½ ounces) unsalted butter, at room temperature

1¼ cups (5 ounces) confectioners' sugar

½ teaspoon granulated sugar

Finely grated zest from 1 lemon

½ teaspoon kosher salt

2 large eggs

1 tablespoon milk

1½ teaspoons all-purpose flour

FOR THE PLUMS

1 cup granulated sugar

½ cup light corn syrup

½ cup verjus, or substitute white wine

10 ripe (but not soft) medium black plums, halved and pit removed

FOR SERVING

White Peach Sorbet (optional; page 283)

FOR THE TART DOUGH: In a stand mixer fitted with the paddle attachment, combine the flour and confectioners' sugar on low speed. Add the butter and mix until the dough looks crumbly. Beat the eggs and ice water together. Add to the dough and mix until just combined. Gather the dough together in a rectangle shape, wrap well in plastic wrap, and refrigerate for at least 1 hour.

FOR THE FILLING: In a stand mixer fitted with the paddle attachment, combine the butter, confectioners' sugar, granulated sugar, lemon zest, and salt on low speed until light and fluffy, about 3 minutes. Beat the eggs with the milk and add that to the bowl. Add the flour and mix until incorporated.

SIMPLE SYRUP IS SIMPLE TO MAKE

You can buy simple syrup, but why bother when it's so easy to make with ingredients, namely granulated sugar and water, that are almost always on hand? Not only is it used in desserts, but it's also a base for many cocktails and is a great way to sweeten iced tea and lemonade. To make it, simply bring equal amounts of water and sugar to a boil over medium-high heat, and cook, stirring, until the sugar is completely dissolved. One cup of each will give you about 1½ cups simple syrup. It will keep, covered tightly and refrigerated, for at least 1 month.

FOR THE PLUMS: Heat a convection oven to 325°F or a conventional oven to 350°F.

In a large ovenproof sauté pan over medium heat, stir together the sugar and corn syrup. Cook, stirring occasionally, until the mixture turns a light caramel color, about 5 minutes. Carefully add the verjus and cook for 15 minutes.

Add the plums, skin side down, and transfer the pan to the oven. Cook, turning the plums over every 5 minutes and swirling the pan so the plums cook evenly, until the plums are very tender but not falling apart, 15 to 20 minutes. If the syrup starts reducing too much, add a little water to the pan. Let the plums cool in their juices in the pan. When cool enough to handle, take the plums out of the pan—reserve the juices—and slice each half into quarters.

To assemble and bake the tart, heat a convection oven to 350°F or a conventional oven to 375°F.

Roll out the tart dough into a 15-inch rectangle about ⅛ inch thick. Lift the dough and transfer it to a 4 x 14-inch tart pan with a removable bottom. Press the dough firmly into the sides of the pan. Trim to the top of the pan by running the rolling pin over the top edge of the tart pan. Poke the dough all over with a fork and bake for about 10 minutes. Let cool.

Spread 1 cup of the filling over the tart shell. Arrange the plums over the filling. Bake for 25 minutes, take the tart out of the oven, brush on the reserved plum juices, and bake for another 5 minutes. Let the tart rest just until cool enough to remove from pan.

Serve warm, or let cool to room temperature and reheat briefly for serving. Slice into 2-inch pieces and serve with reserved plum juice drizzled over it and a scoop of White Peach Sorbet.

WHITE PEACH SORBET

MAKES ABOUT 1 QUART

Frozen white peach purée is available at specialty markets.

2 cups thawed frozen white peach purée

¾ cup simple syrup (see opposite)

2 tablespoons light corn syrup

Juice of ½ lemon

In a blender or with an immersion blender, mix all of the ingredients until combined. Freeze according to your ice-cream maker's instructions.

STRAWBERRY AND BALSAMIC CATALANA

Strawberries and balsamic vinegar is a classic Italian combination, but this custard comes by way of Spain. Instead of brûléeing the custard, as is traditional, we serve it with a crunchy mix of sesame and chocolate, which adds a similar texture. Cacao nibs (the bits of roasted and crushed cocoa beans used to make chocolate) give the dessert that toasty flavor without the need for a blowtorch.

SERVES 8

FOR THE CUSTARD

2 cups heavy cream

½ cup granulated sugar

¼ teaspoon vanilla extract

9 large egg yolks

2 tablespoons balsamic glaze (see Note)

FOR THE STRAWBERRIES

2 cups hulled, chopped fresh strawberries

1 cup granulated sugar

Juice of ½ lemon

1½ teaspoons finely chopped fresh lemon verbena

FOR SERVING

Sesame Crunch (page 287)

Heat a convection oven to 325°F or a conventional oven to 350°F.

FOR THE CUSTARD: In a small saucepan, bring the cream, sugar, and vanilla extract to a simmer over medium heat. In a medium bowl, whisk together the egg yolks and balsamic glaze. Add about 2 tablespoons of the hot cream mixture to the egg yolks and whisk to combine. Add about another 2 tablespoons and whisk again. Slowly whisk the rest of the cream mixture into the egg yolks, then strain though a fine-mesh strainer.

Pour the custard into individual ramekins or other heatproof serving dishes. (At the restaurant, we use heatproof water glasses and fill each with about ½ cup custard.) Put the custards in a roasting pan, add enough water to come halfway up the sides of the ramekins, and cover loosely with aluminum foil. Bake until the custard is mostly set, with a little jiggle left in the center, 35 to 40 minutes depending on the size of your serving dish. Let cool at room temperature, then refrigerate for at least 4 hours and up to 24 hours. The custard will continue to set as it cools.

FOR THE STRAWBERRIES: In a medium bowl, toss the straw-berries with the sugar, lemon juice, and lemon verbena and let sit at room temperature for 1 hour to macerate.

TO SERVE: Top each custard with ¼ cup of the strawberries and 1 to 2 tablespoons of the Sesame Crunch.

NOTE: *Balsamic glaze is vinegar reduced with grape must. Slightly thicker than conventional balsamic vinegar, it's not as harsh and strikes a good balance between sweetness and acidity. Many super-markets carry it, as do Italian markets and specialty food stores.*

SESAME CRUNCH

MAKES 1 CUP

Once you make this crunchy, chocolaty topping, you will think of all kinds of uses for it. Fortunately, it makes more than you need for the Strawberry and Balsamic Catalana, and leftovers keep for 2 weeks refrigerated. You can find cacao nibs, essentially chocolate that hasn't yet been ground and mixed with sugar, near the high-quality chocolate bars at the supermarket and at health food stores.

¼ cup white sesame seeds

2 tablespoons black sesame seeds

⅓ cup cacao nibs

2½ tablespoons confectioners' sugar

¼ cup chopped dark chocolate

Line a small rimmed baking sheet with a silicone liner or parchment paper.

In a small saucepan, toss the white and black sesame seeds, cacao nibs, and confectioners' sugar together. Heat over medium low heat, stirring occasionally, until the sugar melts and the sesame seeds start to pop. Using a rubber spatula, transfer the sesame seed mixture to the baking sheet to cool. Meanwhile, melt the chocolate using a double boiler or the microwave. Pour over the sesame seeds and use the spatula to mix until the sesame seeds and cacao nibs are completely coated. Refrigerate until the chocolate solidifies, then break into smaller pieces. Transfer to an airtight container and refrigerate for up to 2 weeks.

COCONUT PANNA COTTA

This is one of the most popular desserts at Scarpetta. It's light and refreshing and offers contrasts galore: creamy panna cotta, frozen sorbet, a sweet guava sauce, and a crisp cookie.

FOR THE PANNA COTTA

3 gelatin sheets

1 cup heavy cream

⅔ cup whole milk

1¼ cups coconut milk

1 (14-ounce) can sweetened condensed milk

FOR SERVING

Guava Sauce (page 290)

Sugared Pineapple (page 290)

Coconut Sorbet (page 291)

Coconut Tuiles (page 291)

FOR THE PANNA COTTA: Fill a medium bowl with ice water. Add the gelatin sheets and let bloom for 5 to 10 minutes.

Meanwhile, in a medium saucepan over medium-high heat, bring the cream, milk, and coconut milk to a boil. Remove from the heat and skim and discard any skin or foam that formed on top. Stir in the condensed milk.

Remove the gelatin sheets from the water and squeeze to wring out excess water. Add the gelatin to the warm cream and stir to dissolve. Divide the mixture among 6 bowls or ramekins and refrigerate for at least 4 hours to chill and set.

TO SERVE: Pour enough of the Guava Sauce over the panna cotta to create a layer about ⅛ inch thick (about 3 tablespoons each depending on the serving dish). Pile 2 tablespoons of the Sugared Pineapple in the center of each panna cotta. Place a quenelle (see page 79) of the Coconut Sorbet on top of the pineapple, then lay a Coconut Tuile against the sorbet.

GUAVA SAUCE

MAKES 3 CUPS

I love the shock of color this adds to the coconut panna cotta. Its unique flavor also contributes to the refreshing, tropical feel of the dish. Leftover sauce will keep in the refrigerator for up to 5 days and can even be frozen for up to 2 months.

2 cups thawed frozen guava purée

1 cup simple syrup (see page 282)

In a blender or using an immersion blender, combine the purée and the simple syrup. Reserve in the refrigerator until ready to use.

SUGARED PINEAPPLE

MAKES 2 CUPS

This makes more than you need for the panna cotta, but the pineapple will keep up to 5 days, covered and refrigerated; it's delicious on ice cream or swirled into yogurt.

½ cup granulated sugar

2 cups diced (¼-inch) pineapple

In a small saucepan, bring the sugar and ¼ cup water to a boil, and cook just until the sugar has dissolved. Add the pineapple and stir to coat. Remove from the heat and reserve.

COCONUT SORBET

MAKES 1 QUART

If you can find a good-quality coconut sorbet at the market, feel free to substitute that.

2¾ cups granulated sugar

2 tablespoons light corn syrup

2 cups thawed frozen coconut purée

Juice of ½ lemon

In a large saucepan over medium-high heat, mix the sugar and corn syrup with 4½ cups water. Bring to a boil, and boil for 1 minute. Stir in the coconut purée and the lemon juice, take the pan off the heat, and let cool to room temperature. Freeze according to your ice-cream maker's directions.

COCONUT TUILES

MAKES ABOUT 60 *TUILES*

These thin, crispy cookies not only decorate a plate nicely but also add some texture when served with creamy desserts. This recipe makes a lot of cookies, but the batter freezes well, so you can just bake off as many as you want and then freeze the rest in a freezer bag. Let the batter thaw in the refrigerator for a day before using.

1 large egg white

3 tablespoons granulated sugar

½ cup plus 1 tablespoon (1 ounce) finely shredded unsweetened coconut

2 tablespoons (1 ounce) unsalted butter, melted

Whisk together the egg white, sugar, and coconut until well combined. Add the butter and whisk until combined, then refrigerate the batter for 2 hours.

Heat a convection oven to 275°F or a conventional oven to 300°F. Line 2 baking sheets with a silicone liner or parchment paper.

Spoon 1 to 1½ teaspoons batter on a baking sheet. Spread as evenly and thinly as possible into a 4-inch circle or oval (the size won't change much during baking). Repeat with the rest of the batter to make as many cookies as you want. Bake, rotating the pans halfway through baking, until a nice light brown color, about 10 minutes. Cool the *tuiles* on the baking sheet before removing with a thin spatula.

AMEDEI CHOCOLATE CAKE

When I first tried the Amedei brand of chocolate, from Tuscany, I was just blown away by it. I know I wanted to feature it in a dessert that would show it off. This flourless chocolate cake is really all about that chocolate. At the restaurant, we serve it with Burnt Orange Gelato, which helps cut the richness. A crisp cookie and dots of chocolate sauce add interest to the plate but are not crucial to the dessert's success.

SERVES 6

8 tablespoons (4 ounces) unsalted butter

1 cup (5½ ounces) chopped Amedei dark chocolate, preferably Toscano Black 66%

3 large eggs

¾ cup granulated sugar

½ cup unsweetened cocoa powder, sifted

Burnt Orange Gelato (page 294)

Heat a convection oven to 350°F or a conventional oven to 375°F.

Cover the bottoms of six 3-inch ring molds with aluminum foil, folding the excess foil up and around the outside of the ring molds to create a bottom. Alternatively, you can use 6 similar-size ramekins.

In a double boiler or in a heatproof bowl set over, but not touching, simmering water, melt the butter and chocolate together, stirring occasionally.

In a stand mixer fitted with the whisk attachment, whisk the eggs and sugar on medium speed until doubled in volume, 10 to 15 minutes. Turn off the mixer, add the cocoa powder, and mix on low speed until blended. Using a large rubber spatula, fold in the melted butter and chocolate until just combined.

Fill the ring molds about three-quarters full. Bake until the cakes look set but are still a little wiggly in the center, about 10 minutes.

Let the cakes cool, then remove from the molds. (The cakes may be made earlier in the day; let cool completely, then cover and keep at room temperature.)

To serve, reheat the cakes briefly in a warm oven and serve with Burnt Orange Gelato on the side.

BURNT ORANGE GELATO

MAKES 1 QUART

1⅓ cups granulated sugar

½ cup fresh orange juice

2 cups whole milk

2 cups heavy cream

12 large egg yolks

When people have this gelato at the restaurant, they love it, but most can't figure out where its sweet, citrusy, and toasty flavor comes from. Delicious paired with chocolate cake, the gelato is excellent on its own. For the best flavor, be sure to cook the sugar until it's nice and dark.

Fill a large bowl with ice water.

In a large saucepan, heat ⅔ cup of the granulated sugar until it turns dark brown. Remove the sugar from the heat and stir in the orange juice; be careful, as it may spurt. Stir in the milk and heavy cream and return this mixture to the heat. Bring to a boil, then take off the heat.

Meanwhile, in a large bowl, whisk the egg yolks with the remaining ⅔ cup sugar. Slowly pour about ½ cup of the cream mixture into the eggs while whisking to temper them, then pour the egg mixture into the saucepan. Cook, stirring, until the mixture has thickened somewhat and registers 175°F to 180°F on an instant-read thermometer. Immediately strain through a fine-mesh strainer into a bowl. Place the bowl in the ice bath and stir the custard occasionally to cool it quickly, then refrigerate until very cold. Freeze according to your ice-cream maker's directions.

STICKY TOFFEE PUDDING

I love classic British sticky toffee pudding, and though ours is baked instead of steamed, it has that same sweet decadence. The Roasted Banana Gelato we serve with it may seem sacrilege to some, but its flavor goes really well with the pudding and the candied walnut accompaniment.

SERVES 6

FOR THE PUDDING

Cooking spray

8 fresh dates

1 teaspoon baking soda

1 cup plus 2 tablespoons (4½ ounces) all-purpose flour

1 teaspoon baking powder

½ teaspoon kosher salt

4 tablespoons (2 ounces) unsalted butter, softened

¾ cup plus 1 tablespoon granulated sugar

1 large egg

1 teaspoon vanilla extract

¾ teaspoon ground ginger

FOR THE CARAMEL CREAM

3¼ cups heavy cream

2 cups firmly packed dark brown sugar

12 tablespoons (6 ounces) unsalted butter

½ cup Myer's Original Dark Rum

FOR SERVING

Roasted Banana Gelato (page 298)

Candied Walnuts (page 299)

FOR THE PUDDING: Heat a convection oven to 350°F or a conventional oven to 375°F.

Cover the bottoms of six 3-inch ring molds with aluminum foil, folding the excess foil up and around the outside of the ring mold, to create a bottom. Spray the molds generously with cooking spray.

Put the dates in a heatproof bowl and cover with boiling water. Let soak for 5 minutes to loosen the peel, then peel the dates and remove the pits by splitting them in half.

Bring 2 cups water to boil in a medium saucepan. Add the dates, take the pan off the heat, and let sit for 5 minutes. Sprinkle the baking soda over the dates. (The baking soda is said to help break down the fruit's fibers.) Transfer the dates and the liquid to a food processor and pulse until chunky.

In a medium bowl, whisk together the flour, baking powder, and salt.

In another medium bowl, whisk the butter and granulated sugar until lightly creamed. Add the date mixture, egg, vanilla extract, and ginger, and stir well to combine. Add the dry ingredients and mix with your hands until well combined. Divide the mixture among the ring molds, filling them about three-quarters full. Bake until a toothpick or metal cake tester inserted in the middle of the pudding comes out clean, about 25 minutes. Let cool to room temperature.

FOR THE CARAMEL CREAM: In a large saucepan, combine the heavy cream, brown sugar, butter, rum, and ½ cup water. Stir to combine, and bring to a boil over medium-high heat. Cook until the sugar has melted, then take off the heat.

TO SERVE: Remove the puddings from the molds, and then dip each into the caramel cream. Let them sit for 1 hour to soak in the cream, then warm them in a low oven. Serve the pudding with the Roasted Banana Gelato alongside it and some Candied Walnuts sprinkled on the plate.

ROASTED BANANA GELATO

MAKES ABOUT 1 QUART

Roasting bananas intensifies their flavor.

4 bananas (unpeeled)

3 cups whole milk

1⅓ cups heavy cream

¼ cup light corn syrup

½ teaspoon kosher salt

Pinch of nutmeg

8 large egg yolks

¾ cup granulated sugar

Heat a convection oven to 350°F or a conventional oven to 375°F.

Place the bananas on a small rimmed baking sheet and roast until completely soft and the peel is completely black, 30 to 45 minutes. Let cool. Remove the peels and measure 1½ cups of roasted banana. Transfer to a blender and purée with just enough of the milk to make a smooth purée.

Fill a large bowl with ice water.

In a medium saucepan, combine the remaining milk with the purée over medium heat. Stir in the cream, corn syrup, salt, and nutmeg, and bring to a simmer, stirring occasionally.

Meanwhile, in a medium bowl, whisk together the egg yolks and sugar and set aside.

Slowly pour about ½ cup of the cream mixture into the egg yolks while whisking to temper them, then pour the egg mixture into the saucepan and cook over medium heat, stirring, until the mixture has thickened somewhat and registers 175°F to 180°F on an instant-read thermometer. Immediately strain through a fine-mesh strainer into a bowl. Place the bowl in the ice bath and stir the custard occasionally to cool it quickly, then refrigerate until very cold. Freeze according to your ice-cream maker's directions.

CANDIED WALNUTS

MAKES ABOUT 1⅓ CUPS

These sweet toasted nuts add a little crunch to the Sticky Toffee Pudding. This recipe makes more than you will need, but you will want to eat them right off the baking sheet, so it's good to have extra. They're also good chopped and served over ice cream or added to a spinach salad.

1 tablespoon egg whites

1⅓ cups walnuts

1 tablespoon granulated sugar

Heat a convection oven to 350°F or a conventional oven to 375°F.

Line a rimmed baking sheet with a silicone liner or parchment paper. In a medium bowl, whisk the egg whites until frothy. Add the walnuts and sugar and toss well to coat. Spread on the baking sheet and bake for 5 minutes, then stir with a spatula and bake until lightly brown, another 5 minutes. Let cool to room temperature. When completely cool, transfer to an airtight container. (The nuts will keep, covered and refrigerated, for 2 weeks.)

CHOCOLATE TART SOUFFLÉ

A chocolate tart that's also a soufflé—what's not to like? Put simply: This dessert is a crowd-pleaser. This does not require as much last-minute preparation as a conventional soufflé and elements of the dessert may even be made a day ahead of serving.

SERVES 6

FOR THE TART SHELLS

1 cup (4 ounces) bread flour

½ cup almond flour

¼ cup unsweetened cocoa powder

½ teaspoon kosher salt

6 tablespoons (3 ounces) unsalted butter

⅓ cup confectioners' sugar

1 large egg

FOR THE SOUFFLÉ

1 cup chopped 72% dark chocolate

8 tablespoons (4 ounces) unsalted butter

2 large eggs

2 large egg yolks

⅓ cup granulated sugar

⅓ cup all-purpose flour

⅛ teaspoon kosher salt

FOR SERVING

Malt Gelato (page 302)

FOR THE TART SHELLS: In a small bowl, combine the bread flour, almond flour, cocoa powder, and salt. In a stand mixer fitted with the paddle attachment, mix the butter and confectioners' sugar together on low speed until light and fluffy. Add the egg and mix to combine. Add the flour mixture and mix just until combined. Wrap the dough in plastic wrap and refrigerate for 3 hours.

Heat a convection oven to 350°F or a conventional oven to 375°F. Have ready 6 individual tart pans (3½ to 4 inches in diameter), preferably nonstick with removable bottoms.

Roll the dough out ⅛ inch thick. Using a tart pan as a guide, cut out 6 rounds of dough. Transfer a round to the tart pan and press the dough firmly into the bottom and sides of the pan. Trim to the top of the pan by running the rolling pin over the top edge of the tart pan. Repeat with the remaining dough and tart pans. Refrigerate for 30 minutes. Wrap raw rice or beans in plastic wrap to make packages about the same size as the inner part of the tart shell. Place in the tarts and bake for 15 minutes. (The plastic wrap won't melt into the dough, but the rice or beans can no longer be used for cooking; keep them for future blind baking.) Let the tart shells cool. (The shells may be made 1 day ahead; once completely cooled, wrap them in plastic wrap and keep at room temperature.)

FOR THE SOUFFLÉ: In a double boiler or in a heatproof bowl over, but not touching, a pot of simmering water, melt the chocolate and butter together.

In a stand mixer fitted with the whisk attachment, whisk the eggs, egg yolks, and granulated sugar on medium speed until the mixture doubles in volume and turns pale yellow, about 6 minutes. Add the melted chocolate and whisk just until combined. Add the flour and salt and whisk only until just combined so the eggs don't deflate too much.

Fill the tart shells with the soufflé batter (you may have a little bit left over) and refrigerate until set.

Heat a convection oven to 350°F or a conventional oven to 375°F.

Put the soufflés on a rimmed baking sheet and bake until set around the edges but still a little wiggly in the center, about 10 minutes. Carefully remove from the tart pans and serve immediately with the Malt Gelato.

MALT GELATO

MAKES 1 QUART

The malt flavor in this gelato is delicious yet hard to define. It's rich and nutty and has the spirit of chocolate but it's not as overwhelming. It's the perfect flavor to serve with rich chocolate desserts.

2 cups whole milk

2 cups heavy cream

¾ cup plus 1 tablespoon granulated sugar

1 cup malted milk powder

1 teaspoon ground mace

8 large egg yolks

Have ready a large bowl of ice water.

In a medium saucepan over medium heat, combine the milk, cream, and half of the sugar. Cook, stirring, until the sugar has dissolved, then add the malted milk powder and mace and bring to a boil.

Meanwhile, in a large bowl, whisk the egg yolks with the remaining sugar. Slowly pour about ½ cup of the cream mixture into the eggs while whisking to temper them, then pour the egg mixture into the saucepan. Cook, stirring, until the mixture has thickened somewhat and registers 175°F to 180°F on an instant-read thermometer. Immediately strain through a fine-mesh strainer into a bowl. Place the bowl in the ice bath and stir the custard occasionally to cool it quickly, then refrigerate until very cold. Freeze according to your ice-cream maker's directions.

APRICOT SOUFFLÉ

A true soufflé is one of *the* sexiest dishes. Part of that comes from the combination of rich flavor and light as air texture and part is due to the fact that making them is a labor of love. The apricot in this one gives it a slight tang and a little sweetness: Perfection.

FOR THE PASTRY CREAM

1 cup thawed frozen apricot purée

½ cup plus 1 tablespoon granulated sugar

5 large egg yolks

¼ cup plus 2 tablespoons all-purpose flour

1 or 2 drops apricot extract

FOR THE SOUFFLÉ

Unsalted butter, for the soufflé cups

3 tablespoons granulated sugar, plus more as needed

6 large egg whites

FOR SERVING

Olive Oil Gelato (page 304)

FOR THE PASTRY CREAM: In a medium saucepan over medium heat, bring the apricot purée and half of the sugar to a simmer.

In a large bowl, whisk the egg yolks, flour, and the remaining sugar. Add the flour mixture to the apricot purée and cook, whisking constantly, until a very stiff pastry cream forms, about 5 minutes. Strain through a fine-mesh strainer, stir in the apricot extract, and let cool to room temperature. (The pastry cream can be made 1 day ahead, and kept covered and refrigerated. Let come to room temperature before using.)

FOR THE SOUFFLÉ: Butter individual soufflé cups or ramekins, then coat them with granulated sugar, tapping out the excess.

In a double boiler or in a heatproof bowl over, but not touching, a pot of simmering water, whisk the 3 tablespoons sugar and the egg whites until hot. Immediately transfer to a stand mixer fitted with the whisk attachment, and whisk until medium peaks form.

Using a large rubber spatula, fold the egg whites into the pastry cream. Fill the ramekins with this fluffy batter, bake for 10 minutes, and serve immediately with the Olive Oil Gelato alongside.

OLIVE OIL GELATO

MAKES ABOUT 1 QUART

You can really taste the olive oil in this uniquely flavored, lemon-accented gelato.

3¼ cups whole milk

1 cup plus 1 tablespoon heavy cream

1 tablespoon packed finely grated lemon zest

6 large egg yolks

¾ cup plus 2 tablespoons granulated sugar

½ teaspoon kosher salt

¾ cup extra-virgin olive oil

Fill a large bowl with ice water.

In a medium saucepan, bring the milk, heavy cream, and lemon zest to a boil.

Meanwhile, in a medium bowl, whisk the egg yolks with the sugar and salt. Slowly pour about ½ cup of the hot cream mixture into the eggs while whisking to temper them, then pour the egg mixture into the saucepan. Add the olive oil and cook, stirring, until the mixture has thickened somewhat and registers 175°F to 180°F on an instant-read thermometer. Immediately strain through a fine-mesh strainer into a bowl. Place the bowl in the ice bath and stir the custard occasionally to cool it quickly, then refrigerate until very cold. Freeze according to your ice-cream maker's directions.

SCOTT'S SPICED GIANDUJA HOT CHOCOLATE

This thick and rich hot chocolate, flavored with hazelnut and warm spices, is more like a dessert in and of itself, though you could serve it with biscotti or a slice of the Hazelnut and Brown Butter Cake (page 307).

SERVES 6 TO 8

FOR THE SPICES

1 tablespoon whole Szechuan peppercorns

1 tablespoon fennel seeds

1½ teaspoons whole cloves

1 teaspoon crumbled whole cinnamon stick

½ teaspoon whole white peppercorns

5 whole star anise

1 teaspoon flaked sea salt

FOR THE HOT CHOCOLATE

6 cups heavy cream

¾ cup unsweetened cocoa powder

¼ cup plus 2 tablespoons lightly packed light brown sugar

¼ teaspoon vanilla extract

3 ounces dark chocolate, preferably Valrhona 70%, chopped

½ cup gianduja paste (see Note)

⅔ cup Frangelico

FOR SERVING

1 cup heavy cream

2 tablespoons granulated sugar

FOR THE SPICES: Combine all but the salt in a medium sauté pan and toast over medium heat, stirring occasionally, until fragrant, 2 to 3 minutes. Let cool, then grind with the salt in a spice grinder. (The spices will keep, tightly covered, for several weeks.)

FOR THE HOT CHOCOLATE: In a medium saucepan over medium-high heat, combine the cream, cocoa powder, brown sugar, and vanilla extract, and bring to just under a boil, stirring occasionally to help dissolve the sugar.

Meanwhile, put the chocolate, gianduja paste, Frangelico, and 1½ teaspoons of the spices in a medium heatproof bowl. Pour the hot cream over and let sit for 3 minutes to melt the chocolate, then whisk everything together until silky smooth. Transfer the hot chocolate to a clean saucepan and heat gently over low heat.

TO SERVE: Whisk the heavy cream and sugar together until medium-soft peaks form.

Using an immersion blender, froth the hot chocolate. Ladle it into mugs and serve topped with the whipped cream.

NOTE: *Gianduja paste is a delicious mix of chocolate and hazelnuts. Look for it where you buy baking supplies.*

HAZELNUT AND BROWN BUTTER CAKE

This cake, with its subtle toasted-nut flavor and moist, buttery texture, is one of the few things I can't resist, especially when it's still warm from the oven. It's also delicious made with walnuts or almonds in place of the hazelnuts.

2 sticks (8 ounces) unsalted butter, plus more for the pan

4 ounces hazelnuts

¾ cup (3 ounces) all-purpose flour

3 cups (12 ounces) confectioners' sugar, plus more as needed

Pinch of kosher salt

1 cup egg whites (from about 8 large eggs)

In a saucepan, melt the butter over medium heat, and continue to cook it until it turns brown and smells quite nutty, being careful not to let it burn, 10 to 15 minutes. Remove from the heat and let cool almost to room temperature.

Meanwhile, heat a convection oven to 325°F or a conventional oven to 350°F. Butter the bottom of a 10-inch round cake pan and line the bottom of the pan with parchment paper.

Spread the hazelnuts on a rimmed baking sheet and toast them in the oven until lightly browned and fragrant, 10 to 15 minutes. Wrap the hazelnuts in a clean kitchen towel and rub them together vigorously to remove most of the skins. (It's fine if some is left on.)

Chop about ¼ cup of the nuts finely. Grind the rest of the toasted nuts in a food processor until finely ground.

Sift the flour, confectioners' sugar, and salt together into a large bowl. Add the ground nuts and whisk to combine. Add the egg whites and whisk them together well with the dry ingredients. Slowly add the melted butter, whisking constantly until it is completely incorporated and no butter is floating on top of the mixture.

Pour the batter into the prepared pan and sprinkle the top with the reserved chopped nuts. Bake until the cake feels solid but still gives slightly when touched, 40 to 45 minutes. Let the cake cool in the pan for 10 minutes before inverting it onto a serving plate.

THE SCARPETTA PANTRY

WHAT FOLLOWS ARE SOME OF THE RECIPES WE USE in the kitchen as building blocks (stocks), enhancers (spice mixes), and finishes (flavored oils and sauces). Most are used in more than one recipe in the book, and some are used in many of the recipes. And a few, such as the Braised Short Ribs (page 320) and the Scarpetta Tomato Sauce (page 322), which I use on my signature spaghetti, might seem surprising picks for the pantry. But we turn to these staples again and again to use in other recipes. All of these elements can be made well ahead of when they're to be served.

CHICKEN STOCK

Every day we make huge pots of chicken stock. My guys come in, throw a few chickens in a pot, add some carrots, celery, onion, and thyme, fill the pot with water, and put it on the stove, and 2 hours later, it's done. It's not hard to do, and the flavor is so much better than what you will find at the supermarket. Freeze the stock in containers of varying amounts so that you can pull out just what you need.

MAKES ABOUT 2½ QUARTS

2 whole chickens, 3 to 4 pounds each, giblets removed, breasts removed and reserved for another dish

1 carrot, cut into 6 pieces

1 celery stalk, cut into 6 pieces

1 small onion, quartered

4 sprigs fresh thyme

Kosher salt

Put the chickens, carrot, celery, onion, and thyme in a large stockpot. Add cold water to cover (about 4 quarts). Bring to a simmer over high heat, then lower the heat to medium-low and simmer gently for 2 hours. Every so often, skim and discard the scum that floats to the top of the pot.

To tell if it's done, dip a ladle deep into the pot so you can taste the actual broth and not the fat floating on top. Add a little salt to the broth in the ladle and taste. (While no salt is added to the actual stock—it gets seasoned when used in a dish—a little salt is needed when sampling the broth to bring out its flavor.) If it's pleasingly chicken flavored, the broth is done. If not, allow the birds to cook for another half hour or so.

Remove the chicken and strain the broth several times through a fine-mesh strainer. Let cool, then refrigerate. Once chilled, the fat will float to the top; remove about 90 percent of this fat. (A little fat is good for flavor.) The broth can be refrigerated for 2 days or frozen for up to 2 months.

LOBSTER BROTH

Just about any recipe with lobster in it will be better if there is some lobster broth involved, too. See Black Farfalle with Lobster (page 135) and Slow-Cooked Lobster with Ricotta Dumplings (page 197) for just two examples.

MAKES ABOUT 2 QUARTS

1 tablespoon extra-virgin olive oil

2 medium carrots, peeled and thinly sliced

2 medium celery stalks, thinly sliced

1 medium onion, thinly sliced

Lobster shells and small claws from 2 lobsters, body shells chopped lengthwise and then into thirds

3 cloves garlic, 2 cloves lightly smashed, 1 sliced

4 plum tomatoes, chopped

1 cup dry white wine

Heat a convection oven to 350°F or a conventional oven to 375°F.

Heat the olive oil in a small roasting pan over medium-high heat. Add the carrots, celery, and onions, and cook, stirring occasionally until the vegetables are soft and beginning to brown. Add the lobster shells and the 2 smashed garlic cloves. Transfer the pan to the oven and roast the shells, stirring occasionally to make sure everything is roasting evenly, until lightly browned, about 15 minutes. Transfer the pan back to the stove. Add the tomatoes and the sliced garlic and cook over medium-high heat, stirring occasionally, for about 5 minutes. Add the wine and cook until the wine is almost gone, 7 to 10 minutes.

Transfer everything to a large stockpot and add enough water to cover (about 3 quarts). Bring to a boil, then lower the heat to a simmer and cook until the broth is rich and full of flavor, about 45 minutes.

Strain the broth through a fine-mesh strainer. The broth can be refrigerated for 2 days or frozen for up to 2 months.

PRAWN/SHRIMP STOCK

It's easy to make a full-flavored stock using the peeled shells from prawns or shrimp. It freezes beautifully and adds wonderful flavor to shellfish pasta dishes.

MAKES ABOUT 1 CUP

1 tablespoon olive oil

1 small shallot, sliced

2 ounces shrimp shells (from about 10 ounces shrimp)

1 carrot, chopped

½ medium onion, chopped

½ celery stalk, chopped

1 clove garlic, thinly sliced

1 sprig fresh thyme

In a medium saucepan over medium-high heat, heat the olive oil and shallot until the shallot sizzles. Add the shrimp shells and cook, stirring, for 1 minute. Add the carrot, onion, celery, garlic, thyme, and 2 cups water and bring to a boil. Lower the heat to a simmer and cook until reduced by almost half, about 15 minutes.

Strain the stock through a fine-mesh strainer. The stock can be refrigerated for 2 days or frozen for up to 2 months.

TAKING STOCK OF STOCK

A homemade stock is often the difference between what makes a dish good and what makes it great. Most stocks are easy to make but do require some hands-off time. If you can't make your own stock, buy the best-quality stock you can afford. Some gourmet markets make their own in-house and sell it frozen, for example.

CRAB STOCK

Buy the crabs live, if possible. Otherwise, a good frozen product is "gumbo crab," which are blue crabs cleaned and then frozen whole.

MAKES 2 QUARTS

¼ cup extra-virgin olive oil

1 large onion, thinly sliced

1 fennel bulb, trimmed and thinly sliced

2 celery stalks, thinly sliced

2 pounds blue crabs, cut into quarters

3 cloves garlic, smashed lightly

2 sprigs fresh thyme

1 cup dry white wine

Heat a convection oven to 350°F or a conventional oven to 375°F.

Heat the olive oil in a roasting pan over medium-high heat. Add the onion, fennel, and celery and cook, stirring, until the vegetables are lightly browned, about 5 minutes. Add the crabs and garlic, transfer the pan to the oven, and roast until the shells are lightly browned, about 15 minutes. Return the pan to the stove over medium-high heat. Add the thyme and white wine and cook, stirring occasionally, until the pan is dry. Transfer everything to a large stockpot and cover with water. Bring to a boil, then lower the heat to a simmer, and cook for 45 minutes.

Strain the stock through a fine-mesh strainer. The stock can be refrigerated for 3 days or frozen for up to 2 months.

VEGETABLE BROTH

This is so simple to make and so much better than what you can find in a can.

2 teaspoons extra-virgin olive oil

1 cup chopped onion

½ cup chopped carrot

½ cup chopped celery

2 cloves garlic, lightly smashed

Heat the olive oil in a medium saucepan over medium heat. Add the onion, carrot, celery, and garlic, and cook, stirring, until tender but not colored, 5 to 10 minutes. Add 4 cups water and bring to a simmer. Lower the heat to medium-low and cook until flavorful, about 20 minutes.

Strain through a fine-mesh strainer. The broth can be refrigerated for 3 days or frozen for up to 2 months.

CHICKEN REDUCTION

We use this chicken reduction, essentially a brown chicken stock reduced until full bodied and intensely flavorful, in so many of our recipes; it's a crucial element in many of our braises, pasta fillings, and sauces. Freeze it in varying amounts so you can easily pull out just the amount called for in a recipe. Though I highly recommend making this if you want to experience true Scarpetta flavor at home, there is a purchased product that you can substitute with good success (see Note).

6 pounds chicken bones (some meat on them is fine)

3 tablespoons olive oil

2 sprigs fresh rosemary, bruised with the dull side of a chef's knife

1 clove garlic, coarsely chopped

2 celery stalks, coarsely chopped

1 medium onion, coarsely chopped

1 carrot, coarsely chopped

4 whole canned tomatoes, coarsely chopped

2 cups dry white wine

Heat a convection oven to 425°F or a conventional oven to 450°F.

Rinse the chicken bones and pat them dry. Spread them out on two rimmed baking sheets in a single layer with a little room between the bones. Roast until golden brown, about 1 hour, flipping and turning the bones every 15 minutes or so.

In a large stockpot, heat the olive oil over medium heat. Add the rosemary and garlic and cook, stirring, until fragrant, about 1 minute. Add the celery, onion, and carrot, and cook, stirring occasionally, until the vegetables are well browned, about 10 minutes. Add the tomatoes, and cook, stirring, until some of the juices evaporate, 2 to 3 minutes. Add the wine and cook until almost all of it has evaporated. Add the chicken bones (with juices and drippings) to the stockpot, then add enough water to cover everything by about 2 inches (about 6 quarts). Increase the heat to medium-high, bring to a boil, then reduce the heat to medium to cook at a gentle simmer, stirring often to break up the bones and emulsify the fat, until the chicken is falling off the bones and the stock has a full flavor, 2 to 2½ hours.

Remove the chicken bones and strain the broth several times through a chinois or other fine-mesh strainer. If you want to make and use the reduction right away, spoon off any visible fat floating

on top of the stock. Otherwise, chill the stock until the fat solidifies
on top, and then scrape off and discard most of it.

Pour the defatted stock into a saucepan and bring to a boil over
high heat. Reduce the heat slightly so the stock is not boiling so
furiously. As the stock simmers, some of it will remain on the sides
of the saucepan; use a spoon or ladle to pour some of the stock over
this to deglaze it. (This will further increase the intensity of the
flavor.) Continue simmering until the stock has darkened, thickened, and reduced to about 4 cups, about 30 minutes. The reduction can be refrigerated for 3 days or frozen for up to 2 months.

NOTE: *If you don't want to make, or don't have the time to make,
this chicken reduction but want to prepare one of the dishes calling
for it, experiment with some of the commercial chicken reductions out
there. One that I have tried with success is called Glace de Poulet Gold,
by More Than Gourmet brand. A classic reduced chicken stock, it can
be reconstituted to get a flavorful chicken reduction that, while not
exactly what I make, is exceedingly convenient. You can find it at most
supermarkets as well as at specialty food markets.*

TRUCIOLETO SAUCE

We make this sauce in large quantities at the restaurant. It's not too heavy and has a balance of sweetness from caramelized shallots, richness from the Chicken Reduction, and a little tang from the vinegar. It goes well with everything from fish to beef. It's important to use a good-quality vinegar for the sauce, but it doesn't have to be expensive. Because the sauce can be made without relying on pan juices, you can make it well ahead of serving. It will keep, refrigerated, for days and can also be frozen. Consider it your secret weapon for a delicious dinner.

2 tablespoons extra-virgin olive oil

1 cup thinly sliced shallots

2 sprigs fresh thyme

1 clove garlic, thinly sliced

Pinch of crushed red pepper

2 tablespoons red wine vinegar, preferably Trucioleto (see Note)

2 cups Chicken Reduction (page 315)

Heat 1 tablespoon of the olive oil in a medium saucepan over medium-low heat. Add the shallots and cook, stirring occasionally, until well browned, about 15 minutes. Add the thyme, garlic, and crushed red pepper, and cook, stirring, until fragrant, about 1 minute. Add the vinegar and cook until reduced to a glaze. Add the Chicken Reduction, bring to a simmer, and cook for 20 minutes for the flavors to marry.

Strain through a fine-mesh strainer. Transfer to a blender (or use an immersion blender) and, with the blender running, slowly add the remaining 1 tablespoon olive oil until emulsified. Serve right away or let cool to room temperature. Once cooled, cover and refrigerate for up to 2 days or freeze for up to 2 months.

NOTE: *Trucioleto is a red wine vinegar from Emilia-Romagna that is made from the grape's first pressing and is aged in oak. It's not expensive, and it's softer than most red wine vinegars. Whenever a recipe in this book calls for red wine vinegar, this is what we reach for.*

RED WINE SAUCE

Similar to Trucioleto Sauce (page 317) but made with red wine in place of the vinegar, this is a really great sauce to serve with beef.

MAKES ABOUT 1 CUP

1 tablespoon extra-virgin olive oil

1 cup thinly sliced shallots

1 sprig fresh thyme

1 clove garlic, thinly sliced

Pinch of crushed red pepper

½ cup red wine

2 cups Chicken Reduction (page 315)

Heat the olive oil in a medium saucepan over medium-low heat. Add the shallots and cook, stirring occasionally, until well browned, about 15 minutes. Add the thyme, garlic, and crushed red pepper. Cook, stirring, until fragrant, about 1 minute. Add the wine and cook until it thickens. Add the Chicken Reduction, bring to a simmer, and cook for 20 minutes for the flavors to marry.

Strain through a fine-mesh strainer. Serve right away or let cool to room temperature. Once cooled, cover and refrigerate for up to 2 days or freeze for up to 2 months.

BONE MARROW SAUCE

This unctuous sauce is delicious on just about anything. I think I would even have it on toast. The richness from the marrow is countered by the lemon zest, which keeps this luxurious sauce from going over the top.

2 tablespoons extra-virgin olive oil

4 medium shallots, sliced

1 lemon

1 tablespoon fresh thyme leaves

Pinch of crushed red pepper

1 cup Chicken Reduction (page 315)

⅓ cup bone marrow (see Note)

Kosher salt

2 tablespoons chopped fresh chives

Heat the olive oil in a medium saucepan over medium-low heat. Add the shallots and cook, stirring occasionally, until well browned, about 15 minutes. Using a vegetable peeler, zest the lemon in wide strips and add them to the saucepan. Stir in the thyme and crushed red pepper and cook for about 30 seconds. Juice the lemon into the saucepan, add the Chicken Reduction, and bring to a simmer. Stir in the bone marrow and cook for 1 minute. Taste, and season with salt if needed. Remove from the heat, remove the zest, and stir in the chives. Serve right away or let cool to room temperature. Once cooled, cover and refrigerate for up to 2 days or freeze for up to 2 months.

NOTE: *Ask your butcher for bone marrow, or buy beef bones with the marrow inside and heat them in the oven just long enough to loosen the marrow so that you can scoop it out.*

BRAISED SHORT RIBS

It's a little unusual to call something as delicious and main-course worthy as short ribs a pantry recipe, but at Scarpetta, we use the deeply flavored meat, slightly sweetened by balsamic vinegar, in a few different recipes. It stars in an appetizer that pairs slices of it with farro risotto (see page 81). When we make that at the restaurant, the neat slices we cut mean there are lots of ragged (but still delicious) scraps of meat left over, which we use for the Chestnut Soup with Short Rib Daube (page 115) and in the filling for the Short Rib and Bone Marrow Agnolotti (page 161). That doesn't mean you have to reserve it for these purposes only; you can serve these short ribs as a main course with the creamy polenta on page 77.

3½ to 4 pounds beef short ribs

Kosher salt and freshly ground black pepper

Extra-virgin olive oil

1 cup chopped carrot

1 cup chopped celery

1 cup chopped onion

10 cloves garlic, coarsely chopped

¾ cup red wine

½ cup balsamic or red wine vinegar

1 (14-ounce) can chopped tomatoes

2 cups Chicken Reduction (page 315)

4 sprigs fresh thyme

2 sprigs fresh rosemary

Heat a convection oven to 300°F or a conventional oven to 325°F.

Season the short ribs all over with salt and pepper. Heat 2 tablespoons olive oil in a deep, heavy-based Dutch oven or similar pot over medium-high heat. Add the ribs—in two batches if they don't fit in the pot in a single layer—and sear on all sides until well browned all over.

Remove the ribs, wipe out the pan, and add more oil to coat the pan. Add the carrot, celery, onion, and garlic to the pot, and cook over medium heat, stirring occasionally, until nicely browned, 6 to 8 minutes. Add the red wine and the vinegar and cook, stirring and scraping up the bits stuck to the bottom of the pan, until the liquid is reduced by half. Add the tomatoes, Chicken Reduction, thyme, and rosemary. Return the short ribs to the pot, bring the liquid to a boil, cover, and transfer to the oven. Cook, turning the ribs once, until the ribs are fork-tender and the meat is just barely clinging to the bone, 2½ to 3 hours. Remove the ribs from the cooking liquid, then strain and reserve the liquid.

Use a large spoon or ladle to remove as much of the clear fat floating on top of the cooking liquid as possible. (If you are making the ribs ahead, you can remove the fat more easily once the cooking liquid has cooled. Refrigerate the ribs in their cooking liquid, and then remove the hardened fat from the top.) Cook the defatted sauce over medium-high heat until it has reduced somewhat, becoming thicker and more flavorful. (The ribs can be made 2 days ahead; let cool to room temperature, and then cover and refrigerate the ribs in the braising liquid. Reheat gently to serve.)

TO SERVE AS WHOLE RIBS: Reheat the ribs in the reduced braising liquid in a 300°F oven (325°F for a conventional oven).

TO USE IN SHORT RIBS WITH FARRO AND VEGETABLE RISOTTO (PAGE 81): Slice the meat from the ribs across the grain into pieces about ⅓ inch thick. Reserve the slices in the reduced braising liquid.

TO USE FOR THE CHESTNUT SOUP WITH SHORT RIB DAUBE (PAGE 115) OR AS A FILLING FOR PASTA, SUCH AS THE SHORT RIB AND BONE MARROW AGNOLOTTI (PAGE 161): Let the meat cool enough to work with it. Remove the meat from the bones and chop enough of it into small pieces to yield 3 cups. Reserve the chopped meat in the reduced braising liquid.

SCARPETTA TOMATO SAUCE

I know it seems crazy that this sauce, which paired with fresh spaghetti is a signature dish at Scarpetta, is in the pantry chapter of the book. But this is also what we use in every recipe that calls for tomato sauce, whether it's by the tablespoon or the cup. The infused oil is the secret that makes this sauce so great. Not only does it give the sauce a supple texture, but it also reinforces the flavors of the basil and the crushed red pepper while introducing just a hint of garlic. And it's about as easy to make as a cup of tea; you simply let the ingredients steep in the hot oil. For the best consistency, use a potato masher to break up the tomatoes as they cook. It's a trick I learned from watching tomato sauce preparation in my Italian household.

MAKES 3 CUPS

Extra-virgin olive oil

12 plum tomatoes, peeled (see page 22) and seeded, plus any juices from peeling and seeding, strained and reserved (see Note)

Kosher salt

10 cloves garlic

3 sprigs fresh basil (about 24 leaves plus stems)

1 to 1½ teaspoons crushed red pepper flakes

In a wide saucepan, heat 3 tablespoons olive oil over medium-high heat. Add the tomatoes; be careful, as the oil may spurt. Add 1½ teaspoons salt and cook, stirring occasionally, until the tomatoes soften, 2 to 3 minutes. Lower the heat to medium and, using a potato masher, smash the tomatoes, really working the masher to break them up. If the consistency is thick, add the reserved tomato juice to the pan. Cook, occasionally mashing and stirring, for 20 minutes.

Meanwhile, in a small saucepan, heat ½ cup extra-virgin olive oil over medium heat. Add the garlic, basil, and red pepper flakes and cook, stirring occasionally to wilt the basil, until the garlic is golden brown, about 5 minutes. Remove the oil from the heat and let the ingredients steep for 5 minutes.

Strain about half of the oil into the cooked tomatoes. (Strain and reserve the rest of the flavorful oil; it's a great bread-dipping oil.) Stir to combine. Remove the sauce from the heat. Taste and add additional salt, if needed. The sauce may taste spicy on its own, but it gets balanced when used with other ingredients, especially the pasta, butter, and cheese in the Scarpetta Spaghetti (page 121). The sauce will keep, covered and refrigerated, for 2 days. Reheat gently before serving.

NOTE: *If your tomatoes are not ripe, bright, and juicy, reduce the number of fresh tomatoes to 8 and add 4 whole canned San Marzano tomatoes.*

ROASTED CHERRY TOMATOES

I love how these roasted tomatoes punctuate a plate with their intensely sweet flavor, splash of color, and unique texture. Peeling them first is a little work, but the results are worth it, as the peeled tomatoes more readily absorb the flavors of the thyme and garlic and look more elegant.

16 cherry tomatoes, blanched and peeled (see page 22)

2 sprigs fresh thyme

1 clove garlic, thinly sliced

1 tablespoon extra-virgin olive oil

Pinch of kosher salt

Heat a convection oven to 275°F or a conventional oven to 300°F.

On a small rimmed baking sheet, toss all of the ingredients together, and roast until the tomatoes are tender but still hold their shape, about 20 minutes. The tomatoes will keep, covered and refrigerated, for 2 days.

CONCENTRATED TOMATOES

These slow-cooked tomatoes contribute a deep, soulful flavor to whatever they're added to, from our signature Black Cod with Concentrated Tomatoes and Caramelized Fennel (page 186) to salads like the *Stracciatella* with Pickled Eggplant (page 63).

MAKES ABOUT 4 CUPS

Kosher salt

14 plum tomatoes

¼ cup extra-virgin olive oil, plus up to 3 cups if storing in oil

1 teaspoon chopped fresh oregano

1 teaspoon granulated sugar

Freshly ground black pepper

Heat a convection oven to 275°F or a conventional oven to 300°F. Line a rimmed baking sheet with parchment paper.

Fill a medium bowl with ice water. Bring a medium saucepan of lightly salted water to a boil. In batches, blanch the tomatoes for about 45 seconds in the boiling water, then plunge immediately into the ice water. Peel the tomatoes, slice in half lengthwise, and squeeze gently to remove some of the seeds.

Toss the tomatoes with the olive oil to coat them liberally, then lay them cut side down on the baking sheet. Sprinkle the oregano and sugar over the tomatoes and season lightly with salt and black pepper, keeping in mind that the long cooking time will concentrate all of the flavors.

Bake the tomatoes until they are quite concentrated and turn a very deep red color; about 3½ hours; you may need to drizzle additional olive oil over the tomatoes to keep them from browning. You are not trying to dry the tomatoes completely; they should look quite dry on the outside but should retain some moisture within. Let cool to room temperature.

The tomatoes will keep refrigerated for up to 1 week. To keep them supple and flavorful, store them in the following way: Neatly stack them in layers in a plastic storage container, gently pressing them down to remove any air pockets. Cover completely with oil, cover, and refrigerate.

ROASTED CHERRY TOMATOES, PG. 323

CONCENTRATED TOMATOES, OPPOSITE

PARSNIP PURÉE

I love this supple
and subtle purée with
lamb, such as the
Colorado Lamb Chops
on page 257.

MAKES ABOUT 2 CUPS

¼ cup extra-virgin oil

2 medium shallots, thinly
sliced (1 cup)

4 parsnips, peeled and thinly
sliced (about 4 cups)

1½ cups Chicken Stock
(page 310)

1 sprig fresh thyme

In a medium saucepan, heat 1 tablespoon of the olive oil over medium-low heat. Add the shallots and cook, stirring occasionally, until tender but not colored, about 5 minutes. Add the parsnips and cook, stirring occasionally, until just tender, about 5 minutes. Add the stock and thyme, increase the heat to medium-high, and bring to just under a boil. Cook until the parsnips are very soft, about 10 minutes.

Transfer to a blender and purée. With the machine running, slowly add the remaining 3 tablespoons olive oil and blend to emulsify. The purée will keep, covered and refrigerated, for 2 days. Reheat gently before serving.

ABOUT OUR PURÉES

We use vegetable purées in so many of our dishes that it's become a hallmark. Silken, supple, and sauce-like, just a little gets smeared across the plate before the rest of the dish is assembled. It looks great, to be sure, but more important, it adds another layer of flavor and also an interesting texture to the finished dish. I know that when I get a bite of the Colorado Lamb Chops with Rosemary-Lemon Jus, Parsnip Purée, and Hazelnut Crumble (page 257) with some of the parsnip purée on them, I am very happy indeed. The purées on these pages are all basically made in the same fashion and are easy to prepare. But you will need a blender, preferably a good one, to get the best texture. Leftover purée can be thinned slightly with broth or water for a delicious soup.

SUNCHOKE PURÉE

I really like this purée with scallops (see page 64); the two ingredients just have such an affinity for each other.

3 tablespoons extra-virgin olive oil

1 cup sliced shallots

Kosher salt

1 clove garlic, peeled

Pinch of crushed red pepper

8 ounces sunchokes, peeled and thinly sliced

1 sprig fresh thyme

2 cups Chicken Stock (page 310)

Heat 2 tablespoons of the olive oil in a medium saucepan over medium heat. Add the shallots, season lightly with salt, and cook, stirring occasionally, until tender but not colored, about 4 minutes. Stir in the garlic, crushed red pepper, sunchokes, and thyme. Cook, stirring frequently, for 8 minutes. Add the stock, increase the heat to medium-high, and bring to a boil. Lower the heat to a simmer and cook the sunchokes until tender, about 8 minutes.

Remove the thyme sprig, transfer to a blender, and purée until smooth. With the machine running, add the remaining 1 tablespoon olive oil and blend until emulsified. The purée will keep, covered and refrigerated, for 2 days. Reheat gently before serving.

CELERY ROOT PURÉE

I love taking this ugly, earthy vegetable and transforming it into this refined and elegant element. I often serve it under fish, such as the striped bass on page 189.

striped bass on page 189.

MAKES ABOUT 2 CUPS

¼ cup extra-virgin olive oil

8 ounces celery root, peeled and cut into medium dice

2 medium shallots, sliced

2 sprigs fresh thyme

Kosher salt

1 tablespoon mascarpone cheese

In a medium saucepan, heat 2 tablespoons of the olive oil over medium-high heat. Add half of the celery root and cook, stirring occasionally, until browned, about 10 minutes. Add the shallots and thyme, season with a little salt, and cook, stirring, until the shallots are tender and lightly browned, about 4 minutes. Add the rest of the celery root and 2 cups water and bring to a boil. Lower the heat to a simmer and cook until the celery root is soft, about 25 minutes.

Remove the thyme, transfer to a blender, and purée. Add the mascarpone and, with the machine running, the remaining 2 tablespoons olive oil. Pass the purée through a fine-mesh strainer and reserve. The purée will keep, covered and refrigerated, for 2 days. Reheat gently before serving and season to taste with salt.

BUTTERNUT SQUASH PURÉE

The sweetness of butternut squash gets tempered with a pinch of red pepper flakes in this versatile purée. Delicious with pork, it also goes well with roast chicken. You can also thin it with a little broth to make a satisfying soup.

3 tablespoons extra-virgin olive oil

2 medium shallots, sliced

1 sprig fresh thyme

Pinch of crushed red pepper

3 cups diced butternut squash (from 1 large squash)

1½ cups Vegetable Broth (page 314) or water

In a medium saucepan, heat 1 tablespoon of the olive oil over medium-low heat. Add the shallots and cook, stirring occasionally, until tender but not colored, about 5 minutes. Add the thyme and crushed red pepper and cook until fragrant, about 1 minute. Add the squash and cook, stirring occasionally, until just tender, about 5 to 10 minutes. Add the broth and bring to just under a boil. Cook until the squash is very soft, about 10 minutes.

Transfer to a blender, remove the thyme, and purée. With the machine running, slowly add the remaining 2 tablespoons olive oil and blend until emulsified. The purée will keep, covered and refrigerated, for 2 days. Reheat gently before serving.

SALSIFY PURÉE

Salsify has a mild flavor that some say is reminiscent of oysters. Perhaps that's why I like to pair it with seafood.

2 tablespoons extra-virgin olive oil

¼ cup sliced shallots

Kosher salt

2 cups peeled and sliced salsify, submerged in water to keep it from turning brown

1½ to 2 cups Chicken Stock (page 310)

1 sprig fresh thyme

In a small saucepan, heat 1 tablespoon of the olive oil over medium heat. Add the shallots, season with salt, and cook, stirring occasionally, until tender, but not colored, about 5 minutes. Add the salsify and cook, stirring occasionally, until just tender, about 10 minutes. Add the stock and thyme and bring to just under a boil. Cook until the salsify is very soft, about 10 minutes.

Remove the thyme sprig, transfer to a blender, and purée until smooth. With the machine running, add the remaining 1 tablespoon olive oil and blend until emulsified. The purée will keep, covered and refrigerated, for 2 days. Reheat gently before serving.

PICKLED MUSTARD SEEDS

Once you try these, you will want to have them on hand at all times because they add such a fun, tangy pop to dishes like the lentils on page 236 and the sauce for fried whitebait on page 71.

the lentils on page 236 and the sauce for fried whitebait on page 71.

MAKES ABOUT ½ CUP

¾ cup champagne vinegar

½ cup yellow mustard seeds

3 tablespoons granulated sugar

1 teaspoon kosher salt

In a small saucepan, combine the vinegar, mustard seeds, sugar, salt, and ¾ cup water. Bring to a simmer over medium-high heat. Lower the heat and simmer gently for 30 minutes.

Remove from the heat, and let cool to room temperature. Cover and refrigerate for up to 2 months.

PICKLED RED ONIONS

These are quick to make and add a tangy and not too oniony flavor to whatever they are added to. Their bit of crunch is also a welcome textural element.

MAKES ABOUT 1 CUP

1 cup thinly sliced red onion

½ cup red wine vinegar

1 teaspoon kosher salt

Put the onion slices in a small heatproof container. Combine the vinegar, salt, and ½ cup water in a small saucepan over medium-high heat. Bring to a simmer, and pour enough over the onion slices to just cover. Cover and refrigerate for at least 24 hours before using. The onions keep for up to 1 month, covered and refrigerated.

PICKLED MUSTARD SEEDS, PG. 331

PICKLED HON-SHIMEJI MUSHROOMS, PG. 47

PICKLED EGGPLANT, OPPOSITE

PICKLED RED ONIONS, PG. 331

PICKLED EGGPLANT

I grew up eating this stuff, and this is pretty much my mother's recipe. My good friend Mike reminded me of it when we were opening Scarpetta. The tang and texture of the eggplant is just the perfect foil for the creamy *stracciatella* cheese and sweet slow-cooked tomatoes in the salad on page 63. I also love it on sandwiches and to eat as part of an antipasti plate. Though it requires very little labor, the pickled eggplant needs to be started a day or two ahead of when you want to use it.

MAKES ABOUT 2 CUPS

1½ pounds Italian eggplant

2 tablespoons kosher salt

½ cup white wine vinegar, plus more as needed

1½ teaspoons chopped fresh oregano

1 small clove garlic, smashed

½ teaspoon crushed red pepper

1½ cups extra-virgin olive oil, plus more as needed

Peel the eggplant and cut it into a julienne (pieces about ¼ inch thick and 2 inches long).

In a bowl, toss the eggplant with the salt and refrigerate for at least 8 hours and up to 24 hours (the salt draws excess water from the eggplant).

Drain the eggplant and squeeze it to draw out even more liquid. Transfer to a container or bowl and add enough white wine vinegar to cover. Refrigerate for another 8 hours or so.

Lightly squeeze excess vinegar from the eggplant and toss with the oregano, garlic, and crushed red pepper. Put it in a storage container and cover completely with olive oil. Refrigerate for at least 8 hours for the flavors to meld before using. The eggplant will keep for at least 1 month, covered in olive oil and refrigerated.

PICKLED GARLIC

You can always buy pickled garlic to use in the Short Rib Agnolotti on page 161, but it's so easy to make, so why not try it?

page 161

MAKES 20 CLOVES

20 cloves garlic, peeled

1 cup sherry vinegar

1 teaspoon whole black peppercorns

1 dried bay leaf

In a small saucepan, cover the garlic cloves with water, and bring to a simmer. Discard the water, and repeat twice more. (This blanching helps make the garlic less pungent.) Transfer to a heat-proof container.

In a small saucepan, combine the vinegar with 1 cup water. Add the peppercorns and bay leaf and bring to a boil. Pour over the garlic—make sure the cloves are submerged—and let sit at room temperature until cool. Cover and refrigerate for at least 2 days before using. The garlic will keep for up to 1 month, covered and refrigerated.

PICKLED RAMPS

Ramps, with their delicious oniony garlic flavor, are such a brief seasonal treat that when we get them in spring, I use them in as many dishes as possible. A quick pickle using aromatic spices makes them even more intriguing.

¼ pound ramps, trimmed, blanched (see page 194), and diced

½ teaspoon whole black peppercorns

½ teaspoon coriander seeds

½ teaspoon fennel seeds

½ teaspoon dried juniper berries

1 whole star anise

½ stick cinnamon

2 cups Champagne vinegar

¼ cup granulated sugar

Put the ramps in a heatproof quart container or similar size dish or bowl.

Make a sachet by wrapping the peppercorns, coriander, fennel, juniper, star anise, and cinnamon in a 6-inch square of cheesecloth, pouch style, and then tying the pouch closed with kitchen twine. Add the sachet to the ramps.

Combine the vinegar and sugar with 2 cups water in a medium saucepan and bring to a boil over high heat. Reduce the heat and simmer gently for 10 minutes. Pour the hot mixture over the ramps and the sachet. Cool to room temperature, cover, and refrigerate for 24 hours, and then remove the sachet. The ramps will keep, covered and refrigerated, for at least 1 week.

PICKLED LEEKS

A little of these leeks is a great way to add a hit of tangy flavor to a braise or sauce.

2 or 3 leeks, trimmed and diced (white and light green parts; about 1 cup)

1 tablespoon whole black peppercorns

1½ teaspoons coriander seeds

1½ teaspoons fennel seeds

1½ teaspoons yellow mustard seeds

2 cups champagne vinegar

½ cup granulated sugar

1½ teaspoons kosher salt

Put the leeks in a heatproof 1-quart container or similar-size dish or bowl. Make a sachet by wrapping the peppercorns, coriander seeds, fennel seeds, and mustard seeds in a 6-inch square of cheesecloth and tying the pouch closed with kitchen twine. Add the sachet to the leeks.

Combine the vinegar, sugar, salt, and 2 cups water in a medium saucepan and bring to a boil over high heat. Lower the heat and simmer gently for 10 minutes. Pour the hot mixture over the leeks and the sachet. Let cool to room temperature, cover, and refrigerate for 24 hours before using. The leeks will keep, covered and refrigerated, for at least 1 week.

ROASTED BABY CARROTS

We often add just a few baby carrots to a plate for color and sweetness. This recipe, however, is easily multiplied if you want to serve them as a heartier side dish.

SERVES 4 AS AN ACCOMPANIMENT

12 baby carrots, preferably mixed colors, peeled

4 cloves garlic, peeled

4 fresh thyme sprigs

Pinch of crushed red pepper

Extra-virgin olive oil

Kosher salt

Heat a convection oven to 400°F or a conventional oven to 425°F.

On a small rimmed baking sheet, toss the carrots with the garlic, thyme, crushed red pepper, and just enough olive oil to coat lightly. Season with salt and roast, tossing once, until the carrots are tender and nicely browned, about 20 minutes. The carrots will keep, covered and refrigerated, for up to 2 days.

ROASTED BABY BEETS

I love the jewel tones that quartered roasted beets add to a plate. Their deep, earthy, sweet flavor complements roasts and braises, too, and they pair beautifully with my favorite cheese (La Tur) in the salad on page 98. The recipe is easily multiplied.

the salad on page 98.

SERVES 4 AS AN ACCOMPANIMENT

4 baby beets, preferably golden or candy-striped (Chioggia), trimmed

1 tablespoon extra-virgin olive oil

2 sprigs fresh thyme

Kosher salt and freshly ground black pepper

Heat a convection oven to 350°F or a conventional oven to 375°F.

Toss the beets with the oil and thyme and season with salt and black pepper. Lay a piece of aluminum foil large enough to wrap the beets on a rimmed baking sheet. Put the beets on it and wrap them tightly. Bake until tender, 30 to 45 minutes.

Test by inserting a cake tester or knife into a beet; it should go in and out easily. Allow to cool slightly, then peel the beets using a paper towel to rub off the skins. The beets will keep, covered and refrigerated, for 2 days.

ROASTED BABY POTATOES

A few little potatoes as part of a plate not only make it feel more substantial, but also add color and texture. This is an easy recipe to multiply.

SERVES 4 AS AN ACCOMPANIMENT

12 baby potatoes, preferably a mix of colors

2 teaspoons extra-virgin olive oil

2 fresh thyme sprigs

2 cloves garlic, lightly crushed

1 sprig fresh rosemary

¼ teaspoon kosher salt

Pinch of crushed red pepper

Heat a convection oven to 375°F or a conventional oven to 400°F.

On a small rimmed baking sheet, toss the potatoes with the oil, thyme, garlic, rosemary, salt, and crushed red pepper. Roast until tender, 30 to 45 minutes depending on size. The potatoes will keep, covered and refrigerated, for 1 day. Let them come to room temperature before using.

ROASTED CIPOLLINI

Cipollini are small, slightly flattened onions that are cooked whole and look elegant on the plate.

SERVES 4 AS AN ACCOMPANIMENT

2 tablespoons extra-virgin olive oil

12 cipollini onions

2 fresh thyme sprigs

Kosher salt

Heat a convection oven to 350°F or a conventional oven to 375°F.

Heat a medium sauté pan until very hot, add the olive oil, then add the cipollini and cook, turning the onions occasionally, until golden brown on all sides, about 3 minutes.

Add the thyme, season with salt, and add enough water to come a quarter of the way up the sides of the cipollini. Transfer to the oven and cook, turning them once about halfway through cooking, until the onions are tender and the water has evaporated, 12 to 20 minutes depending on size. (If the water evaporates before the onions are tender, add more water to the pan.) Before serving, remove the thyme. The cipollini will keep, covered and refrigerated, for 2 days. Let come to room temperature before using.

SMOKED PAPRIKA OIL

Sweet smoked paprika (*pimentón*) gives this oil a great smoky flavor.

¼ cup plus 3 tablespoons extra-virgin olive oil, preferably a mild-flavored oil

1 tablespoon sweet smoked paprika (pimentón)

In a small saucepan, combine the olive oil and paprika. Heat over low heat until small bubbles start to form. Remove from the heat and let cool. Let sit for at least 2 hours at room temperature for the flavors to infuse. The oil will keep, covered and refrigerated, for 1 month.

CHILE OIL

I am a big fan of crushed red pepper and use it in just about every savory dish I make. Here is another way to impart that warm flavor to food. Even though I use just a few drops of it in my Yellowtail Crudo with Chile and Ginger Oils (page 52), the dish would not be the same without it.

½ cup grapeseed oil

1 tablespoon crushed red pepper

In a small saucepan, combine the oil and the crushed red pepper. Heat over medium heat until small bubbles start to form. Remove from the heat, cover, and let steep for at least 4 hours at room temperature. Strain through a fine-mesh strainer. The oil will keep, covered and refrigerated, for 1 month.

GINGER OIL

Ginger is not exactly an Italian ingredient, but I love it. Infused in an oil, it adds just a subtle flavor that does not take a dish too far in a different direction.

MAKES ABOUT ½ CUP

½ cup grapeseed oil

½ cup sliced fresh ginger

In a small saucepan, combine the oil and ginger. Heat over low heat until small bubbles start to form. Continue cooking over low heat for 30 minutes. Remove from the heat, let cool to room temperature, and strain through a fine-mesh strainer. The oil will keep, covered and refrigerated, for 1 month.

HERB OIL

Composed of herbs with quite different personalities, this herb oil has more depth than one made with just a single herb.

MAKES ABOUT 1 CUP

½ chopped fresh basil

½ cup chopped fresh mint

¼ cup chopped fresh oregano

1 cup extra-virgin olive oil

½ teaspoon kosher salt

Put the herbs in a small bowl or other container and add the olive oil. Season with the salt. Cover and refrigerate to let the flavors meld for at least 24 hours. Strain through a fine-mesh strainer. The oil will keep, covered and refrigerated, for at least 1 week.

BLACK OLIVE OIL, PG. 344

EXTRA-VIRGIN OLIVE OIL

CHILE OIL, PG. 341

BASIL OIL, PG. 345

GINGER OIL, OPPOSITE

SMOKED PAPRIKA OIL, PG. 341

BLACK OLIVE OIL

It's the little things that often matter so much when it comes to cooking. Dehydrating the olives makes their flavor more intense, which makes this flavored oil more potent and intriguing. The dark-colored oil also looks dramatic on the plate. It's not hard to prepare; it just takes some planning.

MAKES ABOUT ½ CUP

1 cup oil-cured black olives, pitted

½ cup extra-virgin olive oil

Pinch of crushed red pepper

If you have a dehydrating machine, dehydrate the olives as the machine directs. Otherwise, bake the olives at your oven's lowest setting until very hard, 8 to 10 hours.

In a blender, combine the olives, olive oil, and crushed red pepper and purée until completely smooth, about 1 minute. The oil will keep, covered and refrigerated, for 2 months.

BASIL OIL

I love this oil because it truly captures that summertime basil flavor, and just a little drizzled on a plate makes a big impact.

MAKES ABOUT ¾ CUP

2 cups fresh basil leaves

½ cup extra-virgin olive oil, preferably a mild-flavored one

½ teaspoon kosher salt

Bring a medium saucepan of water to a rolling boil. Meanwhile, fill a medium bowl with ice water. Put the basil in the boiling water, pressing it gently under the water to submerge, and cook for 1 minute. Quickly remove the basil from the water and plunge it into the ice water. Let cool completely, then squeeze out excess water. Transfer to a blender and add the olive oil and salt. Purée on high speed for 30 seconds. Refrigerate overnight to naturally separate the oil from the solids, or, if using right away, strain through a fine-mesh strainer lined with a coffee filter. The oil will keep, covered and refrigerated, for 2 days.

TARRAGON OIL

This aromatic oil is especially delicious with fish.

MAKES ABOUT 1 CUP

1 bunch fresh tarragon

1 cup extra-virgin olive oil

Combine the tarragon and olive oil in a blender. Purée until completely smooth, and transfer to a storage container. The oil will keep, covered and refrigerated, for 2 days.

POULTRY SPICE

I don't find chicken very interesting to work with, but I do think it's fantastic when sprinkled with a light coating of this spice rub before being roasted or grilled.

5 whole star anise

1 teaspoon whole cloves

1 teaspoon cumin seeds

1½ teaspoons ground nutmeg

In a small sauté pan, toast the star anise, cloves, and cumin over medium heat until fragrant, 2 to 3 minutes. Add the nutmeg and toast briefly. Transfer to a spice grinder and grind finely. Once cool, cover and store at room temperature. The spice mix will keep, stored airtight, for up to 1 month.

MAKE-AHEAD SPICE MIXES

The spice mixes on these pages also appear with specific recipes, but they are such a good thing to have on hand for everyday cooking that I include them here. The spices will keep indefinitely, but they will lose some of their flavor over time.

VEAL SPICE

Roast veal (or veal chops) goes from subtle to spectacular when rubbed with these hot and tingly spices. Be sure to drizzle some of the pan juices on the meat, too. The spices flavor the juices in a fabulous way that should not be wasted.

MAKES ABOUT ¼ CUP

1 tablespoon crushed red pepper

1 tablespoon Szechuan peppercorns

1 tablespoon coriander seeds

1½ teaspoons cumin seeds

1½ teaspoons sweet smoked paprika (pimentón)

2 whole star anise or 1½ teaspoons ground

In a small skillet, toast the crushed red pepper, Szechuan peppercorns, coriander seeds, cumin seeds, smoked paprika, and star anise over medium heat until fragrant, 2 to 3 minutes. Transfer to a spice grinder and grind finely. The spice mix will keep, stored airtight, for up to 1 month.

PORK SPICE

This spice mix works best with pork cuts that have some fat on them, like shoulder, belly, or even ribs.

MAKES ABOUT 2 TABLESPOONS

2 teaspoons cumin seeds

½ teaspoon whole cloves

½ teaspoon yellow mustard seeds

½ teaspoon whole black peppercorns

2 teaspoons sweet paprika

½ teaspoon ground cinnamon

In a small sauté pan, toast the cumin seeds, cloves, mustard seeds, and black peppercorns over medium heat, stirring occasionally, until fragrant, 2 to 3 minutes. Transfer to a spice grinder and grind finely, then transfer to a small bowl and add the paprika and cinnamon. The spice mix will keep, stored airtight, for up to 1 month.

FISH SPICE

The licorice-like notes in this spice mix pair really well with fish as well as with chicken.

MAKES ABOUT 2 TABLESPOONS

1 tablespoon crumbled Dried Lemon Zest (page 351) or high-quality purchased dried lemon zest

1½ teaspoons fennel seeds

1 teaspoon anise seeds (not star anise)

¼ teaspoon crushed red pepper

½ teaspoon fennel pollen (see Note, page 194)

In a small sauté pan, toast the Dried Lemon Zest, fennel seeds, anise seeds, and crushed red pepper over medium heat, stirring occasionally, until fragrant 2 to 3 minutes. Transfer the spices to a spice grinder, add the fennel pollen, and grind finely. The spice mix will keep, stored airtight, for up to 1 month.

BEEF SPICE

The fresh rosemary in this spice mix means that it won't keep as long as others, but that's okay, because the flavor is so fantastic that you will go through it quickly.

1½ teaspoons whole allspice berries

1½ teaspoons cumin seeds

1½ teaspoons yellow mustard seeds

¾ teaspoon Szechuan peppercorns

½ teaspoon crushed red pepper

1 tablespoon plus 1 teaspoon sweet smoked paprika (pimentón)

2 sprigs fresh rosemary

In a small sauté pan, toast the allspice berries, cumin seeds, mustard seeds, Szechuan peppercorns, and crushed red pepper over medium heat, stirring occasionally, until fragrant, 2 to 3 minutes. Take the pan off the heat and add the paprika and the leaves from the rosemary sprigs. Let cool slightly before grinding finely in a spice grinder. The spice mix will keep, stored airtight, for up to 1 week.

DRIED LEMON ZEST/DRIED ORANGE ZEST

You can buy dried lemon and even orange zest, but it's also really easy to make at home in just a few minutes with the help of a microwave. And because it's fresh, it has more flavor than purchased. It will keep indefinitely if stored airtight, but its flavor will dissipate over time.

MAKES ABOUT 1 TABLESPOON

2 lemons, or 1 large orange

If the citrus, such as lemons, is waxed, rinse under warm water and dry.

Using a vegetable peeler, peel the citrus, creating wide strips; try to get just the yellow skin and none of the white pith below. Line a plate with a paper towel and put the strips on the plate. Microwave on high power for 1 minute, then flip the zest over and replace the paper towel with a fresh one. Continue microwaving and flipping the zest, replacing the paper towel as needed, until the zest is dry and crispy, 4 to 6 minutes depending on the strength of the microwave. Let cool. The zest will keep, stored airtight, for up to 1 month.

QUICK PRESERVED LEMON/QUICK PRESERVED ORANGE

Preserved lemons can take weeks to make the traditional way. These have a similar soft skin and salty, tangy flavor but take less than a half hour to make.

1 lemon, orange, or blood orange

6 sprigs fresh thyme

2 shallots, thinly sliced

1½ tablespoons kosher salt

½ teaspoon crushed red pepper

Extra-virgin olive oil

If the citrus, such as lemons, are waxed, rinse them under warm water and dry. Slice the fruit $1/16$ to $1/8$ inch thick.

Line a small flameproof baking dish or ovenproof skillet with a layer of lemon slices. Top with 2 sprigs of the thyme, some of the shallots, a sprinkle of salt, and a pinch of the crushed red pepper. Continue layering until all the ingredients are used up. Cover the lemons completely with olive oil.

Heat the citrus over low heat, shaking the pan occasionally, until the oil reaches about 160°F, about 15 minutes. Using a thermometer is the safest way to gauge the temperature, but all I generally do is stick my finger in the oil occasionally as it heats. As soon as it feels hot enough as to be uncomfortable, I take the pan off the heat. Allow the citrus to cool at room temperature.

If not using right away, cover the citrus (as well as the herbs and shallots) with olive oil and refrigerate for up to 1 month.

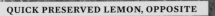

QUICK PRESERVED LEMON, OPPOSITE

CITRUS-HERB OIL, PG. 43

DRIED CITRUS ZEST, PG. 351

QUICK PRESERVED ORANGE, OPPOSITE

BOTTARGA BREAD CRUMBS

The somewhat strong flavor of *bottarga* (dried fish roe) makes these the perfect bread crumbs to use with seafood.

1 cup panko bread crumbs

2 tablespoons extra-virgin olive oil

2 tablespoons freshly grated bottarga or bottarga powder (see Note)

1 tablespoon chopped fresh flat-leaf parsley

Heat a convection oven to 350°F or a conventional oven to 375°F.

On a small rimmed baking sheet, combine the panko, olive oil, *bottarga*, and parsley, and toss to combine well. Toast until the bread crumbs are golden, about 8 minutes. Let cool. The bread crumbs will keep, airtight and frozen, for several weeks.

NOTE: Bottarga *is dried fish roe from either tuna or mullet; at Scarpetta we use mullet, and we buy blocks of it and shave it to order. The powdered form is usually easier to find and also packs a flavorful punch. You can find it at some specialty markets.*

MINTED BREAD CRUMBS

Fresh mint makes these bread crumbs a bright addition to many dishes.

MAKES ABOUT ½ CUP

½ cup panko bread crumbs

1½ teaspoons chopped fresh flat-leaf parsley

1 tablespoon chopped fresh mint

Pinch of crushed red pepper flakes

1 tablespoon extra-virgin olive oil

In a small food processor, pulse the panko, parsley, mint, and crushed red pepper. Add the oil and continue to pulse until the herbs are no longer visible. Let cool. The bread crumbs will keep, airtight and frozen, for several weeks.

HERBED BREAD CRUMBS

This is a good, all-purpose toasted bread crumb. Lightly flavored with parsley, these can be used on fish, for a gratin, or tossed with pasta.

MAKES ABOUT ½ CUP

½ cup panko bread crumbs

2 tablespoons extra-virgin olive oil

1½ teaspoons chopped fresh flat leaf parsley

In a small saucepan, combine the panko, olive oil, and parsley. Toast over medium-high heat, stirring occasionally, until golden brown. Let cool. The bread crumbs will keep, airtight and frozen, for several weeks.

SOURCES

ALMA GOURMET

almagourmet.com

718-433-1616

Features imported Italian products, including Pasta di Gragnano, my favorite dry pasta.

BUON ITALIA

buonitalia.com

212-633-9090

Has a retail outlet in Chelsea Market in New York City, carries many fine Italian products, including Trucioleto, my favorite all-purpose brand of red wine vinegar, and "00" flour.

CHEFS' WAREHOUSE

chefswarehouse.com

718-842-8700

A great resource for all kinds of hard-to-find food items. Look here for *bramata* polenta, squid ink, specialty baking ingredients, and more.

CHOCOSPHERE

chocosphere.com

877-992-4626

An importer of chocolates from around the world and a good source for Amedei chocolate.

D'ARTAGNAN

dartagnan.com

800-327-8246

Sells foie gras, duck, wild boar, venison, and all kinds of gourmet meats.

DEBRAGGA AND SPITLER

debragga.com

646-873-6555

A wholesale butcher that sells restaurant-quality meats, including Australian Wagyu beef.

GUSTIAMO

gustiamo.com

718-860-2949

Imports some of Italy's best foods, and it's my source for *stratto*, the Italian tomato concentrate from Sicily. They carry *bottarga* and a whole host of other great products as well.

LA BOÎTE BISCUITS AND SPICES

laboiteny.com

212-247-4407

Offers high-quality spices and blends.

MORE THAN GOURMET

morethangourmet.com
800-860-9385

Makes delicious reduced sauces, including the Glace de Poulet Gold that I recommend as a substitute for my own Chicken Reduction (page 315) when you don't have time to make it. Their sauces are available at some supermarkets and gourmet groceries, and through the company's Web site.

MURRAY'S CHEESE

murrayscheese.com
888-692-4339

Based in Manhattan, this is my favorite source for cheese; it also has a great selection of cured meats.

PAT LAFREIDA & SON

lafrieda.com
800-876-0898

This rightly famous wholesale meat purveyor sells retail online as well.

SALUMERIA BIELLESE

salumeriabiellese.com
212-736-7376

Sells artisan cured meats such as *lardo*, pancetta, guanciale, *salumi*, and more.

URBANI TRUFFLES

urbani.com
800-281-2330

A great source for truffles and truffle products as well as high-quality wild mushrooms.

INDEX

Page numbers in *italics* refer to photographs.